# THE 30% SOLUTION

## HOW CIVILITY AT WORK INCREASES RETENTION, ENGAGEMENT, AND PROFITABILITY.

## BY LEW BAYER

### WITH CONTRIBUTIONS BY OLEN JUAREZ-LIM

MOtivational PRESS®

LEADERS IN GLOBAL PUBLISHING

Published by Motivational Press, Inc.
1777 Aurora Road
Melbourne, Florida, 32935

www.MotivationalPress.com

Manufactured in the United States of America.

ISBN: 978-1-62865-267-3

# CONTENTS

# DEDICATIONS

To my parents, Ted and Linda Sheard, and Bob and Mariette Bayer, it's the examples all of you have set, the generosity you've each exhibited ongoing to me and to others, and the unrelenting respect, restraint, and responsibility you each exhibit daily that make me believe there is good in the world. Truly, civility starts at home.

To my friend Michelle Painchaud who even while managing incredible challenges in her life, always thinks of others. Michelle, your strength of character, your positivity, and your thoughtfulness never cease to amaze me.

To my brother Stephen Sheard who has endured many incivilities over the years with grace and humanity. Your ability to overcome, to accept people for who they are, and to live and give without judgment inspires me. I'm so grateful to have you in my life.

To my husband Brad Bayer who for twenty plus years has supported me with love and kindness and made countless sacrifices so that I could pursue my professional goals. Bear, thank you for co-authoring my life story and I look forward to what the next chapter brings.

And lastly, to my beautiful daughter Denby Bayer, through your very wise 14 year old eyes, I see the hope and joy the future holds. If I ever need a reason to bring my best self to every opportunity, every conversation, and every interaction, every day- you're it. I love you like crazy cakes.

# ACKNOWLEDGEMENTS

Kent Roberts, Co-founder and Director of the Civility Center **www. civiltycenter.org**. You inspire me with your dedication to building better communities. I am grateful for your mentorship and generosity of spirit.

My admiration and respect to Russ Charvonia, who in choosing civility and taking the road less traveled started a civility movement in his organization.

Justin Sachs, CEO Motivational Press. Thanks to you and your team for your mentorship, patience and support throughout the process of bringing *The 30% Solution* to print. **www.motivationalpress.com**

Kara Wright, Operations Manager at Workplace Education Manitoba, www.wem.mb.ca . Your approach to leadership exemplifies civility. I'm hard pressed to recall a day when I didn't learn something from you.

Sandi Howell, my gratitude for your having taught me the power of Essential Skills and for pushing me to thinking differently. I'm proud to have worked with you.

To Olen Juarez-Lim who has been my trusted friend and colleague for many years, thank you for your contribution on Professional Presence. Truly, one need only be in the room with you to understand that civility is who you are, not just something you do.

# OVERVIEW

*The 30% Solution - How Civility at Work Increases Retention, Engagement and Profitability*, provides essential information, facts, stories, insights from the field, and practical tips related to the business of civility. The book represents a ready-to-use tool kit with practical applications for:

- » Business consultants
- » Performance and productivity analysts
- » Workplace trainers
- » Social and communication training facilitators
- » Customer service experts
- » Business owners, managers, supervisors, and individuals who want to build a better workplace

After reading this book, you can immediately start building a culture of civility in your workplace by incorporating some or all of the tools provided in the book, including:

- » Applying insights from the leading civility experts to your current workplace
- » Identifying and adopting a practical definition of civility
- » Assessing the extent to which incivility is impacting your bottom line
- » Understanding trends and other influences that are impacting how we work
- » Incorporating training plans that build 4 core competencies essential to fostering civility at work

» Reviewing up-to-date resources, recommended reading, and reference materials to help you build your expertise in the area of civility

» Utilizing tip sheets, checklists, quizzes, mini-assessments and other tools provided in the book

## HOW TO USE THIS BOOK:

It is strongly recommended that you read the entire book beginning to end so that you can understand better how all the elements fit together. Then, review the chapters one-by-one and complete any practice sheets or recommended reading that might be included. And take time to review the sources and resources at the end of the book- these will help you as you choose civility for yourself, your team, and your organization.

# WHY THIS BOOK? AND WHY NOW?

*"The mass of men lead lives of quiet desperation."*
- Henry David Thoreau

I f Henry David Thoreau were experiencing life at work today and over the next decade as we make our way towards 2025, I suspect he'd agree with me that the mass of men, and women, are not so quiet in their desperation.

How do I know people are desperate? Because people who are not desperate surely behave better than how a great many men and women are behaving these days. I have to believe there's a good reason for what seems to be wide-spread habitual disregard for others, and for property, and for resources. Of course I realize everyone is entitled to forget his/her manners from time to time or to have a bad day every now and then. It's forgivable that sometimes we crack under pressure, have an occasional outburst, or use poor judgment. These are things I can understand. I can also understand that some people are just plain mean, and that a few others are wholly incapable of kindness.

However, given the scope and frequency of incivility, there has to be some explanation beyond stating that we're *only* human, for all the bad behavior in our workplaces and elsewhere. In case you weren't aware, research focusing on both Canadian and U.S. companies shows that a whopping 98% of people polled have experienced uncivil behavior on the job[1]. And according to the fourth annual study on *Civility in America: A Nationwide Survey*, conducted by global public relations firm Weber Shandwick and public affairs firm Powell Tate in partnership with KRC Research, civility in America continues to erode. This year's study found that 70% of Americans believe incivility has reached crisis proportions. With Americans encountering incivility an average of 2.4 times a day, dealing with incivility has become a way of life for many. Alarmingly, 81% of Americans think that incivility is leading to an increase in violence.[2] Are we surprised?

» 8.5 is the average number of times American's encounter incivility in real life/offline in a week. (I'm sure this isn't too far off for Canadians, or Australians or Brits or Filipinos or any other cultural group, anywhere else in the world.)

» 26% of people have quit a job because it was an uncivil workplace. (Just imagine how many more want to quit- but can't. How do you think that impacts them and/or the organization?)

» In a recent Canadian study of a diverse occupational sample of 180 workers in the Canadian prairies, 40%" polled reported experiencing at least 1 of 45 specific acts indicative of psychological harassment or bullying on a weekly basis for at least 6 months. An additional 10% of the sample reported experiencing 5 or more such acts on a weekly basis for at least 6 months.[3] (Wow, it's a wonder we get any work done at all, as it seems many of us are very busy bullying others or busy being bullied.)

---

1   https://hbr.org/2013/01/the-price-of-incivility/

2   http://www.webershandwick.com/news/article/civility-in-america-2013-incivility-has-reached-crisis-levels

3   http://www.gov.mb.ca/labour/labmgt/emp_standards/submissions/lee.pdf (Lee & Brotheridge, 2005)

Think about this for a minute.

a) You are experiencing psychological harassment and/or bullying on a weekly basis.

b) On top of this harassment and/or bullying, you're also experiencing general rudeness 2.4 times a day.

c) This combination of harassment and bullying carries on for up to 6 months with no end in sight.

d) For a range of reasons, you do not have the option to quit your job.

Do you think you're going to end up feeling desperate?

Do you think this stress might impact your outlook, your communication, your approach to working with others, the extent to which you trust people, and/or your motivation to be nice?

I have absolutely no doubt that it will.

Sadly, in politics, in sports, in our communities, in schools, and in our workplaces, incivility is the new normal. While most of us don't need to see the research to know this is true, there is a growing body of evidence screaming out that incivility is at an all-time high.

And so, temporary lapses in judgment and minor social errors aside, whether it's road rage, theft, disrespect for time, harsh tone in communication, absence of common courtesy, flagrant self-promotion, a general lack of restraint, sloppy dress, quick judgment, petty grievances, assuming the worst, gossip, negativity, and the list goes on... I concur with Thoreau in stating that many of us are desperate. And I suggest that this desperation is a key contributing factor to incivility. I'd like to believe that if we could alleviate the desperation, most of us would behave better, that we really want to be better, but just can't - due to circumstances seemingly beyond our control. The alternative is that we really are just a self-absorbed, immature, lazy, and socially incompetent lot who do not care about anyone but ourselves. I don't want to believe that, so I'm going with desperation.

Again, for the record, I truly believe that most of us would choose civility were it not for our desperation.

## WHERE IS ALL THIS DESPERATION COMING FROM?

If the statistics outlined in this chapter are any indication, WORK seems to be at the root of the problem. The majority of us are physically exhausted, stressed, and over-extended. And many of us are miserable in our jobs. We're worn down and less resilient than we once were. We're burnt out. Our health is at stake, our home lives are suffering. We don't have the time or energy to take care of ourselves, so the idea that we would extend courtesies or consideration to take care of others seems a cost many of us simply cannot bear.

To meet the demands of our fast-paced, demanding, and ever-changing work lives, we've resorted to bad habits. I describe these habits as the "coping selfies"; self-preservation, self-righteousness, self-promotion, self-centeredness, self-pity, self-denial, self-destruction, and so on. These selfies represent many of the "social survival" behaviors desperate people engage in. These habits result in individuals addressing their self-interests at the expense of others. Overall, we're exercising significantly less respect, less restraint, and less responsibility. These are the three tenants that underpin civility- this according to Dr. Pier Forni, Professor at Johns Hopkins, and author of *"Choose Civility"*. Over the past 17 years training, researching, and speaking on civility in the workplace, I am convinced that the conditions and cultures of our workplaces are causing much of the desperation the mass of men and women are experiencing these days.

Notably, 80% of people are dissatisfied with their jobs[4].

25% of employees say work is their main source of stress and 40% say

---

[4]   http://www.businessinsider.com/disturbing-facts-about-your-job-2011-2?op=1#ixzz3XCZH6nbq

their job is "very or extremely stressful"[5]. This stress impacts our health- for example, in the UK over 13 million working days are lost every year because of stress. Stress is believed to trigger 70% of visits to doctors, and 85% of serious illnesses[6].

Work is actually killing us. In Japan, shockingly, 10,000 workers per year literally drop dead at their desks as a result of 60- to 70-hour work weeks in Japan. The phenomenon is known as "karoshi"[7].

Work demands are impacting our work-life balance, for example, each year the average American spends over 100 hours commuting[8], and 64% of Americans canceled vacations last year. One-third did it for work-related reasons even though most felt they were more in need of a vacation than the year before[9]. It's hard to catch up on your life if you're losing time just getting to work, and hard to de-stress if you can't take a vacation.

Stress at work also impacts our relationships. According to the Human Solutions Report, *Under Pressure*, respondents indicated that on average job stress accounted for 73% of their overall life stress. Further, 59% of respondents said that the quality of their home and family life was sometimes impacted by job stress and 16% said that job stress frequently impacted their personal and family life[10].

With a whopping 96% of employees polled in a workplace study conducted by Pearson and Porath[11], experiencing rudeness at work, and knowing that the majority of people say stress at work is the largest contributor to their overall stress, it's not unreasonable to infer that rudeness is contributing to the stress. And, it's easy to see that work simply isn't much fun for a lot of people.

---

5   Quality of Working Life' report from Chartered Management Institute and Workplace Health Connect

6   UK HSE stress statistics

7   http://www.economist.com/node/10329261

8   http://usgovinfo.about.com/od/censusandstatistics/a/commutetimes.htm

9   http://www.businessinsider.com/64-canceled-vacation-this-year-2010-9

10  http://www.grahamlowe.ca/documents/182/Under%20Pressure%2010-06.pdf

11  https://hbr.org/2013/01/the-price-of-incivility/

## SO WHY EXACTLY ARE OUR WORKPLACES SO STRESSFUL?

Good question. And there's not an easy answer. I suspect the reasons vary depending on the workplace and on the people involved.

We can blame change. For example, the factors below could have impact:

» downsizing and restructuring

» labor shortages

» outsourcing

» demographic shifts at work related to generations and cultures that make up the work team

» economic insecurity

» technology – and keeping up with the pace of change

» trends in work style, e.g., mobile executives, job-share programs

Overall, there seems to be much concern about job security. On average, Americans hold seven to eight different jobs before age 30[12]. It's difficult to settle in and build rapport, never mind loyalty, if everyone's constantly got one foot out the door. And difficult for employers to commit to training and long-term work contracts if they perceive a lack of loyalty or longevity in their work team.

Maybe it's a lack of leadership. After all, 25% of managers who admitted to having behaved badly said they were uncivil because their leaders—their own role models—were rude[13]. And, in a survey of 1000 American Executives, Michelle McQuaid, a leader in Positive Psychology interventions, found that only 35% of Americans are happy at their jobs. 65% say a better boss would make them happy. And only 35% say a pay raise will do the same thing[14].

Trust could be the reason. In *Edelman's Trust Barometer,* where results from 31, 000 respondents representing 26 markets around the world

---

12  http://www.businessinsider.com/disturbing-facts-about-your-job-2011-2?op=1#ixzz3XCZfQwgq

13  https://hbr.org/2013/01/the-price-of-incivility/

14  http://www.forbes.com/sites/tykiisel/2012/10/16/65-of-americans-choose-a-better-boss-over-a-raise-heres-why/

were gathered, only 18% of those surveyed trust business leaders to tell the truth. That is just slightly higher than the statistic for trusting government officials, which was only 13%[15].

Or could it be our state of mind? Has all the stress and struggle to balance or get ahead left us physically less hardy and psychologically and emotionally less resilient? Job stress is increasingly recognized as a determinant of employee health and productivity. The experience of chronic stress is used in theoretical models as a predictor of increased risk of mental and physical problems, including chronic conditions such as heart disease, asthma, migraines, and ulcers[16].

Alarmingly, depression will rank second only to heart disease as the leading cause of disability worldwide by the year 2020, which can impact the workplace in areas such as bottom-line production and team work[17].

Is it possible that we are literally too sick and tired to be nice? Maybe.

In my humble opinion, all of these things: leadership, trust, economics, and stress, in endless combinations, are causal factors that impact civility in the workplace. But I also believe that adults at work have the ability to make choices. In many cases, it would seem that we have the power to better manage some of these causal factors, but we choose not to. Instead, we default to "desperate" behavior habits where:

» the immediacy of action overrides the intelligence and/or rele-vance of the action

» our focus is on the act and method of communicating such that what we are actually communicating loses its value

» the quantity of interactions becomes more important than the quality of those interactions

---

15  http://www.edelman.com/insights/intellectual-property/trust-2013/

16  Handbook of Work Stress, Barling, Kelloway and Frone, eds., 2005.

17  J. Samra, M. Gilbert, M. Shain & D. Bilsker. Centre for Applied Research in Mental Health and Addiction (CARMHA).

Some default behavior is a result of laziness. Some of it is due to excuse-making or a lack of accountability, and I'll even allow for a bit of ignorance here and there. But much of it, I believe, is due to a lack of thinking. Dr. Forni, stated in *The Thinking Life*, that "...*deep thinking is the illustrious casualty in the digital revolution....*" I believe this is very true of our time. In this technological age, we are focused on things and neglect people as a result. We seem to care more about connections than connecting and we are often uncivil because we rely on our devices to do our thinking for us, and as a result are in the habit of not thinking for ourselves. We don't consider the impact of our words and actions beyond the short-term, and we don't consider the impact to others. We've stopped thinking, so we've started making bad decisions. And then because we continue not to think, we're not learning from our mistakes, and so the cycle continues.

## ▌ SO, HOW DO WE SOLVE THE PROBLEM OF INCIVILITY AT WORK?

In the *Baltimore Workplace Civility Study*, 83%of respondents agreed that it was "very important" to their well-being, to their health, to their performance, and to their job satisfaction to work in a civil environment[18]. So there's our answer. Civility! Civility is the solution.

> *To solve the incivility problem in our workplaces, we need to change how we work. We need to create workplaces that support a culture of learning where thinking is best practice. We need to build a capacity for civil behavior by giving people the skills they need to make better decisions, and to contribute to reducing the stress and incivility in our workplaces. We need to imbed civility in our workplace policies and procedures, into our organizational values and mission statements, into our job descriptions and codes of conduct, and into our hiring and evaluation practices. Civility has to become a core element*

---

18  https://www.ubalt.edu/jfi/jfi/reports/civility.PDF

*in the character of our organizations. Stated directly, civility in the workplace is a change imperative for organizations expecting to survive, and thrive, in the new world of work.*

Lew Bayer, President, Civility Experts Worldwide

The statement above was the impetus for writing this book. I truly believe civility at work is the solution for reducing desperation and building better workplaces. And I don't believe I am alone in coming to this conclusion.

Dr. Forni, Professor, Johns Hopkins and author of *Choose Civility* states:

*"It's not unreasonable to predict that lower-stress workplaces-workplaces, that is, where a culture of civility makes for better relationships among coworkers-will become very appealing. These are the workplaces where organizations will manage to attract and retain an increasing number of first-rate workers. And this should be a strong incentive for organizations to promote a culture of civility in their workplaces. Encouraging civility in the workplace is becoming one of the fundamental corporate goals in our diverse, hurried, stressed, and litigation-prone society. A civil workplace is good for workers, since the workers' quality of life is improved in such an environment. But a civil workplace is also good for the customers, since the quality of the service they receive form happier and more relaxed service providers is improved.[19]"*

Graham Lowe, Human Solutions states:

*"Employees' quality of work-life is becoming a business issue. Leading employers are recognizing that positive work-life outcomes for employees are key ingredients of a successful business strategy.[20]"*

Kent Roberts and Jay Newman, co-founders of the National Civility Center and authors of *Community Weaving* state:

*"If we are serious about confronting today's challenges, we must also be*

19  https://www.ubalt.edu/jfi/jfi/reports/civility.PDF

20  http://www.grahamlowe.ca/documents/182/Under%20Pressure%2010-06.pdf

*proactive in helping individuals and organizations develop the capacity needed to change their communities' culture and environment. To solve fundamental problems, we must do more than address the symptoms.[21]"*

Roberts and Newman's focus was on communities but I see the workplace as a community of sorts and so agree with their suggestion that capacity building requires that we be proactive versus reactive. In *Community Weaving*, Roberts and Newman illustrate the difference between proactive and reactive response in Figure 2, below.

| Proactive responses focus on…. | Reactive responses focus on…. |
| --- | --- |
| Fundamental problems | Symptoms |
| Underlying issues and structures | Crises and behaviors of concern |
| Long-term solutions | Short-term solutions |
| Results that evolve | Immediate results |
| Changes to culture, environment | No real change |
| Capacity building | Fixing problems |
| Broad citizen involvement | Involvement of service providers |
| Equality | and recipients with divisions |
| Systems thinking Patterns | between experts and clients |
| | Random problem solving |
| | Isolated events |

Figure 2. Source: Community Weaving, page 13, Roberts & Newman, 2003

In *The 30% Solution* we echo the sentiments of Roberts and so offer organizations a proactive civility solution- a structured plan for changing their workplace culture. I maintain that organizations must plan, and then implement, this type of change. Or, in not doing so, they must expect to pay the high costs of incivility in their workplaces.

---

21   Roberts & Newman, Community Weaving, published by National Civility Center, 2003

Through proper assessment, defining civility, applying the Civility Culture Compass®, and training based on the Civility Competency Matrix®, I believe you can create change-ready, socially intelligent, systems-thinking, culturally competent, knowledgeable workers and as a result, better manage the causes of incivility and desperation in your workplaces.

**The benefits of incorporating civility into the workplace, as detailed in research by Weber and Shadwick,[22] include up to 30% more revenue than competitors and four times increased likelihood that employees will be highly engaged. Further, civility training could result in your organization being 20% more likely to report reduced turnover – all of these outcomes are both measurable and significant.**

How the book is organized:

### CHAPTER 1 - TIME FOR CHANGE

» Evidence that Incivility is Rampant

» Civility in the Workplace Initiatives- Changing Workplace Culture

» Elements of a Successful Civility Initiative

» Civility in the Workplace is About Change

» Symptoms of Viral Incivility

» Readiness as an Indicator of Success for Civility Initiatives

» The Civility Initiative Process at a Glance

---

22  http://www.webershandwick.com/uploads/news/files/Civility_in_America_2011.pdf

## CHAPTER 2 - DEFINING CIVILITY

» Outcomes of Civility Training

» Dictionary Definitions of Civility

» Civility Experts Worldwide Definition of Civility

» The Difference Between Civility, Courtesy, Etiquette and Manners

» How Does Civility Relate to Values?

» Isn't Civility the Same Thing as Character?

» How is Being Civil Different from Showing Respect?

» The Difference Between Civility and Ethics

» Civility and Emotional Intelligence

» Civility and Positive Psychology

» Civility and Being Nice

## CHAPTER 3 - THE BUSINESS CASE

» Introducing Value of Civility Training to the Boss

» Strategies for Persuading Others that Civility is Important

» Assertions Made in Presenting Evidence that Civility Training Works

» What are Soft Skills?

» Han's List of Soft Skills

» What the Research Shows About Soft Skills Relative to Technical Skills

» Soft skills are Essential Skills

» Civility requires Essential Skills

» What will Successful Training Look Like?

» Three Parts to Devising an Evaluation Plan

- » Checklist of Personal Values
- » I Choose Civility: Steps to Adopting Civility as a Core Personal Value Worksheet
- » Soft Skills and Civility Checklist
- » Essential Skills Case Study
- » Civility Compass Questionnaire
- » Sample Civility Assessments
- » Civility Self -Assessment
- » Maslow's Needs Chart and Activity
- » Group Temperature Activity
- » Kirkpatrick Model Diagram
- » Continuous Learning Assessment
- » Systems Thinking Overview
- » Cultural Competence Continuum
- » An exercise in Commonality
- » Workplace Toxicity Exercise
- » Civility Culture General Assessment
- » Excerpt on Stress at Work

### SOURCES AND RESOURCES

- » Listing for each Chapter included

If you are a consultant or workplace Trainer who wants to achieve a Civility at Work® Train the Trainer Certificate and/or acquire a License to use the Civility Culture Compass© or the Civility Competency Matrix© training tool and materials, please` contact pr@civilityexperts.com or visit www.civilityexperts.com

# CHAPTER 1

# TIME FOR CHANGE

We are smack in the middle of a civility crises. With research on both Canadian and U.S. companies showing that a whopping 98% of people have experienced uncivil behavior on the job,[1] rudeness in the workplace is systemic and epidemic. Evidence that the incivility virus impacts among other things: our productivity, our ability to work together, our creativity, and our health, is growing every day.

And incivility isn't just a North American problem. A few examples:

A study of British workers found that 40% had experienced incivility or disrespect over a two-year period, with such behavior particularly common in the public sector.[2]

In a study of Australian workers, researchers from Edith Cowan University found that 70% had experienced rudeness or mistreatment by their coworkers.[3]

A Canadian study by Bar-David Consulting and *Canadian HR Reporter* shows incivility affects key business indicators as reported by Human Resource professionals:

---

1   https://hbr.org/2013/01/the-price-of-incivility/

2   http://www.bbc.com/capital/story/20140401-how-rude-why-polite-pays

3   http://www.sciencewa.net.au/topics/social-science/item/2174-reactions-to-workplace-incivili-ty-explored/2174-reactions-to-workplace-incivility-explored

90% say it hurts collaboration

78% say it affects talent retention

52% say it affects brand reputation

92% agree incivility has negative effects on productivity

80% report an impact on absenteeism[4].

Data collected from employees from various organizations in Singapore shows that incivility is not a rare phenomenon in Asian cultures.[5]

Results of study of Korean workplaces offered evidence of a positive relationship between the experience of workplace incivility and the intention to leave the organization. More specifically, it was found that if one experiences workplace incivility, then he/she is more likely to leave the organization.[6]

I'm sure if we kept digging we could find statistics about the negative impact of incivility in workplaces around the globe.

One of the statistics I found particularly concerning was that 43% of Millennials (generation born 1980's to early 2000) reported *expecting* to experience incivility in the next 24 hours. Not surprising really, as the study also showed that regardless of our age, most of us experience incivility an average of 2.4 times a day. It's no wonder then, that more than 50% of people polled said they believe civility will get worse in the next few years.[7]

Yikes....things can get worse? Should we not already be very concerned that a whole generation of future leaders is growing accustomed to living and working in a world where bullying, a lack of respect and restraint, uncivil discourse, racism, and countless other toxic behaviors are the norm? Has the incivility virus become so strong that living with it is easier than fighting it?

---

4   2011 survey on workplace incivility by Bar-David Consulting and Canadian HR Reporter, http://www.benefitscanada.com/benefits/health-wellness/benefits-column-the-impact-of-workplace-incivility-62273

5   http://www.ncbi.nlm.nih.gov/pubmed/21280947

6   http://library.iated.org/view/SHIM2011REL

7   https://www.webershandwick.com/uploads/news/files/Civility_in_America_2013_Exec_Summary.pdf

Given that the average person spends 90,000 hours at work[8] over his/her lifetime, it is not a stretch to surmise that the workplace is where many of us catch the incivility virus. And then we're taking it home and passing it on.

Researchers from Baylor University confirm that people who endure incivility at work often take that stress home with them. And this can have negative effects on their family and marriages -- and even potentially impact their spouses' jobs. The researchers explained that when employees go home stressed and distracted, their partners must often pick up the slack and assume more family responsibilities. These greater demands at home may then interfere with that spouse's performance at work. *"This research underlines the importance of stopping incivility before it starts so that the ripple effect of incivility does not impact the employee's family,"* said study author Merideth Ferguson, assistant professor of management and entrepreneurship at the Baylor University Hankamer School of Business in a university news release. *"Otherwise"*, she said, *"...the toxic atmosphere at work may potentially inflict further damage beyond the workplace...and cross over into the workplace of the partner."*

In surveying 190 full-time workers and their partners, the researchers also found that stress took a toll on the workers' marriages. Complicating matters, they noted that 75% of these couples had children living in their household. The study's authors argued that organizations must address the far-reaching and detrimental effects that ugly behavior in the workplace can have among employees and their families[9].

It's not too difficult to imagine that once the virus is in our homes and our families are infected, that it is then spread to our neighbours and to the people we interact with directly or indirectly at the grocery store or when visiting the school, at church, or on our vacations, etc. If road rage,

---

8    http://www.businessinsider.com/disturbing-facts-about-your-job-2011-2?op=1

9    *https://www.baylor.edu/mediacommunications/news.php?action=story&story=98313;* published online in the Journal of Organizational Behavior.

petty crime, poor customer service, fraud, bullying in the workplace, a lack of restraint in the public forum, parents behaving badly at children's sporting events and so on, are not indications of the contagious aspect of incivility, I don't know what is.

## ▌ EVIDENCE THAT INCIVILITY IS IN FACT RAMPANT:

A recent Civility in America Poll showed that 94% of people believe incivility is a problem in America, with 65% of those agreeing that incivility has risen to crisis levels, and 79% overall agreeing that uncivil behavior leads to increased violence.[10]

In a survey by British Columbia, Canada based Insights West, the majority of respondents had, over the previous month, witnessed public swearing (87%), a child misbehaving without parental intervention (76%), public spitting (72%), and the use of cellphones during a movie (53%).

Poor parenting was cited as a culprit by 93% of respondents, followed by the influence of technology, at 84%. Among Canadians 18 to 34, 70% said someone had written something rude on their Facebook page, directed a mean tweet at them, or been disrespectful to them elsewhere online.

Prior to the Vancouver, Canada Olympics, volunteers participated in a kind of civility boot camp, aimed at fostering such skills as attentive listening and conflict management. And looking to the nation's bleachers, more than 65,000 Canadians have participated in Respect in Sport's parent program, a behavioral training initiative – made mandatory by many sport bodies – designed to prevent infighting among overzealous moms and dads.[11]

At present, both workplace and public incivility have gotten so out of control that we seem unable to manage ourselves, so governments are getting involved. For example, there has been increasing recognition

---

10  Research by Weber Shandwick and public affairs firm Powell Tate with KRC Research, Civility in America Study 2014.

11  http://www.insightswest.com/; http://www.insightswest.com/?s=+civility

in Canada that interpersonal mistreatment – ranging from incivility to harassment to bullying – is highly problematic for organizations, and consequently, legislation forbidding abusive behaviour at work has appeared in several Canadian provinces.[12]

Leaders are now tasked with the goal of creating an organizational climate that prohibits these behaviors, (referencing bullying specifically) but often approach the problem solely from the perspective of regulatory compliance. [13]

To date, 49 American states have anti-bullying laws on the books requiring school districts to adopt anti-bullying policies.[14]

The incivility virus is evidently prevalent beyond North America too. In Australia, as of January 1, 2014, anyone in a constitutionally covered business who perceives he/she is being bullied at work can file a claim with the national workplace relations tribunal, called the Fair Work Commission[15].

Germany's so-called "insult law" not only criminalizes hate speech but also broad conduct showing disrespect for another person – including flipping someone off in traffic. In France, the state-owned railway tasked a team of "polite police" with cracking down on rude passengers after noting a 25% increase in traveler complaints. And in Singapore, a person can be fined for everything from spitting on the sidewalk to not flushing a public toilet.[16]

On October 1, 2013, the Chinese government passed new regulations that require Chinese traveling abroad to watch their manners. Section

---

12  Jana Raver is an Associate Professor and E. Marie Shantz Faculty Fellow in Organizational Behaviour at Queen's School of Business; http://business.queensu.ca/executiveeducation/webinars/workplace_bullying.php

13  Jana Raver is an Associate Professor and E. Marie Shantz Faculty Fellow in Organizational Behaviour at Queen's School of Business, http://business.queensu.ca/executiveeducation/webinars/workplace_bullying.php

14  https://antibullyingsoftware.com/anti-bullying-laws/

15  https://www.fwc.gov.au/resolving-issues-disputes-and-dismissals/workplace-issues-disputes/anti-bullying

16  Compiled and written by Misty Harris, published online. http://o.canada.com/life/rudeness

13 instructs, "Tourists shall respect public order and social morality in tourism activities, respect the local customs, cultural traditions and religious beliefs, take care of tourism resources, protect the ecological environment and respect the norms of civilized tourist behaviours."

Public courtesy is extremely important in Japan. There is for example, Tokyo Metro's "Ie de Yaro" (Do it at Home) poster campaign, which goes some way toward showing how important manners are in Japanese commuting life by depicting various anti-social acts such as falling asleep drunk, taking seats meant for disabled or elderly passengers, or applying make-up on the train, and politely asks "Please do it at home."[17]

In the Philippines, an "Anti-bullying Act"[18] requires all elementary and secondary schools to adopt policies to prevent and address the acts of bullying in their institutions.

On March 1, 2013, Shenzhen in China implemented a Civilized Behavior Promotion Law. Based on this law, government can enforce prohibition of ten specific public behaviors deemed to be uncivilized. These behaviors include spitting in public, smoking in a designated non-smoking area, failing to clean up pets' excrement in public, and damaging public sanitation facilities.[19]

Incivility is almost commonplace in many of our homes, communities, and workplaces. And when you consider that it's also commonplace in homes, cities, and workplaces all over the world, it may be accurate to say that incivility has reached pandemic proportions.

## IT'S TIME FOR CHANGE

Usually I would say that civility starts at home - at least it should - with each of us choosing to be our own best self before expecting the same

---

17  http://www.japantoday.com/category/lifestyle/view/switching-to-manner-mode-the-importance-of-social-etiquette-in-urban-japan

18  http://www.gov.ph/2013/09/12/republic-act-no-10627/

19  http://beijingcream.com/2013/01/shenzhen-rolls-out-legislation-to-enforce-civilized-behavior/

of others. But I recognize that many people do not really know what civility means, and even if they do, they're unsure how to apply it. Or, they know what civility is, but they've given up exhibiting it because they are exhausted and stressed out from working in toxic, uncivil workplaces where their efforts to be civil are neither recognized nor rewarded.

Since work is something most of us can relate to, and because, as referenced earlier, 98% of people reported experiencing incivility on the job, the workplace seems like the right place to start doing things differently.

## CIVILITY IN THE WORKPLACE INITIATIVES – CHANGING ORGANIZATIONAL CULTURES

At Civility Experts Worldwide, our approach is to look at civility in the workplace as a change initiative. In and of itself, this might seem an obvious strategy, but it's not applied as frequently, or instituted as simply, as you might think.

The fact is, when we begin to understand what causes incivility, and when we start to track the nature and frequency of uncivil behavior (as defined for a particular workplace- more on Defining Civility in Chapter 2) we begin to see patterns. Many of these are well-ingrained behaviors and habits of mind. Further, many of these negative and/or uncivil patterns are actually endorsed through, and facilitated by, the organization's processes and procedures.

Expecting that we can change deep-set attitudes, thinking patterns, and behaviors just by posting anti-bullying posters in the lunch room, and/ or requiring employees to attend a 3-8 hour awareness raising seminars, is just not realistic. And to expect these remedies to result in positive change that takes hold quickly, and sticks amidst personnel, workplace priority, and ongoing contextual changes, doesn't seem at all reasonable.

Yes, awareness raising is important but it's not nearly enough.

Unfortunately, this is where many organizations drop the ball. Frequently, efforts to build respect in the workplace consist of the following:

a) Creating, or adopting a ready-made, "Respectful Workplace Policy." These policies usually include:

» Scope of the policy- a description of who it applies to (who can use it).

» Definitions of terms such as: Discriminatory Harassment, Personal Harassment, Accommodation, Bullying, Racism, Respect, Sexism, Hostile Work Environment, Sexual Harassment, etc.

» A list of the goals of the policy which are usually to:

▶ raise awareness of employee and employer rights and obligations

▶ prevent disrespectful and illegal behaviors

▶ set forth fair and consistent procedures related to respect at work

▶ encourage individuals to utilize internal and presumably impartial, supports to resolve complaints

▶ detect signs and symptoms of harassment, bias, and discrimination

» Guidelines for behavior, for example: listings of prohibited behavior and standards outlining expected behavior

» Reference to, and excerpts from, Human Rights Codes, Labour Codes, and other local, provincial, state, and federal legislation

» Details for a complaint process

» Responsibilities and accountabilities, e.g., of management and of individuals related to the policy

» Procedures and protocol for dealing with breeches of the policy

» Contact information for resources inside and outside of the organization

Note: *If you don't have a Respectful Workplace Policy and you would like to devise one, we have include a template created by the Petroleum Human Resources Council of Canada in Chapter 9- Tools You Can Use.

b) Rolling out the aforementioned Respectful Workplace Policy either because the organization is required to have one, or as an after-the-fact response to an increase in harassment or bullying complaints.

c) Requiring employees attend Respect in the Workplace training which is largely about raising awareness that the Policy exists and introducing the terminology and rules outlined in the policy.

d) Failing to teach alternative and pre-emptive behaviors and instead focusing on how to respond to and manage incivility *after* it has become a serious issue, e.g., at the point where you can call it racism or label it as bullying or harassment.

e) Offering generic, catch-all seminars such as emotional intelligence, leadership and values, communication skills, conflict management, and/or how to deal with bullying.

f) Promoting activities or events such as "Anti-bullying Week" or "National Manners Day" concurrent with rolling out a Respectful Workplace Policy.

g) Offering incentives or rewards that celebrate an individual employee and his/her specific behavior but neglect to tie the behavior to superordinate goals and/or to ensure there is measurable impact of the behavior. Examples of this would be things like the "Kindest Co-worker" award or an "I'm a Good Apple" type campaign whereby employees might acknowledge each other for respectful behavior with little red apple lapel pins and the like, but they are not necessarily clear on why these behaviors are useful on the job, or how they benefit the organization.

I'm not saying that these efforts are not of any value. There's no question, for example, that in certain situations conflict management training is necessary and effective. I do think however, that assuming conflict is the root cause and/or an obvious solution to addressing incivility in the workplace can be a mistake. The same goes for assuming that culturally diverse or mixed generation teams who don't work well together *must* need sensitivity training. As stand-alone offerings, my experience has been that many of these traditional training options when applied specifically as solutions to addressing incivility at work offer predominately short-term, incomplete remedies.

Additionally, while I agree that Respect at Work Policies can be helpful. Simply having a respectful workplace policy does not guarantee a more respectful workplace. My view on this is validated by research findings in the *ProActive ReSolutions Workplace Survey*[20] . 8000 employees and managers who were asked to provide feedback related to the effectiveness of their Respectful Workplace Policy. Some of the survey outcomes include:

» 31% of respondents weren't aware of their organization's respectful workplace policies.

» Of the 69% who were aware of the policy, 58% said their organizations hadn't prepared them to respond appropriately when they were being treated with disrespect, specifically:

  ▸ 55% said their organizations had not prepared them to respond appropriately to behavior that made them feel uncomfortable.

  ▸ 58% said their organizations had not prepared them to respond appropriately when they were being treated with disrespect.

  ▸ 64% said their organizations had not prepared them to respond appropriately when they were fearful of being ridiculed or belittled.

» 32% said they were aware of 2-5 past incidents of disrespectful behavior.

---

20  http://proactive-resolutions.com/about/respectful-workplace-policies-facts-statistics/

Again, I would recommend that organizations have Respectful Workplace Policy, but having one is just one part of a comprehensive civility in the workplace plan.

Before implementing such a plan, an organization's leadership must understand that civility at work is at first a *values* (defining character statement) proposition in that the organization has to choose and define civility as a core value. And then it also becomes a *value* (having worth) proposition in that, leadership must be able to devise a persuasive argument as to why employees should buy into the notion of a respectful workplace.

Everyone in the organization has to have some understanding of what civility means in terms of day-to-day life on the job. Ideally every individual in the organization (and at the very least the change-makers) need to be convinced that imbedding a culture of civility into the workplace is of value- to the individual, to the team, to the customer, to the organization, and even to the community. They also have to believe that civility presents the best solution for resolving whatever organizational culture problems may have been identified. The benefits of civility, as well as the costs and consequences of incivility, have to be outlined in detail. (More on the Business Case for Civility in Chapter 3.)

In organizations where there is not a culture of learning, or where incivility has been consciously or unconsciously incorporated into operations and daily activities, training the front-line to be respectful in and of itself rarely results in significant and lasting change. Delivering respectful workplace training alone, without putting the other pieces that make up a comprehensive change initiative in place, is rarely effective in building a better workplace.

The Enterprise & Economic Development Glossary[21] defines a change initiative as *"A series of actions taken to implement a transformation process which should properly begin with planning, then proceeding*

---

21 http://www.findmehere.com/search/dictionary/c/change_process.htm

*with communicating as operational implementation, solving problems, evaluating situations and making decisions."*

Further, they describe change as, *". . . continuous transformation through time, thus keeping all things in a variable state."*

I like this definition because it captures two important points that I believe are fundamental to a successful workplace civility initiative.

## ELEMENTS OF A SUCCESSFUL CIVILITY/CHANGE INITIATIVE

#1: First, we must understand and acknowledge that to take root, a civility change initiative must be strategic, well-planned, and long-term, and there has to be a clarified rationale for civility in the workplace. (This will make more sense after you define civility- more on this in Chapter 2.) Just like most change initiatives, incorporating civility into your workplace culture is going to take some time, money, and energy. You'll likely have to delegate people, and resources and you'll have to manage both the process and the people sides of the change. To be successful, you will have to have a plan that includes identifying stakeholders, assigning roles, completing assessments, setting goals, implementing the plan, delivering alignment communications, planning and delivering training, and evaluating. How complex and costly each of those components are will depend on the context and on your business priorities. To be clear, when we talk about how complex a civility initiative might be, we are referring to how many components are included in the plan. This is different from the level of difficulty or how complicated the initiative might be. Civility as a change initiative might be complex in that there are a lot of components to consider, but it isn't necessarily complicated.

#2: Second, we must understand and acknowledge that the work will be ongoing and continuous. The reality is, due to the fact that the situation, the people, the priorities, and the conditions in a workplace are constantly changing, you are never really finished with civility as a change initiative. Let me repeat that, there is no end point. You are NEVER really finished with civility as a change initiative. And this is an extremely important realization. I believe that this realization is one of the biggest barriers most organizations face in moving forward with civility initiatives. Planning and implementation can be very hard work initially. It is going to cost some time and money and you have to be wholly committed long-term. This can be prohibitive for some. But if you can get past this hurdle, and if use the Civility Culture Compass® - discussed in Chapter 5 as your guide, you will be successful. And the rewards are often immutable, measurable, positive, and significant.

**CIVILITY IN THE WORKPLACE IS ABOUT CHANGE. OKAY. BUT, WE DEAL WITH CHANGE ALL THE TIME, SO WHY IS THIS A BIT DEAL?**

The big deal is that 70% of change initiatives fail.[22] Somewhere along the way, the change management strategies and processes we've been using have become ineffective. 70% is a lot of failure. And a lot of time, a lot of resources, a lot of frustration, and a lot of desperation. (You may recall from the Introduction how problematic desperation can be.)

Where this failure applies to civility initiatives, I've come to understand, that there are two main reasons organizational civility projects fail. This understanding could potentially be applied to other types of change initiatives but for the moment we are of course focusing on civility as a change initiative. The reasons are:

a) Change management processes, efforts regarding application of these processes, and for the most part competencies required to apply the processes, are all rendered less effective, without commitment to the process and more importantly without understanding of both the desired outcome of the change and the value

---

22  As many as 70% of corporate and other organizational change efforts fail, according to research conducted by MC Associates, the change management and leadership development unit of Manchester Partners International.

that outcome. Put simply, **engagement is essential to facilitating lasting, meaningful culture change**, and/or,

b) Many individuals, teams, and organizations simply do not have the capacity- in terms of their skill set to make the required change. **Skills-wise, the organization is not "change ready."**

**Engagement is essential to facilitating lasting, meaningful change. Effective change happens when an organization, and individuals in the organization are "ready" competency-wise, for change.**

Let's first look at point a). What is engagement? For our purposes, "engagement" means that individuals (employees) actively, and consciously choose to contribute to the workplace in a meaningful way. In doing so they show that they believe in the organization, they acknowledge that they as individuals have value and are valued, and they have an understanding of, and share, the organizational values and goals. So engagement goes far beyond attendance. Showing up and doing just what you are required to do is not engagement. Our research has shown that there are factors that definitely impact engagement, these are:

a) How clearly the organizational goals have been communicated

b) The extent to which employees recognize their value and feel valued

c) Whether or not the day to day contributions of employees are properly aligned with the organizational goals- this creates a shared purpose

These three factors contribute to overall levels of trust and help create workplace culture. (More on this in Chapter 5.) When any or all of the above factors are not in place, we start to see disengagement and other symptoms of incivility begin to emerge.

Imagine a workplace where some or all of the **Symptoms of Viral**

---

**Incivility** are present. (A version of this assessment is included in Chapter 9- Tools You Can Use.)

» Persistent miscommunication, such as non-responsiveness, mis-understandings, arguments, withholding of information, diminished morale and/or mood, negative attitudes, lack of energy, poor engagement, lowered confidence, and measurable lack of accountability

» Decreased productivity, increased lateness and laziness, reduced quality and quantity of output, diminished collaborative effort

» Increased customer service complaints, visible decrease in product and/or service standards

» Growing gap in alignment between personal or corporate goals and leadership's abilities, lack of integrity and ethics

» Inability to adapt effectively to change

» Inability to navigate cultural and communication barriers

» Increased difficulty recruiting and hiring competent personnel

» Difficulty identifying and practicing core values

» Lowered common sense, failure to attend to social cues and follow social conventions

» Increased disengagement, difficulty maintaining relationships, less involvement in social, civic and community events

Over the years we have learned that the more symptoms there are present, and the greater the frequency of observance of the symptoms, the more these symptoms support the statistics referenced in the Introduction which suggested that 80% of people are dissatisfied with their work. Dissatisfied means that employees do not feel valued, they don't feel adequately compensated, they don't feel safe at work, they are experiencing unmanageable stress, they are being bullied, they don't feel secure, or do not trust their boss, etc. If employees are dissatisfied, it is unlikely that they are focused on skill-building and productivity. They are more likely focused on those desperate "coping selfies" we referenced earlier– the social survival behaviors; self-preservation, self-promotion, self-indulgence, self-absorption, self-pity, self-interest, and so on. Self-focus does not lend well to team-orientation or collective goals.

An organization might implement respectful workplace or conflict management training in an effort to alleviate one of the incivility symptoms, and this training might even be deemed "good" because employees gain some knowledge or skill. But employees may not be inclined to transfer that skill and knowledge to the workplace in a meaningful way because they are not sufficiently engaged. Most employers would agree that it doesn't matter how much people learn if they cannot connect and use their new knowledge and skills effectively on the job. Unfortunately, a lot of time and money is often spent on good but ineffective training before leadership realizes there hasn't been sufficient transfer of learning. Without transfer of learning, there likely won't be much measurable impact or benefit to the workplace. And you need engagement to ensure meaningful transfer of learning.

When building a culture of civility in the workplace is the goal, much of the conflict management, general communication, and diversity training delivered in workplaces these days constitute good -but ineffective- solutions. If employees are not engaged, it doesn't matter how many conflict resolution strategies, how much cultural knowledge, or how many communication courses you offer them, you will likely not experience a significant decrease in incivility in your workplace.

Full engagement means employees are willing and wanting, not only to participate, but also to contribute through that participation in a way that is useful and valuable- beyond meeting the minimum requirements to stay employed. Activity does not equal engagement. Attendance is not necessarily an indication of engagement. Buy-in, trust, and active, conscious, meaningful contribution – these are indicators of engagement.

## READINESS AS AN INDICATOR OF SUCCESS FOR CIVILITY INITIATIVES

That individuals, teams, and/or the organization overall are not "change ready" skills-wise is the second reason we (the team at Civility Experts Worldwide) find that many civility initiatives fail. By "change readiness" we are referring to competency in specific skills that underpin the ability to exhibit civility at work. We have identified four core competency areas necessary to change uncivil workplaces into positive, healthy, civil organizations. These four competence areas are; social intelligence, cultural competence, systems thinking, and continuous learning. These are discussed in detail in Chapter 7- *The Civility Competency Matrix.*

The basic idea is that while we hope and expect that people who adopt civility as a core value will necessarily adopt a positive, proactive attitude, attitude change is not enough. We need behavior change too. We need everyone in the organization to be able to exhibit skills that reflect their civil attitude.

One of my favorite quotes is by Alan Watts, "...the *word* water doesn't make you wet." Similarly, thinking about, and talking about civility is one thing, but being civil and exhibiting civility is quite another.

Building competency in the four key skill areas outlined in the *Civility Matrix*® enables individuals, teams, and organizations to behave more consistently in ways that support a culture of civility in a workplace.

In Chapter 5 when we introduce the *Civility Culture Compass*®, we are also going to talk about general organizational "readiness" which for our purposes refers to the organizations ability to adapt to change financially and logistically.

## THE CIVILITY INITIATIVE PROCESS AT A GLANCE.

As you make your way through the next few chapters of this book you will come to understand how to devise and implement a civility initiative in your workplace. If you are not yet clear on what civility is, Chapter

2- Defining Civility should be helpful. And if you are not yet sure about the benefits of starting a civility initiative, we present the business case in Chapter 3.

Please note Figure 1 below which outlines a general 3-step process for devising a civility initiative.

**Figure 1.**

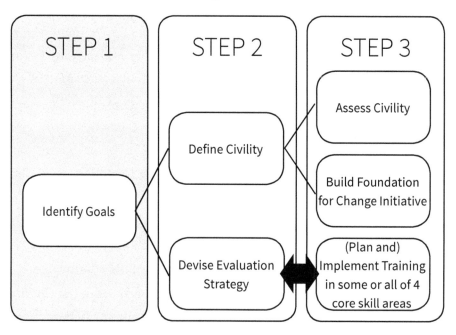

There are just three general steps in the civility initiative process, seems easy enough, right!

**Step 1** in the process **is identifying your goals**. This means starting with the end in mind. In the case of devising a civility initiative, we know in advance that because of the nature of change in our workplaces, and because civility competencies are soft skills that are never fully developed, we are ALWAYS going to identify some need related to one or more of four core skill areas. And based on 18 years in the field combined with the research, we also know that training in the civility competency areas does result in specific outcomes- and these outcomes are most likely on your "end in mind" wish list. You'll have to trust me on this, but I promise it will make sense to you after you get through Chapters 6-7. With civility initiatives, we always start with the end in mind.

To begin, ask yourself (or work with your team to answer) the questions below. If you don't have an answer for each, you are not ready to move on to Step 2:

1. **What exactly do you want to happen as a result of the initiative?** Stated differently, what is the purpose of building a culture of civility? E.g., reduced turnover, higher productivity, increased engagement, more collaboration etc. Sometimes using a tool like the *Symptoms of Viral Incivility Checklist* referenced earlier can help you identify what you don't want. And/or, review of the list of 32 possible positive outcomes of civility training included at the beginning of Chapter 2 can help you identify what you do want.

2. **Why do you want whatever it is that you want?** Think about how, and if, a successful civility initiative is something you should invest your time and money in. If your immediate response is something like: "Because it seems the right thing to do", or "We have a lot of bullying and legal issues and this seems like a necessary next step", or "We don't want to be the only company without one", please take some additional time to think about whether these motivators will be enough to propel you through the process. In the past, when organizations adopt civility as a means of running away from something as opposed to running towards something, we frequently don't get past the first two stages of the process.

3. **What specifically is the benefit or impact to the employee(s), and/or to the organization, if you get what you want?** For example, if you say you want more collaboration, why would this be good for employees? How does it benefit the organization? And what if you get what you want? Will you actually do something with it? Will you be able to manage it? Will increasing collabora-

tion, for example, potentially result in any unforeseen costs? Will it require employees work differently and can you support that? Is the management team on board?

4. **What evidence do you have that the outcome you want could, or would, in fact result from the initiative?** We want to be sure that we can clarify what exactly civility will look like in the workplace. This enables us to measure success. Consider doing a comprehensive situational analysis so that you can understand the current situation and recognize factors that could hinder or facilitate the impact of your civility training plan. (The Civility Culture Compass® can help you with this.)

5. **Are there any drawbacks or unfavorable consequences to you, the team or the organization if you get what you want?** Are you prepared if the outcomes are different than you expected? As an example, what if employees start to work better as a team? What will you do with the potential time savings? What if the teams are even 10% more productive? Positive change typically results in more positive change and you have to be prepared to manage these changes ongoing. As an example, if people become more competent, do you have to pay bonuses? Will you have to secure more accounts to keep up with increased productivity? Will you end up laying off employees because production is more efficient? Be sure to consider the trends, changes, and other influences impacting the organization, and forecast any impacts that could influence change in your workplace over the next five years at minimum.

6. **Are your goals realistic, e.g., SMARTER; specific, measurable, attainable, realistic, time-set and/or timely, evaluated, and rewarding/rewarded?** Do you have a goal that is clearly defined? This is going to drive the whole process so it is important to take some time to devise this SMARTER goal.

## CHAPTER SNAPSHOT

» Civility in the workplace is an issue all around the world.

» There is an increasing body of research suggesting that incivility in the workplace is systemic and epidemic and it's time for a change.

» To successfully imbed civility into your workplace culture, it is necessary to approach civility in the workplace as a change initiative.

» While a Respectful Workplace Policy may be required, and can be useful, the policy in and of itself does not guarantee a respectful workplace.

» 70% of change initiatives fail.

» Engagement is essential to facilitating lasting, meaningful culture change and in order for a civility initiative to be successful, organizations must be "change-ready" skills-wise. This means employees must be competent in four skill areas that underpin the ability to exhibit civility at work.

» The first step in the 3-step civility plan is have an end in mind. Goal setting is based on this desired outcome and your SMARTER goal will drive the civility initiative process.

# CHAPTER 2

# DEFINING CIVILITY

What if I told you that I could offer your organization a customized training solution that would result in some or all of the outcomes below? Go ahead, take a look. And take your time, it's a long list.

## OUTCOMES OF CIVILITY TRAINING

- » Increased retention
- » Greater individual and organizational adaptive capacity
- » Employee autonomy
- » Individual skills mastery and increased confidence
- » More effective goal setting
- » Better alignment of daily activity with organizational goals
- » More accountability
- » Greater consistency in service delivery
- » Increased respect in the workplace
- » More frequent exhibition of common courtesies

» Generalized reciprocity
» More civil discourse
» Increased acceptance of diversity
» Greater team-orientation
» More collaboration
» Increased innovation
» Improved thinking skills
» Improved self-respect
» More self-directed learning
» Improved culture of learning
» Greater change readiness
» Improved engagement
» Higher understanding of shared purpose
» Increased trust
» More responsibility-taking
» Higher self-rated happy at work scores
» Employee hardiness
» Increased psychological safety
» Better stress management
» Increased exercising of restraint
» Improved morale
» More efficient communication

Pretty impressive, right?

Wouldn't you like to experience some of these outcomes in your workplace? Take a minute and put a mental check mark beside the items that represent the top three improvements you'd like to see. And then, think about the impact to the bottom line if we could in fact achieve these improvements. I'm telling you we **CAN** do this. And the impact would be measurable! This miraculous training solution is, CIVILITY at WORK training.

I already know what you're thinking, and I can picture your face. You don't believe me. I know this to be true because over the last 17 years I've seen that very same face literally hundreds of times. It's the, *"You have got to be kidding me. Manners? Really? She is a complete nut-bar if she thinks I'm going to pay her to teach my executive team about handshakes and being nice. Please lady, do not waste my time,"* face.

Ladies and gentlemen, it's that face and the inevitable assumption that when we use the word civility, we are *just* talking about manners, that presents an enormous roadblock for civility trainers, and it's likely the reason there aren't that many of us out there.

It's also likely that the inability to get past this assumption is why even though the research shows that the stress of incivility costs US businesses alone more than $300 billion a year[1], many organizations are still not compelled to engage in civility training.

Alan W. Watts, British Philosopher, said that, *"We seldom realize, for example that our most private thoughts and emotions are not actually our own. For we think in terms of languages and images which we did not invent, but which were given to us by our society."*

In reviewing several dictionary definitions of civility, it seems to me that Mr. Watts is right- at least when it comes to defining civility. Many people have adopted a dictionary definition and understand the word to mean "politeness" or "manners," or "reasonable behavior." This might be okay in terms of day to day interactions but when discussing civility in the workplace, these oversimplified definitions of civility allow for far too much subjectivity to be useful. And if your image of civility relates only to the language of politeness, you likely only see old fashioned etiquette, white gloves, and teacups when you hear the term civility. If

---

1    The Cost of Bad Behavior: How Incivility Is Damaging Your Business and What You Can do About It By Christine Pearson, Christine Porath

this is the case, it comes as no surprise that you won't, or don't, consider civility as having immediate and significant impact on your bottom line.

## SOME DICTIONARY DEFINITIONS OF CIVILITY:

Oxford Dictionary Online: Civility - Formal politeness and courtesy in behavior or speech[2]

Merriam Webster Online: Civility - Polite, reasonable, and respectful behavior[3]

Dictionary.com: Civility - Courtesy; politeness[4]

Cambridge Dictionary Online: Civility- the quality of being polite[5]

None of these definitions capture the attitudinal and values components that are so important to the practical applications of civility. From a workplace training point of view, when civility is reduced to politeness, it's often categorized along with other social courtesies such as thank you notes, hygiene, eye contact, and handshakes – and in many organizational contexts these are considered "nice to have." Even if politeness is understood to be an important element of customer service, or maybe courtesy is recognized as one aspect of working well with others, it's still not usually deemed important enough as a stand-alone skill to warrant spending time, money, and energy on it.

This dismissal can have BIG consequences. In spite of the growing evidence that civility in the workplace can be a game-changer, if you are a training professional, a human resources manager, or even a gung-ho on site supervisor whose excited about civility training, good luck selling it to the top brass if you (or they) are defining it as "nice to have" skills.

---

2   http://www.oxforddictionaries.com/us/?gclid=CjwKEAjwucmoBRDmysGsgbDr5j0SJAAxL9abyw-Mob-33GgbdmeuL_MrBGvySpPo7dN4WNsJUK_6wGhoC4tvw_wcB

3   http://www.merriam-webster.com/

4   http://dictionary.reference.com/

5   http://dictionary.cambridge.org/us/

The fact is, words matter. And so to ensure people recognize civility training as a real solution, I've found it helpful to define the term civility in a way that expands the thoughts and emotions that using the word typically conjures.

Civility must be defined in a way that is comprehensive enough to makes people think differently. And at the same time it has to have immediate personal relevance for people, given whatever environment or situation they happen to be in. When a person hears the word, he/she needs to see the possibilities and imagine some of the outcomes that I have come to know are absolutely possible, e.g., the long list at the beginning of this chapter. The definition has to include elements that expand it from a vague, subjective notion, to a practical, measurable concept with applications for skill development in a range of different contexts.

I'm not alone in thinking that dictionary definitions of civility are not sufficient. Many civility advocates devise their own definitions of civility to make it meaningful for their specific application. As examples:

Gary Burgess, Ph.D. and Heidi Burgess, Ph.D. Co-Directors, Conflict Research Consortium, University of Colorado state, *"...Clearly, civility has to mean something more than mere politeness. The movement will have accomplished little if all it does is get people to say, 'Excuse me please,' while they (figuratively) stab you in the back. Civility also cannot mean 'roll over and play dead.' People need to be able to raise tough questions and present their cases when they feel their vital interests are being threatened. A civil society cannot avoid tough but important issues, simply because they are unpleasant to address. There must also be more to civility than a scrupulous adherence to the laws governing public-policy decision making...In our work at the University of Colorado's Conflict Research Consortium, we have been developing an approach which we call 'constructive confrontation.' This approach combines an understanding of conflict processes, dispute resolution, and advocacy strategies to help disputants better advance their interests. In addition to explaining why the politeness embodied in conventional definitions of 'civility' is important, we also identify a number of other areas in which adversaries, decision makers, and those caught in the middle can work individually and collectively to increase the constructiveness of public debate...."* [6]

*Tomas Spath and Cassandra Dahnke, Founders of the Institute for Civility in Government state, "Civility is claiming and caring for one's identity, needs and beliefs without degrading someone else's in the process."* On the Institute's webpage, you'll find a notation explaining the definition: *"Civility is about more than just politeness, although politeness is a necessary first step. It is about disagreeing without disrespect, seeking common ground as a starting point for dialogue about differences, listening past one's preconceptions, and teaching others to do the same. Civility is the hard work of staying present even with those with whom we have deep-rooted and fierce disagreements. It is political in the sense that it is a necessary prerequisite for civic action. But it is political, too, in the sense that it is about negotiating interpersonal power such that everyone's voice is heard, and nobody's is ignored. And civility begins with us."* [7]

Purdue University Calumet places a priority on student learning. Extracted from their website, "We value the inherent worth and dignity of every person, thereby fostering a community of mutual respect. We believe that in order to achieve these ideals, all Purdue University Calumet students are expected, while in the role as student or representative of the university, to exhibit and practice civil behaviors, defined as behaviors that:

1. Respect faculty, staff, fellow students, guests, and all university property, policies, rules and regulations

2. Take responsibility for one's choices and actions

3. Accept consequences of one's inappropriate choices and actions

4. Communicate in a professional and courteous manner in all forms, and at all times, whether verbal, non-verbal or written [8]

---

6    http://www.colorado.edu/conflict/civility.htm

7    http://www.instituteforcivility.org/who-we-are/what-is-civility/

8    http://webs.purduecal.edu/deanofstudents/toward-a-model-of-community-civility-stu-dent-guide-12006/

From Dr. Pier Forni, Johns Hopkins- considering the leading US researcher and author on civility- *"Building on the notion of 'civilitas,' here is a possible definition of civility for our times: The civil person is someone who cares for his or her community and who looks at others with a benevolent disposition rooted in the belief that their claim to well-being and happiness is as valid as his or her own. More Americans are discerning with increasing clarity the connections between civility and ethics, civility and health, and civility and quality of life. In fact a consensus is developing around the notion that a vigorous civility is necessary for the survival of society as we know it."* [9]

According to Stephen L. Carter, author of *Civility: Manners, Morals, and the Etiquette of Democracy*, *"Civility is the sum of the many sacrifices we are called to make for the sake of living together."* [10]

Dr. Cindy Clark, a Professor at Boise State who co-developed the *The Organizational Civility Scale*® defines civility as, *"Authentic respect for others requiring time, presence, engagement, and an intention to seek common ground."* [11]

And from Kent Roberts and Jay Newman, co-founders of The National Civility Center, a not for profit organization established in 2000 to help people make their communities better places to live, *"Civility builds on the Golden Rule: Always treat others as you would like to be treated. When true civil dialogue takes place, a high-minded, self-sacrificing behavior often emerges. Those simple building blocks create positive relationships and raise levels of trust between people and institutions. And without trust, nothing of value can happen."* [12]

As you can see in reviewing these examples, there are some reoccurring themes threaded through the definitions. And while politeness and

---

9   http://www.dallasnews.com/opinion/sunday-commentary/20100723-p.m.-forni-why-civility-is-necessary-for-society_s-survival.ece

10  *Civility: Manners, Morals and the Etiquette of Democracy,* Stephen Carter, 1998.

11  http://hs.boisestate.edu/civilitymatters/

12  Community Weaving, published in 2003 by the National Civility Center, authors Kent Roberts and Jay Newman.

courtesy are included in most them, they are not the focus. Instead the *impact* of civility is highlighted, references to: living together, creating positive relationships, building trust, well-being and happiness, taking responsibility, valuing worth and dignity, staying present, seeking common ground, starting point for dialogue, and constructive confrontation.

It is this same end in mind approach that we used at Civility Experts Worldwide when we worked to define the term. Some of the considerations we applied in devising our definition were:

a) The definition would have practical applications for workplaces- generally, but that could be expanded or adapted to individual and/or specific workplaces as well.

b) Because we have affiliates all over the world, we needed to have a definition that would be meaningful when translated, and that would resonate with our affiliates regardless of what culture they represented.

c) We needed a definition that could inform our training and tie in to what we had come to understand as skills that underpinned overall civility competencies.

d) We wanted to build on- and in some small way offer tribute- to the good work of civility experts who had inspired and mentored us. For example when I first started my civility journey, works by Dr. Pier Forni, Dr. Karl Albrecht and Benet Davetian were top of my reading list.

e) We wanted the definition to reflect our own personal values, so that we could truly buy in and feel confident and comfortable that in choosing civility as our work, we could actually live our values.

---

**AT CIVILITY EXPERTS WORLDWIDE, WE DEFINE CIVILITY AS.....**

» *A **conscious awareness** of the impact of one's thoughts, actions, words and intentions on others; combined with,*

> » A **continuous acknowledgement** of one's responsibility to ease the experience of others (e.g., through restraint, kindness, non-judgment, respect, and courtesy); and,

> » A **consistent effort** to adopt and exhibit civil behavior as a non-negotiable point of one's character.

In our definition, **conscious awareness** is intended to make the point that it's not enough to extend courtesy out of habit, and it's not a good enough excuse when you do not extend appropriate consideration to say you weren't aware, or weren't paying attention. When we are conscious of the impact of our thoughts and words and actions, when we focus and attend to our surroundings, we are reminded that we have the power to impact people and situations and communications. In attending, we become thoughtful and when we are thoughtful, we become thinkers, As Dr. Forni says in his latest book, *The Thinking Life-How to Thrive in the Age of Distraction, "You are thoughtful if you are a thinker, but you are also thoughtful if you are considerate. To be considerate you need first of all, to pay attention to other people...you need to think about them and their well-being."* [13] Very few could argue that we do not live in an age of distraction. As such, that someone is deliberate in thinking before he/she acts or speaks, and that he/she then intentionally chooses a civil action, even when it may not be comfortable, cost-free, or convenient to do so, speaks volumes about that individual's character. Sadly, many of us are too caught up in ourselves to look up and attend to what is going on around us. And when we do have occasion to look up, many of us are distracted and often not present to, or caring about anyone. To me, the breadth of incivility we experience every day is a good indication that thinking is not as common a pursuit as it once was.

As an aside, and just as one example of how powerful a few minutes of paying attention can be, a short excerpt that captures the humanity and gratitude aspects of civility is included in Chapter 9-Tools You Can Use. It was written by my friend and colleague, Anjali Handa, Author *of I Choose Blissful*[14].

---

13  The Thinking Life, Dr. P. Forni, St. Martens Press, 2011, page 150.

14  http://www.ichooseblissful.com/people-watching-i-thank-him-for-being-him/

---

When we talk about a "**continuous acknowledgement of one's responsibility**" we are referencing ethics and the inherent human dignity of others. Easing the experience of others echoes the *do no harm* principle that has been the bedrock of Eastern and Western religious traditions alike. In the workplace, this responsibility ties to accountability and includes obligations related to common courtesy, non-judgment, and restraint, regardless of whether they are written into a job description or code of conduct.

"**Consistent effort**" relates to the point that when standards are at issue, as happens in most workplaces, being civil some of the time isn't enough. Civility must be an everyday, all day endeavor. This is essential to building trust. Choosing civility has to become our default thinking pattern. It must become imbedded in the workplace culture such that it becomes a key part of the character of the organization and a reflection of the character of the people who make up the organization. This element of our definition also suggests the ongoing hard work and commitment that is required to build a culture of civility. Truly, if it were easy to choose civility, wouldn't everyone would be doing it?

We will be referencing this definition throughout this book. In the past 17 years designing and co-delivering civility initiatives, assessments, and training, this definition has served as the basis for the majority of the decisions we've made in our organization and it offers a framework for the programs, strategies, and training materials we develop and use daily.

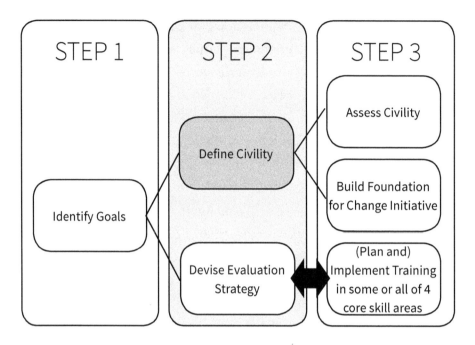

Step 2 in the 3 Step Civility Initiative Process is to **Define Civility** and to **Devise an Evaluation Strategy**. You can't devise an evaluation strategy until you know what you are measuring and this is why it is critical to define civility. We will talk more about evaluation in Chapter 3, but for now, a couple of important comments about defining civility:

1. I encourage every individual to reflect on his/her own values and to arrive at a definition of civility that is meaningful to himself/herself. I actually think going through the exercise of identifying one's personal values is hugely important as a way of being self-aware, being emotionally intelligent, and for setting personal standards- this has value independent of defining civility.

   A great site to learn more about values is www.values.com and we've included a values activity in the Tools You Can Use section of Chapter 9.

2. I also encourage, no *insist* is a better word, that organizations we work with at Civility Experts Worldwide spend the time to come up with a definition of civility that properly reflects their

organizational values, goals, and workplace culture. If you plan to use the Civility Culture Compass® or the Civility Competency Matrix®, you will need to define civility for your organization.

3. As part of a workplace civility initiative, an organization must be able to articulate what civility looks like in terms of day-to-day life in the workplace. An organization's leadership must be able to clearly communicate that civility is a core value and what that means in practice. Next the organization has to find the courage to require individuals to take on the organizational values including their definition of civility, and the leadership has to create a workplace culture where employees can actually give them what they're asking for behavior-wise.

4. I believe it's always a good idea for individuals to find out if their personal definition of civility (and other values as well) aligns with the organization's definition. This because in my experience, things tend not to go well if there is great disparity between these important values definitions.

It does happen that people, and you may be one of them, resist defining civility for others and prefer that each individual interpret or define the term on his/her own. A word of caution about this. It is true that each person behaving and making decisions based on the language and image he/she has for what civility is, can work for a little while, and/or this might work well for individuals in their personal lives.

However, when it comes to civility at work, where presumably people will be held accountable, and where equality is expected, we need to be able to measure behavior based on a set, well-defined standard. In this case, I don't find individual definitions of civility useful because it's hard to measure subjective standards. Inevitably, a values gap is perceived by one or more parties and then miscommunications and even conflict ensue. And when/where one or more of these personal definitions collides with the organizational definition, all sorts of complicated scenarios can arise.

In order to evaluate employees' performance we have to initiate clear standards with established and specific behavioral indicators that we can measure. For standards to be useful, we need to ensure that everyone is using the same frame of reference and defining terms related to these standards based on a commonly understood context. To illustrate this point, I often do a short activity called "Draw a House." Details about this activity are provided in Chapter 9.

You will see that having a clear definition of civility for application in a specific context will help get the change makers and leadership on board. The definition will also set the groundwork for achieving some of those positive outcomes we introduced you to at the beginning of this chapter.

Before we move on to how to assess and how to build civility in your workplace, let's briefly discuss civility relative to some other terms and concepts that are closely related and will likely come up in your civility conversations and training.

## WHAT'S THE DIFFERENCE BETWEEN CIVILITY, ETIQUETTE, COURTESY, AND MANNERS?

Etiquette guidelines, which incorporate manners, represent the rules or conventions that apply to a situation, a time, a culture or a country. Courtesy represents a demeanor, an attitude of respectfulness or reverence for a specific set of social rules. And manners are the polite behaviors we use to express courtesy. Manners are frequently dictated by etiquette rules and relate to what is expected for a given situation, e.g., wedding etiquette, funeral etiquette, dining etiquette, golf etiquette and so on. I believe you don't have to know or follow etiquette rules to be civil. And following prescribed social conventions out of some sense of obligation, or being courteous just because you are directed to do so by some person or circumstance, *without* some measure of understanding and good intention, is not nearly the same as choosing and practicing civility.

Put simply, courtesy is about convention and civility is about conscience.

Etiquette helps us get along better together and manners foster social decorum so there is that. But in the grand scheme of things, I personally care more about you paying me some focused attention and making me feel valued in your presence, than I care about which fork you use or whether you wear white after Labor Day.

Regarding the relationship between incivility and rudeness, rudeness is certainly uncivil but it relates more to a behavior that breeches a known rule. And you can unconsciously break the rules. Incivility is more about behaviors that breech values and/or ethics, so incivility incorporates both behavior and intention or attitude  and this type of breech requires conscious awareness.

In *Choose Civility*, Dr. Forni, describes rudeness as follows:

» Rudeness diminishes and demeans others. It is taking without giving.

» Unfocused rudeness is done in obliviousness.

» Focused rudeness is mean-spirited. Continued focused rudeness can be bullying or harassment.

» Rudeness damages others by creating stress, eroding self-esteem, creating problems in relationships, making things difficult at work and escalating into violence. Rudeness leaves us vulnerable to self-doubt and anxiety. People who are treated rudely can with-draw or become aggressive.


As a side note, "protocol" is an assigned process, approach or procedure, for a specific context. Protocol is often dictated by regulated or written rules and these are more rigid than etiquette rules which really function as guidelines. Protocol is to be followed without deviation, sometimes for safety reasons, e.g., military protocol or medical protocol. But when following etiquette guidelines, you are expected to consider the circumstances and sometimes it's appropriate to break the rule. As an example, in North America it is considered good business etiquette to extend your hand for a handshake when you first meet someone. However, if you note that a person has his/her hands full, or that he/she does not appear comfortable with a handshake, you would be expected to know that breaking the etiquette rule to ensure the other party is not embarrassed or uncomfortable is the courteous thing to do.

## HOW DOES CIVILITY RELATE TO VALUES?

Civility is a values proposition. Choosing civility means that civility (defined however you prefer) represents a personal principle or value. A value is a standard or code that we, as individuals and/or as a collective (may be a family and organization or a community) lives by. Our values impact how we make decisions, and how we determine what is important to us. When groups of individuals share the same core values, those values create the character or culture of a family, an organization, and even a nation. When you do not have clearly defined values, it is difficult to establish personal standards, and so it is easier to choose popular actions based on convenience rather than choose civility based on conscience. The end result is incivility.

## ISN'T CIVILITY THE SAME THING AS CHARACTER?

Allan Greenspan, Former Chairman, U.S. Federal Reserve said, *"Rules cannot take the place of character."* I agree. Following this line of thought, if you are defining civility as etiquette, following these mannerly rules is not the same as having character. Choosing the right action, weighing the potential impact of choices against one's own values, and being accountable for the outcomes of those choices are what builds character. And, it's character that distinguishes mannerly actions from civility.

In his new book *Return on Character*, Fred Kiel, defines character as *"An individual's unique combination of beliefs and character habits that motivate and shape how he or she relates to others. Our character is defined by out behavior- the way we treat others is character in action."*[15] Kiel goes on to suggest that there are four keystone character habits: integrity, responsibility, forgiveness and compassion. According to Kiel, these character habits are the direct expression of our innate moral intuitions. These intuitions not only make us uniquely human, but the habitual demonstration of the principles they foster is essential to the kind of strong, principled character we associate with what he calls "Virtuoso" leadership.

Abraham Lincoln said, *"Reputation is the shadow. Character is the tree."* Civility is a gesture or communication that is perceived as meaningful to someone else. This belief is an aspect of your true self, part of your character, whereas manners can easily and often be exhibited simply as a means of sending a positive impression or appearing to be good.

## HOW IS BEING CIVIL DIFFERENT FROM SHOWING RESPECT?

In my mind, being civil is not exactly the same as showing respect. However, the two are very closely related. The difference is most easily explained in saying that the recipient of an action – not the action taker – decides whether that action is civil. Civility is perceived as a gesture or communication that is meaningful to someone else. And so to be civil, there is usually some consciousness or awareness of what the other person might need or want. And so to be civil is usually something intentional. For example, in speaking of civility, many people have adopt-

---

15    Return on Character; The Real Reason Leaders and Their Companies Win, Fred Kiel, Harvard
      Business Review Press, 2015, page 17.

ed what is described as "The Platinum Rule" over "The Golden Rule." Where the Golden Rule says that we should do unto others as we would have done to us, (this means assuming others want what we want or expect), the Platinum Rule, according to Tony Alessandra[16] says that we should treat someone as he/she wishes to be treated. To follow the Platinum rule you have to set assumptions aside and consider the perspectives of others. In doing so, you adopt an "other-focus" and in this way, I believe that in being civil, one necessarily conveys a service-orientation. But respect isn't necessarily about serving others.

I believe that showing respect is a way of honoring someone's humanness. And you shouldn't have to know that person or share his/her perspective, or understand what he/she wants or believes or feels, to respect him/her. Respect is something that should be automatically, spontaneously, and easily given. Put simply, respect is something you feel towards someone, and this is often unconscious. Where civility is something you consciously choose – this is one of the reasons I believe you can teach civility, but it's much harder to teach respect. Sure I can explain what respect looks like, but that's not the same as teaching how to truly feel respect in one's heart. This requires setting aside bias and prejudice for example, and this can be a difficult endeavor.

The reality is that someone could perceive him or herself as being treated in a respectful way or see him or herself having been treated civilly merely as a result of someone else extending a courtesy – and this can be a mistake. In actuality, that someone says something kind or does what the rules say he/she should do e.g., gives a gift, sends a thank you note, and shows up on time, etc. does not mean that this person is civil. And it does not necessarily mean that the person respects us. Frequently people can have respect for the rules and so exhibit them, and still not have respect for the people they are following the rules for.

Respectfulness is absolutely a part of being civil. When a person is truly civil, he/she understands that respect is something that should be given

---

16   The Platinum Rule http://www.platinumrule.com/whatistheplatinumrule.html

with no expectation of return. Respecting others just because they're human, and in being human they are deserving of our respect, and deserving of their dignity, shows a civil attitude. This civil attitude is an indication that we are not judgmental, and that we recognize everyone as equal. That I would say, or think, that someone needs to earn my respect for example, suggests that I am not civil. I would argue that often when we say we don't respect someone, we actually mean we don't trust him/her. Similarly when someone doesn't seem to give us respect without measuring our value, we don't trust that person.

When you explain respect as above, it is easier to understand how someone could respect the rules, but not trust the person making them. Or how you can respect someone on a basic human level and at the same time be discourteous (break a social rule) to that person. I can respect myself, but not trust myself. I can respect you, but not trust you.

I can be civil- that is choose not to judge you, and be courteous (be polite) and respect you (accept you for who you are and treat you as equal) and at the same time have different views, live differently, and potentially behave in a way that you perceive as rude. Maybe you call this rudeness disrespectful, and maybe you don't trust me as a result of it. But, even when you are rude, while I don't appreciate your behavior, I can still respect you as a person. And if you are civil, you will still respect me too, even if you behave rudely towards me. The fact that I breeched a rule that you adhere value to, doesn't make me an uncivil person. Rude, maybe. Impolite, sure. But not uncivil.

## WHAT'S THE DIFFERENCE BETWEEN CIVILITY AND ETHICS?

Almost every civility expert that I've encountered agrees that civility is closely aligned with ethics. But this debate can get messy. Much depends on how you define ethics. Another example of how words matter.

Dr. P. Forni, in *Choosing Civility*, developed four principles about civility:

(1) Civility is complex; (2) Civility is good; (3) Whatever civility might be it has to do with courtesy, politeness, and manners; (4) Civility belongs in the realm of ethics.[17] And he goes on to say, *"What gives true civility depth and importance is, first of all, its connection with ethics. Just look at the Principle of Respect for Persons, a cornerstone of all ethical systems known to history. It states that we are to treat others as ends in themselves rather than as means for the furthering of our personal advantage. In other words, our behavior must be informed by empathy."*[18]

In his book, *Ethical Intelligence*, Bruce Weinstein describes five simple principles that help us make the best decisions – no matter who is looking at a problem. I'm hard pressed to think of a civility training session where some or all of these terms didn't enter in, they are:

>  Do No Harm

>  Make Things Better

>  Respect Others

>  Be Fair

>  Be Loving

Weinstein suggests that we know these principles already, they're the basis of both religious traditions and secular societies, and they're tremendously hard to live by. Further, he states, "...all five principles mentioned above provide excellent guidelines for making the best possible decisions in every area of your life. These principles have legal, financial, and psychological implications; *but they* are first and foremost principles of ethics and they form the core of what I call *ethical intelligence."*

There is no question that alignment between civility and these five principles, for example, Mr. Weinstein states in his book that "do no

---

17  https://books.google.ca/books?id=_xYSXM-kDp4C&printsec=frontcover&dq=choose+ci-vility,+forni&hl=en&sa=X&ei=LMkWVYDbJNDTgwSlkIGoBw&ved=0CCsQ6AEwAA#v=onep-age&q=choose%20civility%2C%20forni&f=false

18  http://www.dallasnews.com/opinion/sunday-commentary/20100723-p.m.-forni-why-civili-ty-is-necessary-for-society_s-survival.ece

harm" is largely a principle of restraint. And restraint is a notion that comes up frequently in civility conversations. For example, Dr. Pier Forni, considered one of the leading scholars in the field, suggests that the three key tenants of civility are: respect, restraint, and responsibility.

Additionally, when discussing principle #3- Respect Others, Weinstein explains that *"...respect is not just a matter of etiquette. Rude or offensive behavior is a breach of etiquette. But behavior that is harmful or violates another person's rights is a breach of ethics. Ethically intelligent people show respect in the deeper sense by honoring the values, preferences, and, most important, the rights of others.... Rights speak to the inherent dignity inhuman beings...these rights never change. They are the basis of legal rights but they exist even when not codified by law."*

Another term that has come up now and again in civility class when the conversation turns to ethics is "moral turpitude." The question I've been asked is whether incivility "let run rampant" results in a permissiveness that enables moral turpitude. I've also been asked if I believe that a person's consistent exhibition of incivility is a precursor to, or an indication of, a greater evil lurking below the surface.

Moral Turpitude is a legal concept dating back to the 19th century and so I asked Russ Charvonia, Grand Master Masonic Grand Lodge of California, who is actively involved in the Freemason's Civility Task Force, and on the Board of the Civility Center, but also a lawyer, to comment. Russ provided a definition of moral turpitude and offered an excerpt from the California Masonic Code.

Moral Turpitude is *"Any act of baseness, vileness or depravity during a violation of the moral law, even though not necessarily a criminal offense. For conduct to involve moral turpitude, it normally must be accompanied by an inherently evil intent. The most common examples of this inherently evil intent are:*

*A. An intent to defraud;*

*B. An intent to take a thing unlawfully (larceny); and*

*C. An intent to harm a person or a thing."*

Interpretation of Section 100.075 of the *California Masonic Code*. Moral Turpitude (2009 G.M. Decision No. 2)

Conduct involving moral turpitude can be broken down into three general categories: actions against property, actions against people and actions against government.

When asked whether he felt teaching civility could decrease the incidence of moral turpitude, Mr. Charvonia, stated, *"I think crimes of moral turpitude reflect incivility in the way the perpetrator treats his/ her fellow citizen. While I have no expectation that our efforts to restore civility in society will reach every person who is inclined to this type of behavior, it is my hope that it may reach and influence those whose conscious is making them reconsider their poor choices."*

In my view, ethics relate to what is right and wrong, independent of what regulations, workplace codes of conduct or legislations might state. This is where conversations about moral conduct and human rights begin. While some people have an absolute personal line in terms of what is ethical, there are many influencing, and ever-changing factors and sometimes culture, religion, law, and context come into play. Ongoing debates about abortion, assisted suicide, and human cloning for example, represent ethical questions that are not likely to be resolved any time soon. Over the years I've come to understand that what is civil is frequently ethical but not always. And being ethical does not always include being civil, at least not the way I define it. It occurs to me that in determining what is civil, we look inward and rely on conscience. Where in determining what is ethical, we tend to look outward and rely more on the expectations of our community and society. I'm also inclined to say that civility is the *kind* thing-regardless of the rules, where Ethics is the *right* thing- with a direct correlation to inherent human dignity, (for some people, this dignity and rights extend to all living things). With regard to the questions about whether I think rampant permissive incivility enables moral turpitude – my view is that where there is no conscience, there are likely no ethics and so it is a lack of conscience that enables evil in the form of moral turpitude and not permissible incivility that causes it.

## CIVILITY AND EMOTIONAL INTELLIGENCE

In 1995, Daniel Goleman wrote a book on Emotional Intelligence or EQ.[19] Ground-breaking at the time, Goleman suggested that the ability to discern how you and others feel (and what might be the root cause of those feelings) regardless of what you may be outwardly presenting to the world, for example through your demeanor or body language, was essential to building relationships and a key component of success. The essential premise of EQ is that to be successful requires the effective awareness, control and management of one's own emotions, and those of other people. According to Goleman, EQ embraces two aspects of intelligence:

» Understanding yourself, your goals, intentions, responses, behavior and all.
» Understanding others, and their feelings.

While I agree with the esteemed Dr. Goleman that there is tremendous value in knowing oneself and in having the ability to be aware of, control, and manage one's own emotions and the emotions of others, I'm not convinced that building emotional intelligence is the most important intelligence for workplace.

As was included in our definition of civility, awareness of the impact of your thoughts, feelings, words and actions on others is important for civility in the workplace. My opinion is that focus on internal drivers and feelings end up putting more importance on the intent and

---

19  Daniel Goleman, *Emotional Intelligence, 10th Anniversary Edition,* Bantam, 2005

motivation for doing and feeling, and this is contrary to the other focus we need to build civility in the workplace. Further, my view is that this self-development and reflective work is what the individual should take responsibility for, independent of the workplace. I don't believe that beyond the regulated psychological safety elements, it should be the employer's responsibility to delve into each employees emotional issues and sort out what makes him or her tick. As an employer, this is not where I would put my training dollars. Some exceptions would be if we're working in a sector where empathy and emotion are an important part of the job, such as healthcare or childcare. In Chapter 7 we're going to discuss how another type of intelligence- Social Intelligence, may in fact be more useful in building civility as a core competence.

## CIVILITY AND POSITIVE PSYCHOLOGY

There has been a lot of buzz lately about "positive psychology." Positive psychology is the study of happiness. Martin Seligman and Mihaly Csikszentmihalyi describe this term in the following way: *"We believe that a psychology of positive human functioning will arise that achieves a scientific understanding and effective interventions to build thriving in individuals, families, and communities."*[20] Positive psychology is tied to civility in that the research shows positive psychology promotes character development, positive interactions, stress-reduction, gratitude and altruism.[21] These outcomes echo what we see when there is a culture of civility imbedded in workplaces. A related term is "Positive Intelligence." Positive Intelligence can be measured as the percentage of the time your mind works for you instead of against you. There is a tug of war constantly raging inside your mind between your Saboteurs – the mental patterns that sabotage your success and wellbeing – and your Sage – the mental patterns that serve Positive Intelligence

---

20  http://psychology.about.com/od/branchesofpsycholog1/a/positive-psychology.htm

21  Peterson, C. (2006). A Primer in Positive Psychology. New York: Oxford University Press.

is the groundbreaking new science and practice of stress-free peak performance. The scientific foundation of Positive Intelligence is a synthesis of breakthrough original research by Shirzad Chamine. [22]

The greatest differentiators in performance and achievement are "soft skills" and mindset, such as Emotional Intelligence. Positive Intelligence builds on the principles of Emotional Intelligence and goes a step further by addressing a missing component of Emotional Intelligence training – mastery over the internal Saboteurs.

Recent scientific studies have established that Positive Intelligence is a significant determinant of how much of your potential for both happiness and professional success you actually achieve. Positive Intelligence has been directly linked to a wide range of measurable benefits:

» Sales people sell 37% more

» Teams perform 31% better with high-PQ leaders

» Creative output increases 3x

» People live as much as 10 years longer[23]

---

### CIVILITY AND BEING NICE OR BEING KIND

Renowned Lebanese Poet Kahil Gilbran said, *"Tenderness and kindness are not signs of weakness and despair, but manifestations of strength and resolution."* Based on the Civility Experts Worldwide definition of civility, kindness is one of the ways we can ease the experience of others. Kindness often takes planning, and sometimes discipline. Additionally, being kind frequently requires restraint. Further, I believe kindness is a precursor to generosity. True, heartfelt, spontaneous kindness is given as civility should be- with no expectation of return. Getting to the point where you can give your time, money, energy, or attention, without monitoring the cost of doing same is very difficult to achieve.

---

22  http://positiveintelligence.com/overview/science/

23  http://positiveintelligence.com/overview/science/

It's not easy to be kind, especially when you are surrounded by unkind. Indeed these days, choosing civility takes courage, strength and resolution.

In her book, *Saving Civility; 52 Ways to Tame Rude, Crude and Attitude for a Polite Planet* Sarah Hacala describes kindness as, *"...charity, generosity, compassion, and empathy...as it applies to good behavior, it is an almost inclusive antidote to disrespect, inconsideration and rudeness. If we were simply kind to everyone, a host of other negative behaviors would fall by the wayside."* [24]

## CHAPTER SNAPSHOT

» At Civility Experts Worldwide, we define civility as.....

▶ A conscious awareness of the impact of one's thoughts, actions, words and intentions on others; combined with,

▶ A continuous acknowledgement of one's responsibility to ease the experience of others (e.g., through restraint, kindness, non-judgment, respect, and courtesy); and,

▶ A consistent effort to adopt and exhibit civil behavior as a non-negotiable point of one's character.

There is growing evidence that civility can have tremendous positive and measurable impacts on organizations, including:

▶ Engagement, Morale, and Retention

▶ Confidence, Continuous Learning, and Competency

▶ Respect, Restraint, and Responsibility

▶ Psychological Safety, Stress Management, and Resilience

▶ Change Readiness, Adaptive Capacity and Profitability

» Step 2 in the process for creating a workplace civility initiative has

---

24  Saving Civility: 52 Ways to Tame Rude, Crude, & Attitude for a Polite Planet, Sara Hacala,

2 sub-steps: Sub-step #1 is to define civility. Your definition should support your "Hedgehog Concept" which is to Choose Civility so it will likely be an expanded, SMARTER version of a basic goal to "build a better workplace." The definition must be specific to your workplace context, and you must include behavioral indicators- these are descriptions of what exactly civility looks like on the job.

» Sub-step 2 is to devise an evaluation strategy. You have to define civility – so you know exactly what behaviors you are looking for, before you can outline a strategy for evaluating whether or not, and how, those behaviors are being exhibited, and whether or not, and how, this is benefiting the organization.

» Civility is not the same as courtesy, or the same as manners, or etiquette; these are all related but different.

## CHAPTER 3

# THE BUSINESS CASE FOR CIVILITY TRAINING

**You to the boss:** Boss, what would you do with 30% more revenue?

**Boss to you:** I could do a lot, what do you know that I don't?

**You to the boss:** I know that companies that openly promote civil communication among employees earn 30% more revenue than competitors.[1]

**Boss to you:** Really? So tell me again...why aren't we doing civility training?

**You to the boss:** Just say when Boss, shouldn't be too hard a sell the idea of civility training to the team as 67% of employees who responded to a Civility in America poll said they believe there is a strong need for civility training.[2]

**Boss to you:** Offering training that 67 percent of employees say they want, as a means of achieving 30 percent more revenue...seems like a no brainer to me, let's get started!

Are *you* convinced yet? After reviewing the Introduction, Chapter 1

---

1    http://www.webershandwick.com/uploads/news/files/Civility_in_America_2011.pdf

2    http://www.webershandwick.com/uploads/news/files/Civility_in_America_2011.pdf

and Chapter 2, you should have a clearer idea of what civility is and hopefully you agree with the research showing that most organizations are dealing with incivility in the workplace to some degree. By the end this chapter, we hope you will also see that based on the business case, implementing a civility initiative the workplace is more than just a good idea. **"A Civility Initiative is a change imperative for organizations that want to succeed in the new world of work."** (Further, we want to provide you with the information you need to persuade your leadership and teams to choose civility and support your workplace civility initiative. Approaching civility at work as a change initiative is one way to manage the impact of incivility in the workplace and change your overall organizational culture for the better.

Please do reference some of the worksheets in Chapter 9. And it's never too soon to start working on your own definition of civility. Although you may not be able to finalize a definition, the goal is that you would be able to at least describe for the naysayers and skeptical decision-makers what civility is *not*. If you are able to at least define what civility means to you personally, you can fall back on this definition as a way of illustrating to others what civility looks like in practice, as well as what it means relative to other commonly associated terms such as manners, ethics, courtesy, morals, etc.

If you have a personal interest in civility but aren't quite ready to introduce the concept in your workplace, you might benefit from the *I Choose Civility: Steps to Adopting Civility as a Core Personal Value* worksheet in Chapter 9- Tools You Can Use.

If you are a decision-maker who has reviewed that long list of potential positive outcomes at the beginning of Chapter 2, you may already be considering civility training for your organization. In this case, extracting facts and stats and other information provided in this chapter will help you present the business case for civility training to your team.

## STRATEGIES FOR PERSUADING OTHERS THAT CIVILITY AT WORK IS IMPORTANT

Whatever your role is in your organization, unless you have access to a pot of unallocated funds that you're free to spend on whatever training you can get your hands on, you will need to persuade others to get on board. There are two issues to consider in achieving this:

1. You have to figure out how to get over **the "civility = manners= soft skills, and soft skills are nice to have but not necessary skills" hurdle**. Even if we take manners out of the equation, civility still equals soft skills to most people, and this can be problematic when it comes to training decisions and budgeting.

2. You have to know your audience. **What will convince your team that civility training is worthwhile? Will it be a focus on costs, benefits, or consequences?** Because I feel it is actually contrary to civility to engage in ongoing conversations about negative behavior, my approach to making the business case is _always to focus on the benefits_ (see the long list at the beginning of Chapter 2) and the research verifying the positive impacts of civility. Having said that, if fear and consequences are what motivate you and your team, please see Sources and Resources/Chapter 3 where we have included a section of statistics and facts about the costs and consequences of incivility.

Before we get into the business case for civility training, some assertions we're making in presenting the evidence that civility training works.

## ASSERTIONS MADE WHEN PRESENTING EVIDENCE THAT CIVILITY TRAINING WORKS:

» Civility is...

▶ A conscious awareness of the impact of one's thoughts, actions, words and intentions on others; combined with,

» A continuous acknowledgement of one's responsibility to ease the experience of others (e.g., through restraint, kindness, non-judgment, respect, and courtesy); and,

» A consistent effort to adopt and exhibit civil behavior as a non-negotiable point of one's character.

(This is the Civility Experts Worldwide definition)

▶ On the surface, civility is perceived to be largely attitudinal but as per the definition above is also understood to encompass a range of "soft" skills

▶ Soft skills are proving to be equally, or more important than, technical skills (This is especially true in the new world of work- we talk about this in Chapter 4.)

▶ Soft skills- as per Han's definitions enable individuals to effectively apply technical skills and exhibiting soft skills requires some technical abilities; soft and technical skills are not necessarily useful independent of each other

▶ Soft skills also include in part, what are described as "Essential Skills" or foundational skills (More on this further into chapter.)

▶ Every job in every sector requires some Essential Skills

Note: If you are using a different definition of civility than the one presented above, please consider whether your definition includes a soft skills element. If not, aspects of the *Civility Culture Compass*® **may not work for you.**

## WHAT ARE SOFT SKILLS?

Soft skills can be described as a cluster of personal qualities that include things like:

» Approach to communication

» Cooperative attitude

» Personal habits

» Emotional intelligence

» Social style... and so on.

These are non-technical skills, sometimes intangible, and often hard to measure because they tend to be more related to willingness, attitude, personality, and social intelligence than they are related to physical ability or intellectual capacity.

You'll see in Chapter 7 when we talk about competencies that support a culture of civility that I believe there are four measurable skills that as a collective make up what we at Civility Experts refer to as the "*Civility Competency Matrix*®." These skills support an individual's ability to exhibit civility generally, but on the job specifically.

Lei Han, Stanford engineer, Wharton MBA offers clarification on what soft skills are versus people skills, and what she calls "tribal" skills. For a skill to be considered soft, it needs to have three characteristics.

1. Rules for mastering this skill are not black and white – Unlike hard skills, like math, where the rule for doing it perfectly is always the same, how effective you are at a soft skill changes depends on your emotional state, external circumstance, and the type of people you interact with.

2. This skill is portable and valuable to any job/career – Because soft skills are about your inner strength and interpersonal effectiveness, as long as you work with people, these skills are valuable to your career.

3. Mastering this skill is an ongoing journey – You can reach a level of competency in it but you can always encounter new situations or people that will test your soft skills and push you to learn more.

## HAN'S SOFT SKILLS LIST PART A: SELF-MANAGEMENT SKILLS

Self-Management Skills address how you perceive yourself and others, manage your emotions, and react to adverse situations. Only when you build an inner excellence can you have a strong mental and emotional foundation to succeed in your career.

1.  **Growth mindset** – Looking at any situation, especially difficult ones, as an opportunity for you to learn, grow, and change for the better. Focusing your attention on improving yourself instead of changing others or blaming anyone.

2.  **Self-awareness** – Knowing and understanding what drives, angers, motivates, embarrasses, frustrates, and inspires you. Being able to observe yourself objectively in a difficult situation and understand how your perceptions of yourself, others, and the situation are driving your actions.

3.  **Emotion regulation** – Being able to manage your emotions, especially negative ones, at work (e.g. anger, frustration, embarrassment) so you can think clearly and objectively, and act accordingly.

4.  **Self-confidence** – Believing in yourself and your ability to accomplish anything. Knowing that all you need is within you now. "Those who believe in themselves have access to unlimited power" – wisdom from Kung Fu Panda.

5.  **Stress management** – Being able to stay healthy, calm, and balanced in any challenging situations. Knowing how to reduce your stress level will increase your productivity, prepare you for new challenges and support your physical and emotional health, all of which you need for a fulfilling, successful career.

6.  **Resilience** – Being able to bounce back after a disappointment or set back, big or small, and continue to move onward and upward.

7.  **Skills to forgive and forget** –Being able to forgive yourself for making a mistake, forgive others that wronged you, and move on

without "mental or emotional baggage." Freeing your mind from the past so you can focus 100% of your mental energy on your short and long-term career goals.

8. **Persistence and perseverance** – Being able to maintain the same energy and dedication in your effort to learn, do, and achieve in your career despite difficulties, failures, and oppositions.

9. **Patience** – Being able to step back in a seemingly rushed or crisis situation, so you can think clearly and take action that fulfills your long term goals.

10. **Perceptiveness** – Giving attention and understanding to the unspoken cues and underlying nuance of other people's communication and actions. Oftentimes, we are too busy thinking about ourselves and what we are saying, so we leave little room to watch and understand others' action and intentions. If you misinterpret others' intention, you can easily encounter difficulties dealing with people and not even know why. (FYI, you will note in Chapter 7 under the Social Intelligence section, that Han's self-management skills make up much of what we reference as *social style* and they are inter-woven with *social radar*.)

## HAN'S SOFT SKILLS LIST PART B: PEOPLE SKILLS

People Skills address how to best interact and work with others so you can build meaningful work relationships, influence others' perception of you and your work, and motivate their actions. I have split them into two sections – Conventional and Tribal

**People Skills Sub-group 1: Conventional Skills**– List of people skills you can find in most job descriptions and you will be assessed on some or all of these in your performance reviews depending on your level. (FYI, you will not in Chapter 7 when we reference the *written rules and social knowledge*, many of the skills on Han's conventional skills list require high social radar, and are influenced by etiquette and contextual rules.)

1. **Communication skills** – Being able to actively listen to others and articulate your ideas in writing and verbally to any audience in a way where you are heard and you achieve the goals you intended with that communication.

2. **Teamwork skills** – Being able to work effectively with anyone with different skill sets, personalities, work styles, or motivation levels to achieve a better team result.

3. **Interpersonal relationship skills** – Effective at building trust, finding common ground, having empathy, and ultimately building strong relationships with people at work and in your network. This skill is closely related to Communication Skills. As Maya Angelou said *"I have learned people will forget what you said. People will forget what you did, but people will never forget how you make them feel."*

4. **Presentation skills** – Effectively presenting your work results and ideas formally to an audience that captivates their attention, engage their input, and motivates them to act in accordance to your desired outcome. While presentation skills are a form of communication skills, they are listed separately given that the ability to present plays a huge role in any business profession, especially as you move up in your career.

5. **Meeting management skills** – Leading a meeting to efficiently and effectively reach productive results. At least 50% of meetings today are a waste of time.

6. **Facilitating skills** – Being able to coordinate and solicit well represented opinions and feedback from a group with diverse perspectives to reach a common, best solution.

7. **Selling skills -** Building buy-in to an idea, a decision, an action, a product, or a service. This is not just for people in sales.

8. **Management skills** – Creating and motivating a high performing team with people of varied skills, personalities, motivations, and work styles.

9. **Leadership skills** – Defining and communicating vision and ideas that inspire others to follow with commitment and dedication.

10. **Mentoring / coaching skills -** Providing constructive wisdom, guidance, and/or feedback that can help others further their career development

**People Skills Sub-group 2: "Tribal" Skills** – List of people skills that you will not typically find in job descriptions. They are also important to your career success. Han calls them "tribal" because they are more "insider knowledge" that you gain from work experience or from mentors. Some people can go through their entire career and not be aware of some of these skills. (FYI, you will see in Chapter 7 in the section on Social Intelligence section that Han's tribal skills are in large part what we reference as *the unwritten rules* component of social knowledge.)

11. **Managing upwards** – Proactively managing your relationship with your boss, his or her expectations of your work, and his or her perception of your performance. Whether you are challenged, given opportunities, or recognized at work heavily depends on your ability to communicate, manage expectations, and build a good relationship with your boss.

12. **Self-promotion skills** – Proactively and subtly promoting your skills and work results to people of power or influence in your organization and network. It is not enough that your boss knows you do great work. You need to subtly build your reputation with all key people that can influence your performance review. This is because hard work alone does not guarantee success.

13. **Skills in dealing with difficult personalities** – Being able to achieve the work result needed while working with someone whom you find difficult.

14. **Skills in dealing with difficult/unexpected situations** – Being able to stay calm and still are effective when faced with an

unexpected or difficult situation. This includes being able to think on your feet and articulate thoughts in an organized manner even when you are not prepared for the discussion or situation you are in.

15. **Savvy in handling office politics** – Being able to understand and proactively deal with the unspoken nuances of office and people dynamics so you can protect yourself from unfairness as well as further your career. Office politics are a fact of life. If you don't choose to play, they can play you.

16. **Influence/persuasion skills** - Being able to influence perspectives or decision making but still have the people you influence think they made up their own minds.

17. **Negotiation skills** - Being able to understand the other side's motivations and leverage and reach a win-win resolution that you find favorably satisfies both sides, and maintains relationships for future interactions.

18. **Networking skills** - Being able to be interesting and interested in business conversations that motivate people to want to be in your network. The bigger and stronger the network you have, the more easily you can get things done (e.g., find a job, get advice, find business partners, find customers, etc....)[3]

As you can see upon reviewing Ms. Han's definitions, every single soft skill, whether indicated as self-managed, people or tribal includes one or more aspects of conscious awareness, consistent acknowledgement, and consistency- the three key elements in our definition of civility. We'll get into this in more depth in Chapter 7- Competencies that Support Civility in the Workplace. A checklist of Ms. Han's soft skills with the civility definition elements indicated in includes in Chapter 9- Tools You Can Use.

---

3   https://bemycareercoach.com/soft-skills/list-soft-skills.html#comment-79983

## WHAT THE RESEARCH SHOWS ABOUT SOFT SKILLS RELATIVE TO TECHNICAL SKILLS

Research carried out by the Carnegie Institute of Technology shows that 85 percent of your financial success is due to skills in "human engineering," your personality and ability to communicate, negotiate, and lead. Shockingly, only 15 percent is due to technical knowledge.[4]

Dr. John Fleenor of the Center for Creative Leadership explains that the CEO's "soft" skills make all the difference. To be successful, individuals must be good listeners, consensus builders, team players and empathizers. Hence, to climb the corporate ladder quickly, it is essential for executives to possess more of soft skills and less of hard skills. We can compare soft skills with emotional intelligence quotient (EQ) and hard skills with intelligence quotient (IQ). Succinctly, soft skills are twice as important as IQ or technical skills for the success of senior executives. Studies have shown that individuals with high emotional quotient are highly appreciated in the workplace and they tend to grow rapidly in the corporate ladder. [5]

To Daniel Goleman, author of several books on relational intelligence, soft skills are a combination of competencies that contribute to a person's ability to manage him/herself and relate to other people. These are the skills, abilities, and traits concerning the personality, attitude, and behavior of a person. They are the human skills that make a huge difference for your professional success. They are needed for good leaders to become great leaders. In contrast, hard skills are about your technical competence and domain expertise. Sometimes soft skills are equated with teamwork while hard skills with execution. Hence, executives must proportionately blend the soft and hard skills with leadership to excel as successful leaders. However, as they gain more experience they need more of soft skills because they work less on their hard skills and more on interpersonal skills. They are mostly into

---

4   http://web.mit.edu/~jwk/www/docs/Mann%201918%20Study_of_Engineering_Educ.pdf

5   http://www.ccl.org/leadership/news/2002/softskillssurvey.aspx?pageId=694

visioning, troubleshooting, and managing several stakeholders which demands soft skills and leadership skills.[6]

Nobel Prize winning psychologist Daniel Kahneman found that people would rather do business with a person they like and trust rather than someone they don't, even if the person they don't like is offering a better price or higher quality product.[7] The ability to build trust is largely based on soft skills.

## SOFT SKILLS ARE "ESSENTIAL" SKILLS

Over the past 8 or so years, I've had the privilege of doing some contract work with Workplace Education Manitoba (WEM). WEM is a nonprofit organization, funded by the Province of Manitoba and the Government of Canada. For the past 26 years, Workplace Education Manitoba has been providing Essential Skills training solutions to Manitoba's small and medium-sized businesses.

Essential Skills are needed for work, learning, and life. They provide the foundation for learning all other skills and enable people to evolve with their jobs and adapt to workplace change.[8] Since 1994, the Canadian Government has surveyed more than 3000 Canadians in workplaces in all sectors and of all types and sizes of organizations. Research participants were asked what workplace skills they felt were needed in order for workers to be most effective, efficient, and productive.

The result has been the identification of the following nine *Essential Skills* for workplace:

1. Reading

2. Document Use

3. Numeracy

---

6   http://under30ceo.com/acquire-soft-skills-fast-track-career-success/

7   Thinking, Fast and Slow, Daniel Kahneman

8   http://www.llsc.on.ca/literacy-essential-skills/what-are-essential-skills

4. Writing

5. Oral Communication

6. Working with Others

7. Thinking

8. Digital Technology

9. Continuous Learning

Essential Skills are used in different combinations, in different applications, in every occupation. They are the foundational skills you use to carry out your work tasks and they're the building blocks you use to learn new ones. The importance of, and need for, employees to have appropriate levels of workplace Essential Skills is clear and strong.

## SO WHAT DOES THIS HAVE TO DO WITH CIVILITY?

It turns out each of the 4 skills we identify in the *Civility Competency Matrix*® **(Chapter 7)** fits into one of these broader 9 Essential Skill categories. The four skills in the Matrix are: Social Intelligence, Cultural Competence, Continuous Learning, and Systems Thinking. Details about this categorization are included in the Soft Skills Definition Checklist provided in Chapter 9. Generally, the four core skills that support civility at work fit under the Essential Skills Categories of:

**Working with Others** is the ability to lead, coordinate or collaborate with others on work activities. We use this skill when we work as a member of a team or jointly with a partner (whether in person or at a distance), and when we engage in supervisory or leadership activities.

**Oral Communication** is the ability to talk with others to give and exchange information & ideas, such as: ask questions, give directions, coordinate work tasks, explain & persuade.

**Thinking** is the ability to engage in the process of problem solving, job task planning and organizing, finding information, critical thinking, significant use of memory and decision-making. We use a thinking process to solve problems, organize and plan, find needed information, be logical, remember things and make decisions.

**Continuous Learning** is the ability to apply strategies which support learning and the ability to adapt to change. We use this skill when we learn as part of regular work or from co-workers and when we access training in the workplace or off-site.

Once a person understands the foundational aspect of Essential Skills it is easy to see how these skills underpin almost every technical skill in every job. Frequently a few hours spent on strategic training in these foundational skills can increase uptake, shorten learning curves, and save training time and resources, related to technical training. This is because learners often have technical knowledge but they don't have the foundational skills that enable them to use what they know in a meaningful way. Or, they have technical skills, but they don't have the Essential Skills needed to help them transfer elements of their skills to different contexts and/or to build on their technical knowledge and skills.

### WHAT WILL SUCCESSFUL CIVILITY TRAINING LOOK LIKE?

Okay, so once you understand that soft skills are essential and that the skills that underpin the ability to be civil are soft skills, you will presumably include a reference to soft skills in your definition of civility. Having a clear definition will enable you to outline performance indicators specific to your workplace and this will provide a means for measuring behavior change on the job- that is, the transfer of new knowledge and skills to the workplace. And once you can see the skills applied to the job, you will have a way to measure the overall impact of the skill gain and subsequent behavior change on the job. Specifically, you should be able to understand if, and how, the training benefited not only the individual, but also the organization. This will show your return on investment.

## THREE PARTS TO DEVISING AN EVALUATION STRATEGY

There are at least three parts to devising an evaluation strategy:

1. **Outlining performance indicators**. Performance Indicators will be specific to the organization, to the role of the employee(s) being trained, and to the skill(s) being addressed. As an example of an indicator, let's say we choose a skill statement like "show respect for time." Performance indicators for this skill would include behaviors such as:

   a) Adhere to workplace policy stating that "on time" means ready to work at the designated start time

   b) Use email protocol where up to 3 issues, questions, or notations are included in one email, rather than 1 email for each, as a means of saving the reader time

   c) Schedule meetings with a 10 minute closing buffer to enable meeting attendees to get to their next meetings on time, e.g., do not schedule meetings immediately back to back; 3pm-4pm and then 4pm to 5pm

   d) Reserve social communications for non-designated work time, e.g., breaks and lunch hour, as a means of maximizing productivity during designated work time

2. **Monitoring transfer of skills** – Monitoring transfer of skills means looking for, and tracking, transfer of knowledge and skill gain to the workplace. For each desired behavior that will become part of the workplace standard, you need to outline specific examples- we call these "indicators." For example, for a skill called "communicate effectively via email," we would include indicators such as "use email protocol where up to 3 issues, questions, or notations are included in one email." This protocol might include instructing trainees to write subject lines in a specific way, e.g., "3 issues" or "Response required; 3 questions." After the training we would be able to monitor if/and how frequently trainees are

writing subject lines in this way- relative to how many times they were doing this before the training. As part of your evaluation strategy you'll need to determine what will be measured, and when, and how, and by whom.

3. **Measuring bottom line impact(s)**. Again, using "show respect for time" as an example, we would have identified why this skill is important in building a culture of civility (time wasting is considered one of the more disrespectful workplace behaviors) and also would have identified how not wasting time will benefit the individual (greater efficiency, potentially less stress) and the employer (increased productivity and time is money- so potentially cost saving). To measure impact to the bottom line, we could attach a monetary value to each email, e.g., via survey or feedback from trainees, we determine that to read and respond to general/typical email might take on average 1 minute. Then we audit or survey and establish that prior to training employees/ trainees were getting on average 150 emails a day. At 1 minute per email they are spending on average 2.5 hours a day on email. At a wage of say $45/hour, this equals a cost of .75 cents per email. If we see that as a result of using the new email protocol, most employees reduce their overall number of email by even 10%, we can calculate a savings of 15 minutes per employee per day at a value of $11.25. If you've got 100 employees for example, that can equal an estimated monthly cost savings of just under $23,000.00 – and that's just the measurable bottom line impact. It will be harder to measure the decrease in stress levels but it's possible to devise a strategy to do that too.

What I can tell you for sure, is that over the past 18 years, we have worked with many organizations that have experienced at least one, but often several of the measurable bottom line and other impacts listed at the beginning of chapter 2 as outcomes of civility training.

Once we know what success will look like, and we know what we plan to measure, we can align these desired and expected outcomes with our training plan.

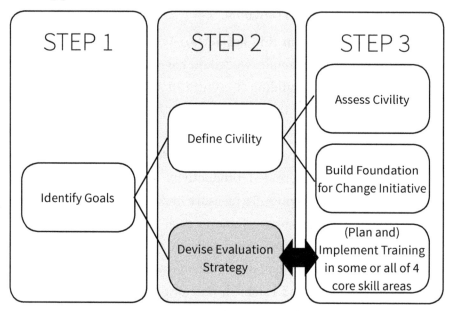

Understanding that sometimes decision makers need evidence that the outcomes we are saying can be achieved through soft skills training have actually been realized, some research to support you in that discussion is provided below.

## IMPACT OF ESSENTIAL SKILLS TRAINING

People with strong Essential Skills are:

» More employable. They find work 29 weeks faster than people with poor Essential Skills.

» Wealthier. They earn more money. In Canada, about 28 percent of what we earn is directly related to our level of Essential Skills. Nothing else - not even education and experience - contributes as much to income.

>> More productive. They make fewer mistakes and better decisions.

>> Safer. They are less likely to injure themselves or others on the job.

>> Fast learners. They learn technical skills for work, like how to operate equipment, faster.

>> Better at adapting to change. They apply what they've learned in the past to new situations and need less retraining.[9]

Workplace Education Manitoba has 25 years of positive feedback and input/evaluation data from over 500 organizations showing various measureable improvements based on Essential Skills training. As an example, Christiane Devlin, Human Resources Manager at The Kleyson Group, a Transportation Company head-quartered in Winnipeg, Manitoba, Canada stated – re outcomes of an ongoing Essential Skills training initiative designed to support Dispatchers working under very high stress conditions and interacting with diverse teams, *"...the training was an overall success in that both the intended AND unintended outcomes were achieved... there have been less errors in scheduling observed and managers are reporting a notable increase in teamwork, with dispatchers offering more help to drivers and vice versa. Managers also say they're having to spend less time refereeing problems, and a decline in customer service complaints suggests issues are being resolved at the appropriate levels."[10]*

A copy of an Essential Skills Case Study about Kleysen Transport is included in Chapter 9- Tools You Can Use.

## THE BUSINESS CASE - IMPACT OF CIVILITY TRAINING

Increased Revenue and Engagement

>> Companies that openly promote civil communication among employees earn 30% more revenue than competitors, are four times more likely to have highly engaged employees, and are 20% more

---

9   http://en.careers.essentialskillsgroup.com/?p=important

10  Workplace Education Manitoba, WPG.KT.1-6, 2015 www.wem.mb.ca

likely to report reduced turnover. Watson Wyatt Civility Survey.[11]

» In addition to skills gains, program participants in the UpSkills – Essentials to Excell, (focused on Essential Skills for Hospitality) conducted by the Social Research and Demonstration Corporation, experienced significant improvements in job performance that were accompanied by a number of positive effects for businesses. A greater breadth of service quality and improved relations with customers were observed, leading to increased customer loyalty, repeat sales, and higher revenues. Increased task efficiency and accuracy led to fewer errors and lower costs of supervision. Ultimately, improved performance was accompanied by greater job retention, leading to higher earnings for employees and lower turnover costs for employers.[12]

## INCREASED MORALE, PHYSICAL AND MENTAL HEALTH, AND HAPPINESS AT WORK

» According to the American Psychological Association, when employees feel valued by their employer, 92% say they are satisfied with their job, 91% say they are motivated to do their best, and 89% are more likely to report being in good psychological health.[13]

» In a Civility, Respect, and Engagement in the Workplace (CREW) intervention, a six-month process that fosters civil interactions between employees. Participants in the intervention experienced increases in civility with decreases in workplace distress and incivility after completing CREW. These improvements continued to increase one year after the intervention ended.[14]

---

11  http://www.towerswatson.com/

12  http://www.srdc.org/news/new-study-shows-net-benefits-of-essential-skills-training-in-the-workplace.aspx

13  http://www.apaexcellence.org/assets/general/2015-phwa-oea-magazine.pdf

14  Leiter, M. P., Day, A., Oore, D. G., & Laschinger, H. K. S. (2012). Getting better and staying better: Assessing civility, incivility, distress, and job attitudes one year after a civility intervention. Journal of Occupational Health Psychology, 17(4), 425-434.

---

## INCREASED PERFORMANCE AND PRODUCTIVITY

» The greatest differentiators in performance and achievement are "soft skills" and mindset. Recent scientific studies have established that Positive Intelligence (PQ) is a significant determinant of how much of your potential for both happiness and professional success you actually achieve. Positive Intelligence has been directly linked to a wide range of measurable benefits[15]:

- ▸ Sales people sell 37% more

- ▸ Teams perform 31% better with high-PQ leaders

- ▸ Creative output increases 3x

- ▸ People live as much as 10 years longer

» A study of workplace hiring practices by L'Oreal showed that salespeople hired based on their emotional intelligence made $90,000 more annually than those hired through traditional methods.[16]

» Behaviors involving persistence, self-discipline, effort and compliance are likely to increase individual worker effectiveness.[17]

## INCREASED TEAM ORIENTATION AND ABILITY TO WORK WELL WITH OTHERS

» The high (Emotionally Intelligent) EI individual, relative to others, is less apt to engage in problem behaviors, and avoids self-destructive, negative behaviors such as smoking, excessive drinking, drug abuse, or violent episodes with others. The high EI person is more likely to have possessions of sentimental attachment around the home and to have more positive social interactions, particularly if the individual scored highly on emotional management. Such individuals may also be more adept at describing motivational goals, aims, and missions. [18]

---

15  http://positiveintelligence.com/overview/science/

16  https://www.academia.edu/1293046/The_Business_Case_for_Emotional_Intelligence

17  https://www.questia.com/read/1G1-397579873/taking-the-good-with-the-bad-measuring-civility-and (Motowidlo, Borman, & Schmit, 1997; Podsakoff & MacKenzie, 1997).

18  http://www.unh.edu/emotional_intelligence/EI%20Assets/Reprints...EI%20Proper/EI2004Mayer-SaloveyCarusotarget.pdf

While it is true that there seems to be a greater focus on the research that proves the negative aspects of incivility, (See examples in Chapter 10/Sources and Resources for Chapter 3- Costs and Consequences of Incivility), there is also compelling evidence to support the positive impacts. I encourage you to focus on these.

As discussed in Chapter 2-Defining Civility, once you've gotten your team to agree that a key organizational goal is to build a better workplace, you will plan to implement a civility initiative. Then you'll have to work together to define civility in the context of your organization and understand what it looks like.

Completing these first steps are in fact the hardest pieces in the civility at work puzzle. But you have to do it. Without clarifying what civility means in your workplace, it will be very difficult to assess civility, to identify where your training needs are, and to evaluate your success. And without setting a clear, superordinate and overriding goal, it will be difficult to know how specifically to empower your teams to choose civility and/or to justify to various stakeholders why their support of this goal is important, and how it will benefit everyone.

## CHAPTER SNAPSHOT

» A Civility Initiative is a change imperative for companies that want to thrive in the new world of work.

» Companies that openly promote civil communication among employees earn 30% more revenue than competitors, are four times more likely to have highly engaged employees, and are 20% more likely to report reduced turnover.[19]

» If an increase in revenue isn't incentive enough, there are two other issues to consider when you need to persuade your leadership or team to support your civility initiative, they are:

---

19  http://www.webershandwick.com/uploads/news/files/Civility_in_America_2011.pdf

i.   How to get over **the "civility = manners= soft skills, and soft skills are nice to have but not necessary skills" hurdle**, and...

ii.  What will convince your team that civility training is worthwhile- will it be the costs, benefits, or consequences of civility/incivility in the workplace?

Your ability to explain what civility is relative to skills and competencies at work, combined with your ability to identify which proven outcomes of civility will be most meaningful to your stakeholders, will impact the likelihood that your organization will choose civility. Some helpful information in this regard...

» There is increasing evidence that skills once presumed to be "soft" or nice to have are in fact critical to long term success.

» Soft skills can be described as a cluster of personal qualities related to willingness, attitude, personality, and social intelligence.

» Soft skills incorporate "Essential Skills"- these are the skills and abilities needed for work, learning, and life. Essential skills provide the foundation for learning all other skills and enable people to evolve with their jobs and adapt to workplace change.

» Exhibiting civility requires incorporating a range of soft and essential skills in different combinations.

» Research shows that the majority of one's financial success is due to skills in "human engineering." Human engineering includes elements of your personality and your ability to communicate, negotiate, and lead. Human engineering is less reliant on technical knowledge- as previously understood, and more reliant on soft skills.

» Once you have defined civility, you can establish performance indicators, monitor transfer of learning on the job, and evaluate the impact of training to the business.

» There is evidence that civility in the workplace results in:

- ▶ Increased Revenue and Engagement
- ▶ Increased Morale, Physical and Mental Health, and Happiness at Work
- ▶ Increased Team Orientation and Ability to Work Well with Others
- ▶ Increased Performance and Productivity

## CHAPTER 4

# CIVILITY AT WORK - A CHANGE IMPERATIVE

*"....let us use this occasion to expand our moral imaginations, to listen to each other more carefully, to sharpen our instincts for empathy, and remind ourselves of all the ways our hopes and dreams are bound together..."*

President Obama speech at the memorial for the Arizona shooting victims.

The world is changing. The way people respond to stress and other situations seems different than even five years ago. The way we value each other, and how we act in public has also changed and without question, the way we live and work has changed too. And all this change continues at a rapid rate. Sometimes the change can be frightening, or difficult, or sad. But as President Obama suggests in the quote above, we need to change our mindset about what we're experiencing. We need to see change as an opportunity to learn. And this is especially true of changes in the workplace.

An ongoing challenge for businesses today is to manage themselves effectively in times of change, to remain in control when unexpected change arises, and to leverage the positive impact of change. The American Management Association commissioned the Human Resource Institute to conduct a global, in-depth study on strategic agility and resilience. The Institute's series of "Major Issues" surveys showed that "managing change" was perennially ranked among the top workforce management issues throughout the 1990s and into this past decade. Some of the main findings were:

» The vast majority of respondents (82%) report that the pace of change experienced by their organizations has increased compared with five years ago.

» A majority (69%) say that their organizations had experienced disruptive change- that is, severe surprises or unanticipated shocks- over the previous 12 months.

» There are meaningful differences among surveyed organizations in the highest- and lowest- performing categories. Compared with their lower-performing counterparts, higher performers were more likely to:

▶ View themselves as agile and resistant

▶ See change as an opportunity

▶ Say that the pace of change has gotten faster but remains predictable

▶ View themselves as having better change capacities at the individual, team, and organizational levels

▶ Engage in strategies such as training to improve managers' change-management skills[1]

Additionally, the Conference Board of Canada found that CEOs around the globe identify "speed, flexibility, and adaptability to change" as among

---

1    Source: American Management Association; A Global Study of Current Trends and Human Possibilities, 2006-2010. Introduction.

their greatest concerns. "Adapt or die" seems to be a prevailing attitude. Accordingly, companies of the future will benefit by finding good ways of measuring their capacity to manage change; that is, their "adaptive capacity." These organizations will be able to gauge their current agility and resilience and then determine additional needs. When gauging adaptive capacity, organizations will look at four different levels:

» the individual employee

» the team

» the organization

» the industry [2]

## WHAT DOES CHANGE HAVE TO DO WITH CIVILITY?

To survive and thrive in the new world of work, we need to learn continuously and we need to do so at the pace of change. And what does this have to do with civility? Well, clearly, implementing a civility initiative in your workplace is going to require change. People, processes, codes of conduct, how you recruit and hire, the way you evaluate performance, etc. Many of these things are going to change.

One very important aspect workplace civility programs that isn't true of all change "initiatives", is that the process and the work related to civility will necessarily go on for a long, long, time- maybe even forever! Remember in Chapter 1 where we talked about how when you approach civility as a change initiative you are never really done?

For some, this realization is going to be an insurmountable barrier to implementing civility as a change initiative. But others, as I was, may instead be inspired to learn more about change and identify ways to overcome barriers to change. Understanding what it takes to achieve positive culture change in workplaces has been a long-term pursuit

---

2    The Conference Board (2005) found that Eos around the globe identify "speed, flexibility, adaptability to change" as among their greatest concerns.

for me and it's been key in helping me discover that the best model for building a culture of civility in the workplace is a "change readiness" model- and so the *Civility Culture Compass*® was born. More on this in Chapter 7- but for now, some general discussion on change.

## THE STRESS OF CHANGE CAN BE POSITIVE

We know from our own experiences that change can be stressful. And research shows that stress impacts behavior and how we think. Of note:

a) Stress is the number one health threat in the US[3]

b) 70-90% of doctor visits are due to stress-related issue[4]

c) Stress is linked to the six leading causes of death[5]

While these risks are real, recent research is showing that work strain, when managed correctly, can actually have a positive impact on productivity and performance.[6] When driving change toward a culture of civility, the trick is to change participants' mindsets such that what might be perceived as negative stress becomes good stress e.g., anxiety becomes excitement; fear becomes enthusiasm, etc.

The fact is, stress is unavoidable. *"We live in a world of ongoing worry, change, and uncertainty. You have to get used to it,"* says Justin Menkes, an expert in the field of C-suite talent evaluation and the author of *Better Under Pressure: How Great Leaders Bring Out the Best in Themselves and Others. "Stress is an inevitable part of work and life, but the effect of stress upon us is far from inevitable,"* says Shawn Achor, an expert in positive psychology and the founder of Good Think, Inc. Both Achor and Menkes agree that altering your approach to stress can yield positive effects. *"Stress can be good or bad depending on how you use it,"* says Achor. In fact, how you manage pressures can distinguish you as a leader and give you a career advantage.

---

3    http://www.stress.org/americas-1-health-problem/

4    http://www.webmd.com/balance/stress-management/effects-of-stress-on-your-body

5    http://psychcentral.com/lib/how-does-stress-affect-us/0001130

6    http://blogs.hbr.org/cs/2011/02/make_stress_work_for_you.html

Positive impacts- stress can:

» Cause the human brain to use more of its capabilities

» Improve memory and intelligence

» Increase productivity

» Speed recovery from things like knee surgery

» And even at high levels, stress can:

» Create greater mental toughness

» Help build deeper relationships

» Heighten awareness

» Foster new perspectives

» Provide a sense of mastery

» Build a greater appreciation for life

» Give people a heightened sense of meaning

» Strengthened priorities

The findings of Harvard researchers Achor and Menkes (2011) were significant:

a) When an individual thought about stress as enhancing, instead of debilitating, they embraced the reality of their current stress level and used it to their advantage.

b) Positive-minded individuals reported significantly fewer physical symptoms associated with distress (such as headaches, backaches, fatigue).

c) On a scale of 1 to 4, productivity assessment moved from 1.9 to 2.6 — a significant shift.

d) Life satisfaction scores also increased, which in previous studies has been found to be one of the greatest predictors of productivity and happiness at work.[7]

---

7   Source: http://blogs.hbr.org/cs/2011/02/make_stress_work_for_you.html

## ▍CHANGE = LEARNING

Since many people have a visceral reaction and assume the worst when they hear the word "change," we recommend encouraging everyone involved in a workplace civility initiative to replace the word *change* with the word *learning* and to focus on the positive, as well as on the end in mind goals and outcomes, of the initiative. For example:

-Avoid calling your initiative a change initiative, call it a Ready to Learn, or XYZ Workplace Civility Project. Maybe it's an Employee Engagement Program or your Building a Better Workplace Initiative, whatever you like, just try not to put the word change in the title.

-Instead of saying, "As a result of market changes and global trends, we all have to change. We need to work faster and be more agile", say, "We can build on our current skills and take this opportunity to learn as we adapt to trends and market shifts."

-Don't say, "You need to change how you work," say, "Learning how to work differently will make you more efficient."

-Rather than saying, "You are all required to attend Change Management training," say, "The Continuous Learning course we're all taking, is going to help us manage whatever comes our way."

-Employees are more inclined to get excited about learning opportunities versus requirements to change, and people usually like knowing what the benefit of the change/learning will be, e.g., Say, "We can all reduce our daily stress by learning how to manage our time better. Attendance requested: Learning opportunity for Supervisors, every Tuesday 9-11am," versus saying, "We are wasting too much time and have to do things differently. Mandatory training for supervisors. Time Management training 6 consecutive Tuesday mornings 9-11am."

When you review Chapter 7- Competencies that Support Civility in the Workplace, you'll learn more about how specific skills such as Systems Thinking and Continuous Learning enable you to learn amid constant change. And you'll see how Social Intelligence and Cultural

Competence skill development can help individual employees and your overall organization be to be both resilient and adaptive, to foster effective communications, and to overcome the challenges that new changes bring. These abilities all support a culture of civility. You may note as you continue on in the chapter how frequently we reference "Learning" versus "Change." Think about how doing the same in your conversations about change might shift attitudes about change in your work group.

Speaking of attitudes about change, one quick exercise you can do with training participants is distribute a short perspectives on change survey.

## PERSPECTIVES ON CHANGE

| I Believe that.... | YES | Somewhat | NO |
|---|---|---|---|
| 1. Change is inevitable | | | |
| 2. Change is ongoing | | | |
| 3. Change is mostly good | | | |
| 4. Change is something I have no control over | | | |
| 5. Change is something that happens to me | | | |
| 6. Change is something I choose to actively participate in | | | |
| 7. Change is always hard | | | |
| 8. Change must be managed to be effective | | | |
| 9. A person can never prepare enough for change | | | |
| 10. Change always presents opportunities | | | |

You can also ask general questions about perspectives on civility and on learning. Sample surveys are provided in Chapter 9- Tools You Can Use.

The responses you get to these short surveys will be an indication of overall levels of resistance to change, insight into participant's general understanding of civility, and an idea of your teams' general attitudes about learning. With a civility initiative, these three elements are intertwined.

You can also get a sense of how confident participants are about their ability to handle change, e.g., often negative perceptions related to change are due to fearfulness about some perceived hardship or stress that may occur as a result of a specific change. If we can pinpoint where there is the most fear and resistance, we can intentionally address these issues and try shift these perceptions in advance of rolling out training.

It's not that we won't engage in a more comprehensive organizational and individual assessment process, but these three short, simple surveys are great tools for starting the conversation in a low-stress, non-threatening way.

## THE NEW WORLD OF WORK

While we're talking about change, and before we get too far into planning our civility initiative, it seems prudent to have a look at some trends and influences that may be impacting our workplaces, currently, or in the near future. You'll see when we look at the *Civility Culture Compass*® Model shortly that these are insights that can help you navigate potentially barriers when starting and managing a workplace civility initiative.

## RESEARCH AND RESOURCES ON TRENDS IMPACTING THE WAY WE WORK.

**Social Trends**

- » When and where employees work is changing due to mobile devices: they work at home, during their commute, and on weekends.
- » We see an emergence of the 24 hour shift (62% work before office commute,
- » 37% each evening at home, 49% in middle of the night if they cannot sleep).
- » "Trivialization" of place – employees can work anywhere, anytime, thus much more freedom.

» Many employees have smart phones and tablets and use both for work/personal.[8]

## HOW DO THESE SOCIAL TRENDS IMPACT HOW WE WORK?

We're not working face to face as much, we're on the go, and we're communicating via technology so we may lose our ability to read nonverbal and verbal cues. Plus, we may use time differently and this can be a problem if someone has a different idea of "respect for time." We may be relying on our devises and not thinking as much.

## EMPLOYMENT ISSUES

» An increase in non-standard jobs with non-traditional working arrangements

» A decrease in "middle class" jobs such as middle management with a commensurate increase in "good" jobs (professional, white-collar) and "bad" jobs (unskilled, semiskilled- cashiers, cooks), increases in downsizing and restructuring of organizations

» A definite increase in multitasking and multiskilling (expanding the range of duties and increasing responsibilities) in the modern workplace

» An increase in contract work and part time

» Moving away from job specialists to job generalists

» Management hierarchies generally are flattening

» The combination of changes in market dynamics and a shortage of available talent_create an environment where organizations will continually be asked to do even more with less and respond even faster to changes in their industry and economy" [9]

---

8  "How Work shifting is Changing the Way We Work" by Rieva Lesonsky (Sept 2011) (article)

9  "10 Trends: A Study of Senior Executives' Views on the Future" by Corey Criswell and

How do these employment trends impact how we work?

These trends can result in stress related to:

- » fewer opportunities for advancement
- » decreased employee loyalty and motivation
- » change fatigue
- » mental and physical health issues, e.g., depression, longer periods of unemployment between job changes, longer work terms before retirement resulting in multi-generations at work
- » underemployment due to necessity to take whatever job is available
- » over work and labour shortages
- » job insecurity
- » low morale
- » Workforce aging (tension between generations, retirement age, disability concerns), population aging (eldercare pressures for employees), population more ethnically diverse

Also, due to pressures of globalization, the employment relationship is increasingly fragmented, interrelated (networked) and unstable (ongoing mergers and acquisitions). [10]

## TECHNOLOGY AND HOW WE DO BUSINESS

- » Mobility, cloud computing, business intelligence and social media are transforming business: consumer behavior more value driven, business pace accelerating to "real-time," and new digital economy (due to technology) creating need for business to become more networked, less hierarchical[11]

Andre Martin for Center for Creative Leadership (CCL) (2007)

10 "The Future of Workplace Relations" by Sarah Podoro for ACAS Policy Discussion Papers (2011)

11 "The New Digital Economy: How It Will Transform Business" by Oxford Economics (June 2011)

» Changes in the structure and composition of IT: toward cloud computing (by 2020, IT computing will be almost entirely outsourced to the "cloud")[12]

» More flexibility for business in creating IT solutions for use, application and storage of information[13]

» An increase in the number of employees working at home, 90% of companies surveyed plan to invest heavily in productivity-enabling technology such as voice-activation and video conferencing, trend toward increasing mobility and use of smart phones, ongoing blurring between business and personal technology[14]

» Almost half of U.S, workforce employed in information technology industry – computer technology will continue to cause swift and extensive change in workplaces: like increasing numbers of employees working from home[15]

» Effect of social media (defined as "the use of web-based and mobile technologies to turn communication into interactive dialogue") in workplace. enhance ability of organizations to collaborate, access and learn info more quickly[16]

» The Internet is transforming the global marketplace-changing consumer behaviour and creating new business models[17]

» Industries are transforming due to the application of information technology, business pace is accelerating – "real-time" business intelligence and predictive analysis will be required for faster decision making, and coping with unexpected market risks and opportunities, and business is reorganizing to embrace the new

---

12 "10 Trends: A Study of Senior Executives` Views on the Future" by Corey Criswell and Andre Martin for Center for Creative Leadership (CCL) (2007)

13 InfoWorld (website): "Cloud Computing" (article)

14 "Workplace of the Future: How Technology Will Change the Way We Work" by Erika Chickowski (Nov 16 2011)

15 U.S. Dept of Labour "Futureworks" study (1999)

16 "Impact of Social Media in the Workplace" by Marci Paino

17 Oxford Economics "New Digital Economy"

digital economy- toward a network structure and away from hierarchy[18]

<u>How do these technology trends impact how we work?</u>

Work has intensified, through application of technology: processes move swiftly, more tasks are expected, pressure to meet productivity targets increasing. And work is becoming more dependent upon technical competence, so if you are not tech savvy or digitally competent, this can become a very big problem. Technology has enabled all sorts of non-traditional, flexible work arrangements which impact how, when and if we socialize and how we collaborate. Additionally, working effectively from home requires employees be more autonomous, make decisions and problem-solve more often without ready access to support, find information, and manage themselves and time in different ways than when operating in a workplace full-time. Networking, communication and the nature of social interaction skills need to be learned and honed for new work at home applications.

## ECONOMIC TRENDS

» "The recession and financial crisis that ended in 2009 caused a seismic shift that has reshaped the global business landscape. The world economy is now characterized by sluggish growth in the West, a shift in power to the East, and value-driven customers and rising risks everywhere. At the same time, the downturn has hastened the adoption of key technologies – mobility, cloud computing, business intelligence and social media- that are transforming business and sparking a new wave of wealth creation..."[19]

---

18  "The New Digital Economy: How It Will Transform Business" by Oxford Economics (June 2011)

19  "The New Digital Economy: How It Will Transform Business" by Oxford Economics (June 2011)

» There has been an increase in "complex challenges": globalization, market dynamics/regulation, and shortage in qualified talent, increasing competition, proliferation of new technologies, increased customer expectations, mergers and acquisitions.[20]

» Globalization, facilitated by technology, has increasingly: allowed fragmentation and outsourcing of production generally, created networked organization (joint partnership arrangements which increase efficiency and decrease costs e.g. - bringing in specialist knowledge and expertise at competitive prices), and facilitated/necessitated ongoing mergers and acquisitions.[21]

How do these Economic trends impact how we work?

We need to understand how our little piece of the world, our work etc., impact and are impacted by the rest of the world. This requires systems thinking and an ability to connect and collaborate with others as a means of accessing ideas, information and solutions that might not be immediately accessible from inside our little world. Increasingly, I would say that collaboration is currency, and you have to be a knowledgeable worker to manage the impact of these economic trends.

**▌ DEMOGRAPHIC SHIFTS**

Canadians are aging and the birth rate is falling: by 2031, 25% of Canadians will be over 65 (up from 13% currently). The Canadian population will rise to 36 million in 2026 and fall thereafter - by 2030 there will be 40 retirees for every 100 working persons. It will be more difficult over next 10-20 years to attract immigrants due to competition from other countries, and historical immigrant pools are aging also - After 2030 all Canadian population growth will be from immigration – Canadian im-

---

20 "10 Trends: A Study of Senior Executives' Views on the Future" by Corey Criswell and Andre Martin for Center for Creative Leadership (CCL) (2007)

21 "The Future of Workplace Relations" by Sarah Podoro for ACAS Policy Discussion Papers (2011)

migrants increasingly from Asian and Middle eastern countries.[22]

While the insights provided reference demographic outlook in Canada specifically, there is little doubt that other countries are experiencing similar demographic shifts.

*Gov't efforts directed to keeping older workers in the workforce (including proposed changes to human rights legislation)

*World population continues to grow overall (U.S. Census Bureau, International Database, and World Population Trends 2011)

How do these demographic trends impact how we work?

Having the ability to work well with others and to understand the impact of cultural and generational issues will be increasingly important. Employers will need to understand how to integrate their organizational culture with the growing number of legal requirements related to accommodation in the workplace. We will all have to build our social skills and communication competencies to overcome gender, generational, cultural, experiential, and communication barriers in the workplace.

## WHAT LEADERSHIP LOOKS LIKE IN 2020?

» Checklist of CEO Imperatives in "New Digital Economy" indicates leaders need to be: flexible, forward-thinking, resilient, adaptive, creative, and conversant with social media.[23]

» For leadership competency in future, the focus "....should be on key emerging business revolutions: agility (speed in anticipating change), authenticity (must create clarity: articulate a vision, cre-

---

22  Gov't of Canada: Report of the Standing Committee on Banking, Trade and Commerce, "The Demographic Time Bomb: Mitigating the Effects of Demographic Change in Canada" (June 2006)

23  "10 Trends: A Study of Senior Executives' Views on the Future" by Corey Criswell and Andre Martin for Center for Creative Leadership (CCL) (2007)

ate sense of purpose, build confidence and trust in their teams), talent (develop, engage, motivate), and sustainability (balancing business results with concern for greater good). "The winners of tomorrow....will use their skills to remain at the ready, anticipate and harness the power of change, and stay ahead of the shifting business environment."[24]

» "As globalization increases, organizations are continually asked to bridge cultural, geographical and functional boundaries effectively and efficiently."[25]

» Leaders need to create emotional resonance with and impact on others.[26]

» "Most organizations will not need a 'Lone Ranger' type of leader as much as a leader who can motivate and coordinate a team-based approach."[27]

» Future leaders will need to be conversant with doing business internationally and conceiving strategies on a global basis.[28]

» Leaders will need to cultivate resilience in their workforces to navigate change effectively and mitigate effects of employee stress.[29]

How do these trends in leadership style and skill impact how we work?

Leaders need to be able to identify stressors and engagement issues accurately and in a timely fashion. They, themselves, need to be resilient and adaptive. They need to have high social intelligence, and continually increase their cultural competence as well as always apply systems thinking.

---

24  "How Leadership Must Change to Meet the Future" p. 23 by PriceWaterhouseCooper (March 2008) (research paper)

25  "10 Trends: A Study of Senior Executives` Views on the Future" by Corey Criswell and Andre Martin for Center for Creative Leadership (CCL) (2007)

26  "Leadership Development: Past, Present and Future" by Hernez-Broome, Hughes for Center for Creative Leadership

27  "Leadership Development: Past, Present and Future" by Hernez-Broome, Hughes for Center for Creative Leadership

28  "Leadership Development: Past, Present and Future" by Hernez-Broome, Hughes for Center for Creative Leadership

29  "Why You Need a Resilient Workforce in Today`s Economy" by David Lee (2008) (article

## ADDITIONAL "INFLUENCERS"

A new pattern of work is emerging as the knowledge economy realizes the potential of new technologies and new organizational models. The changes are occurring in the areas of:

*Cognitive competence (increased range of tasks and abilities needed, and ability to sort and manage huge amounts of info)

*Social and interactive competence (excellence in conflict management and negotiation skills needed due to increased teamwork/collaboration)

*Changes in process and place (work becoming mobile)

*A new "psychological contract" between employers and employees (expectation of competency development, continuous training, work/life balance[30])

Oxford Economics: The New Digital Economy research paper co-produced by AT&T, Cisco, Citi, PwC & SAP[31] identified six dramatic shifts for which organizations need to prepare:

» The global digital economy comes of age

» Industries undergo a digital transformation

» The digital divide reverses

» The emerging-market customer takes center stage

» Business shifts into hyper drive

» Firms reorganize to embrace the digital economy

A great many of these trends and influences were considered in creating the *Civility Culture Compass*®. I encourage you to take some time to consider if and how some of these trends might already be evident in your workplace and/or how they might impact you in the future. Your answers are going to help you identify and predict skills gaps – and this

---

30  "The Changing Nature of Organizations, Work, and Workplace" by Judith Heerwagen Ph.D. (Dec 2010) (article)

31  "The New Digital Economy: How It Will Transform Business" by Oxford Economics (June 2011)

information will be very useful when you are outlining a civility competencies training plan.

## THE MYTH OF CHANGE

One of my current favorite books is *Good to Great* by Jim Collins. If you haven't read it, I highly recommend it. Collins talks about the "myths of change." He says, *"I want to give you a lobotomy about change. I want you to forget everything you've ever learned about what it takes to create great results. I want you to realize that nearly all operating prescriptions for creating large-scale corporate change are nothing but myths."*[32]

Generally, Mr. Collins talks about how in the companies that his team observed making the leap from good to great, *"... there was no miracle moment. Instead, a down-to-earth, pragmatic, committed-to-excellence process—a framework—kept each company, its leaders, and its people on track for the long haul."* And this is often how it is with civility as a change initiative. Rarely are there obvious breakthrough moments with civility initiatives. Instead, it's through the subtle day-to-day shifts in attitude, through a few extra minutes of paying attention, and through incremental modifications to each individual's way of living in the workplace, that civility takes hold.

In civility training I often reference the notion of 212 degrees- how you can be watching the pot of warm water heat up and you know something's happening but you can't always see it. There's simmering under the surface but the water is just warm- not exciting to watch, but you know that if you just keep the pot on the heat, eventually something will happen. And then it does. With one small increment, the 1 degree difference from 211 to 212, suddenly the water's boiling. One degree makes all the difference. With one last little effort you see big change. Powerful change. You can do a lot with boiling water, cook, sanitize etc. and there are beneficial side effects too. One of the side effects of boiling water is steam and you can move a locomotive with steam!

---

32   Good to Great, Jim Collins, Harper Business 2001

This is how it is with civility in the workplace. You don't always see immediate impact, but things are brewing beneath the surface. People are starting to think differently. They are starting to respond differently, starting to be more attentive. And then suddenly there's a boiling point and all those individual efforts come together to create powerful change. And there are beneficial side effects too. In addition to the obvious culture changes such as increased morale, fewer sick days, higher productivity, etc., we may also see employees taking civility home with them, being more polite to their neighbor, social capital increasing in the communities where employees live, and so on.

Collings goes on to list 7 commonly held notions about organizational change and explains how they are *"wrong, wrong, wrong, wrong, wrong, wrong, totally wrong."* His statements are based on research involving over 1400 companies over 5 years. In the end there were 5 companies that made the leap from Good to Great and Collins goes on to explain why. The myths are:

1. The Myth of the Change Program: This approach comes with the launch event, the tag line, and the cascading activities.

2. The Myth of the Burning Platform: This one says that change starts only when there's a crisis that persuades "unmotivated" employees to accept the need for change.

3. The Myth of Stock Options: Stock options, high salaries, and bonuses are incentives that grease the wheels of change.

4. The Myth of Fear-Driven Change: The fear of being left behind, the fear of watching others win, the fear of presiding over monumental failure—all are drivers of change, we're told.

5. The Myth of Acquisitions: You can buy your way to growth, so it figures that you can buy your way to greatness.

6. The Myth of Technology-Driven Change: The breakthrough that you're looking for can be achieved by using technology to leapfrog the competition.

7. The Myth of Revolution: Big change has to be wrenching, extreme, and painful—one big, discontinuous, shattering break.

Myths #1, 2, 4, and 7 can most undermine civility initiative efforts in many workplaces.

Regarding Myth 1, The Myth of a Change Program, I also agree with Collins that you don't necessarily need a "launch" event to initiate the change. With civility initiatives, grand introductions are often actually detrimental to building civility. You need to roll out the plan, sure, but without some immediate evidence of real change taking hold, hype, bandwagon campaigns, politics, and lip service, don't really contribute much to building better workplaces. Often we see workplaces spending more time and money on the launch than they actually spend on planning and rolling out the initiative. Civility ends up being perceived as the flavor of the month, and employees simply are not buying in anymore.

With regard to Myth 2, The Myth of the Burning Platform: Collins says that many people believe that change starts only when there's a crisis that persuades "unmotivated" employees to accept the need for change. The fact is, we're in the middle of a civility crisis in most workplaces-incivility is ongoing. It's already happening, and so we're well beyond waiting for an alarm to go off, the bells have been ringing and ringing and ringing. Employees are unmotivated to change *precisely* because they've been in crisis for a long time. I believe most are dumb and numb already. By this I mean that incivility is well-enough ingrained in daily work life that many employees don't even recognize it anymore. They're numb and desensitized. And where/when they recognize incivility they remain quiet- dumb, unable or unwilling to raise the issue; tired of talking about it, or incapable of navigating the often difficult conversations required to address it.

This leads us into Myth #4- the Myth of Fear as a Motivator. Yes, fear is a motivator alright, but not a motivator to be more civil. Remember, people are desperate. Fear in uncivil workplaces tends to drive desperation not motivation. And many desperate people are very afraid of change. Eliminating workplace stress, being healthy, being treated with respect, autonomy, self-mastery, shared purpose.....when it comes to fostering civility, these are the real motivators, and fear is not!

Lastly, Myth #7, The Myth of Revolution: Big change has to be wrenching, extreme, and painful—one big, discontinuous, shattering break. This is absolutely NOT true of civility initiatives. When done properly, imbedding civility is about implementing a series of subtle process changes, it's about incremental shifts- many of which are actually easy to achieve, don't cost much, and end up being self-directed by engaged individuals who are empowered and encouraged to bring their best selves to work every day.

Collins also references an ancient Greek parable that distinguishes between foxes, which know many small things, and hedgehogs, which know one big thing. He states, *"All good-to-great leaders, it turns out, are hedgehogs. They know how to simplify a complex world into a single, organizing idea, the kind of basic principle that unifies, organizes, and guides all decisions. That's not to say hedgehogs are simplistic. Like great thinkers, who take complexities and boil them down into simple, yet profound, ideas. Leaders of good-to-great companies develop a Hedgehog Concept that is simple but that reflects penetrating insight and deep understanding."* When I read this excerpt, I was validated. For years and years I have been trying to explain to clients and others how building a culture of civility is maybe complex in process but that the overall concept is simple- you want to build a better workplace. Sometimes they get it, sometimes they don't. But if you're looking to create change that will increase engagement, performance, and profitability in your workplace, your "Hedgehog Concept," the basic principle that will unify, organize and guide decisions, is not complicated. "Choose Civility." That's it. It's really a very simple concept.

## CHAPTER SNAPSHOT

» To survive and to thrive in the new world, and the new world of work, we need to learn continuously and we need to learn at the pace of change.

» To be competent in the 4 skills (Social Intelligence, Continuous Learning, Cultural Competence and Systems Thinking) that build a culture of civility and/or enable an individual to exercise civility ongoing, you need to be able to adapt to change.

» When managed properly, the stress of change can be positive, e.g., cause the human brain to use more of its capabilities, improve memory, intelligence and even increase productivity.

» Change can be frightening, but it's not so scary if you change your perspective and see it as an opportunity to learn.

» You don't need a grand launch or a catchy tag line for your civility initiative.

» The crises have already happened, incivility is likely already impacting your bottom line.

» Fear is not a good motivator- for a lot of things, but especially not when it comes to fostering civility.

» Building a culture of civility does not have to be an abrupt, painful process. When done properly making the change from uncivil to civil is a continuous process where small, subtle, painless processes enable people to think and act differently.

» Take a page from Jim Collins book *Good to Great* – literally. Be a hedgehog not a fox. If your goal is to build a better workplace, CHOOSE CIVILITY- that's your Hedgehog Concept.

# CHAPTER 5

# THE CIVILITY CULTURE COMPASS

*"The hardest decision we have to make is whether we live in a friendly universe or a hostile universe..."*

*Albert Einstein*

We've already established that civility is a values proposition (Chapter 2). It's something that you believe in that becomes a point of character. With consistency of practice, civility becomes who you are, more so than something you do. Civility is what motivates you to do the good and right thing, and what helps you determine what the good and right thing is. When applied practically, civility as a core value drives your decision-making. It influences how you communicate and directs how you behave. For most of us, learning to be civil is at first an experiential exercise, that is, our attitudes about kindness, and respect, and compassion, and graciousness, and generosity etc., develop as a result of our childhood experiences and upbringing. Influenced by our frame of reference, we develop certain perspectives on respect and related values, about our self-worth and our place in the world, and these attitudes certainly influence how we interact with our families and/or in early relationships at school and socially. It's reasonable to presume that we carry these attitudes forward into our workplaces and communities.

Unfortunately, given the high incidence of incivility in the workplace and the frequency and extent to which most of us are exposed to toxic behavior, it would seem that even those of us who grew up in civil environments are taking on the unruly behavior and negative attitudes that uncivil workplace cultures foster. How is this happening?

What is causing these lovely, polite, respectful people to turn into office bullies?

What is causing our internal civility compass to veer off a path of respectfulness and move towards incivility and negativity?

How can we get back on track?

## WHAT COMES FIRST, UNCIVIL ATTITUDE OR UNCIVIL BEHAVIOR?

This is a long-debated question when it comes to civility. What's your opinion? If you read the Introduction you already know my views on this issue. I believe that for most people, circumstances result in uncivil behavior (and desperation) which result in negative thinking and then, because we don't experience the positive impact of civility often enough, we end up with uncivil attitudes. These attitudes manifest as thinking patterns and they direct and guide our behavior.

## ABOUT ATTITUDE

In his book, *The Conditions of Learning*, Robert Gagne, defines attitude as *"A mental state that predisposes a learner to choose to behave in a certain way."* So, when we devise attitudinal training, the goals typically include asking training participants to choose to do something, or to choose to think something. In the workplace, the choices we want the participants to make would usually relate to some key organizational value proposition. Changing attitudes requires changing a person's experience so that his/her perceptions and opinions change. Then, as a result of these shifts, the individual will choose to adopt a new attitude and this results in new behavior.

Regardless of which comes first, uncivil behavior or uncivil attitude, many of us navigate through life, or at least our work life, with our internal compass veering off in negative directions because it's our habit to do so and that's the terrain we're familiar with. I like to think of this internal force, akin to the magnet that directs a compass needle, as a person's morality, conscience, and/or values. While it's allowable to be human and to make some mistakes, I believe as adults we are responsible for our choices - ultimately we have the power to choose what we do and how we think, where we go and who we go with, how we act and what we say. We need only decide to set our compass in the right direction and choose civility. Albert Einstein said that *"...the hardest decision we'll have to make is whether we live in a friendly universe or a hostile universe..."* I believe it's that once you make this decision, the second decision you have to make is whether you will contribute to the universe you choose in a positive or negative way.

Sometimes our "compass" points us in the wrong direction. This doesn't mean we're bad people. It just means we're making poor choices. And in some workplace contexts, we're inclined to behave badly more often because the pull towards incivility is very strong.

## WHY ARE PEOPLE RUDE AT WORK?

In many workplaces, this negative force towards incivility gets stronger because:

a) Choosing incivility is easier than choosing civility - when you're tired and busy and stressed, there's little time or energy left over for thinking about others

b) In many workplaces, it seems there are more rewards than consequences for being uncivil

c) Some of us haven't experienced civility enough to recognize it – we aren't learning to be civil through our experiences and interactions at work, and without experiencing civility, it's difficult to understand the benefits of it

d) The written and unwritten rules have changed so much, and are changing ongoing, so many of us just aren't sure of the current expectations and so we mirror the behavior of whomever seems to be leading at a specific time, in a specific context

e) Civility in the workplace has been dismissed for a very long time as something "nice to have" and so it is rarely strategically or formally taught. We focus on what we consider to be "need to have" skills which typically don't include "soft" skills like sensing the mood of others, being empathetic, monitoring our emotions, interpreting nonverbal cues, showing appreciation, practicing restraint, etc.

f) Even when they know what civility is, many people simply don't have the skills they need to exhibit civility in an ever-changing workplace.

Time and time again, the outcomes of workplace civility audits conducted by the Civility Experts Worldwide team reinforce my view that where incivility has become a problem, it's usually *not* because employers and/or employees don't want a civil workplace. And it's usually *not* because either or both the employee group and the employer aren't willing to do the work to make their workplace civil. Instead, in most workplaces, disrespectful behavior has simply been adopted as habit. Over time these bad habits, behaviors such as "abuse of time and resources", inappropriate tone of voice, language that fosters negativity, and poor e-communication skills as examples, become the norm in the workplace. These norms are often so well-ingrained that changing them seems an impossible endeavor. Further, people have lived with the uncivil behavior so long that they often don't even know what "civil" looks like anymore. They give up, they disengage, and they stop believing that a better workplace is even a reasonable expectation.

Wayne Dyer, a well-known author and motivational speaker, said in reference to love and kindness, *"You can only give away what you have to give."* Similarly, I believe you have to experience civility in order to be able to extend it to others. Many people don't experience civility often enough to recognize it so they are unable to extend it to others. They would be willing to think, act, and speak differently, but they don't know what is expected and so it's hard to know where to begin to change things.

It's actually quite astonishing how, as an outsider looking into a workplace, you can see all kinds of overtly uncivil behavior that people living in the organization don't even identify as uncivil. The fact that employees would say for example that chronic lateness, inappropriate language, poor communication skills and the like are just something they live with at work so it doesn't bother them much anymore, explains why even when people are sick more often, or less productive overall, they still don't see the connection between toxic workplace culture and their physical and/or mental conditions. We see too how people can exhibit a toxic behavior out of habit for a long time before even realizing they too are contributing to incivility at work. In fact, accepting incivility is contributing to incivility. If the realization that a particular behavior has changed what used to be a positive attitude into a negative one isn't enough to compel a person to change the behavior, or if the individual benefits by being uncivil, we know then that the incivility virus has taken hold. When the workplace conditions actually support incivility, rude behavior becomes a part of the fabric or personality that makes up the organizational culture.

In terms of changing workplace culture, many people assume (As mentioned in Chapter 2- Defining Civility), that behaviors described as uncivil *always* reflect an uncivil attitude. Because it can be extremely difficult to change adults' attitudes, it is also then assumed that there is very little we can actually do about incivility at work. As a result, many organizations put in place strategies such as a Respectful Workplace Policy which are strictly designed to manage behavior.

In my view, there are two potential problems with this approach. First, exhibiting a particular behavior out of habit does not necessarily reflect a specific attitude. And in cases where this is true, behavior modification can be an unnecessary and costly approach. Sometimes awareness raising is enough to bring a positive attitude back to consciousness and change a toxic behavior. Second, in and of itself, I don't find that Respectful Workplace Policies are effective tools for changing uncivil behavior because they often just "talk" about what should or could happen *after* the incivility has occurred. It's as though we are saying, "Accept that incivility is going to happen. You can't stop it, so just learn how to deal with it." It seems to me that through this approach, we are perpetuating a sort of learned helplessness and in many ways co-developing a culture of mistrust and disengagement.

If, as per Stephen R. Covey's insight quoted at the beginning of Chapter 7, *you can't TALK yourself out of problems you've BEHAVED yourself into,* the problem of incivility can only be resolved by being, thinking, and acting differently- this so that the incivility doesn't happen in the first place. One way to do this is by creating workplace environments where incivility cannot survive and certainly cannot thrive.

In a workplace context, where incivility can be attributed to a lack of experiential education, I find that people are usually not behaving civilly because they don't know any better. Or, they have specific attitudes about respect and civility based on what they may NOT have experienced. And so the plan for fostering a culture of civility in the workplace is to change their experience. We do this by:

a) creating an environment where positive change (learning) is required and supported- this to replace an environment where bad habits and negativity have been endorsed over positive change/learning

b) encouraging (and in fact requiring by way of policy and procedure) this positive change in the form of behavior in four key skill areas that underpin an ability to be civil

Then, due to the measurable benefits of the new civil behaviors being exhibited consistently and more frequently, we can change peoples' experiences. These positive experiences often result in attitudinal changes and when we can shift paradigms, we can change organizational culture. We'll be getting into this in more detail in Chapter 7- Competencies that Support a Culture of Civility.

The *Civility Culture Compass*® offers a model for a creating a culture of civility in your workplace. The Compass outlines a proactive, competency-based approach to shifting organizational culture from toxic and negative to respectful and positive.

If you are following the 3-step process for implementing a civility initiative, our discussion here is the first sub-step in Step 3. (Please see chart below)

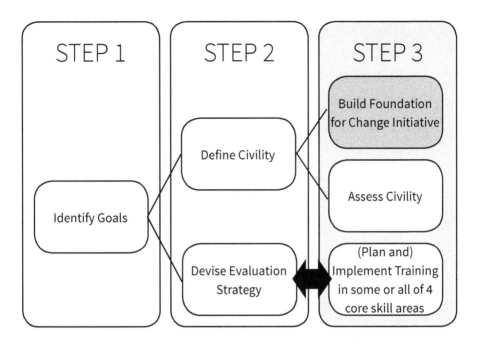

## WHAT IS ORGANIZATIONAL CULTURE?

Culture is an anthropological concept. But in the field of organizations it refers to the values, beliefs, activities, style of communication and interaction, and rituals that determine an organization's character or "personality." A company's culture can support or hinder the realization of its own vision and objectives, encourage or stifle collaboration and creativity, make it more difficult or easier to accomplish great things by its people, and so on. The organization's culture has the power to shape people's practices and behavior within it, but fortunately, we also can shape our organizations' culture by our determined understanding of cultural dynamics, and by taking action to mold the culture in a way that reflects our vision and values.[1]

As discussed in Chapter 4, it is our understanding that because we are looking to change behavior and attitude to effect organizational culture in a positive way, that imbedding civility in your workplace is a change initiative.

---

1    Extracted from HumanNext LLC www.humannext.com Cultural Competence Profile

Here is an overview of how this works:

» A Civility Change Initiative is a 3-step process (chart above), that utilizes the *Civility Culture Compass*® Model to build a foundation – that is, create conditions- that support a culture of civility.

» Once the foundation is in place – you will have identified, assessed, and addressed:

▸ Change- the past, current, and future situation

▸ Alignment- the clarity and cohesiveness of your goals and understanding of the same across the leadership team

▸ Engagement of work team

▸ Readiness- "competency-wise"

» Building on the foundation, you will devise a training plan to build civility competencies. The civility competency training plan is based on the *Civility Competency Matrix*® which details skills required in 4 key areas related to competency in civility.

» In implementing the civility initiative, you will use a range of tools such as assessments, evaluation strategies, training plans, etc. and you will engage in various activities including assigning tasks to various stakeholders.

You may be tempted to use some of these tools as stand-alone solutions and while they may be useful to some degree independently, it is important to recognize that the tools in and of themselves, are not enough to facilitate real, long-lasting change. This recognition comes as a result of our experience with past civility initiatives but also through the experience of others.

As an example, "...*like time management tools alone won't solve your time management issues, change management tools and techniques are not enough to ensure organizational change success. Leaders must shift their thinking about how change is facilitated in their organizations and integrate an understanding of the change process into all their leadership practices. In an age where there is an 'app' for everything, it is not surprising that leaders often look at organizational change from the perspective of the tools. However, there are three potential risks when you view change from this perspective:*

1. *You lose sight of the intended outcome, focusing instead on getting the tools or technology implemented.*

2. *You place the right tool in the wrong hands, thus negating its value to your organization.*

3. *You compartmentalize the change from the wider context of your organization, thus limiting your ability to increase your organization's capacity for change."*

Research has shown compartmentalizing the change and focusing on the tools and techniques instead of the leadership and management of the change is one reason for the high failure rate.[2]

Successfully changing uncivil, negative workplace cultures to civil, positive workplaces comes as a result of all the components of the model fitting together in a specific way.

## SKILLS VS COMPETENCIES. WHAT'S THE DIFFERENCE?

Once suitable conditions for implementing a civility initiative have been achieved, the next step will be to devise a training plan to build competency in civility. When individuals across an organization reach a baseline level of competency in civility, the resulting attitudes and behaviors begin to create a culture of civility. For our purposes in this book, we are making an assumption that, barring any psychological or physical barriers, every person has an inherent capacity to be civil.

Civility as a core competency requires that an individual can exhibit certain measurable, and related knowledge, skills, abilities, and

2   *Karp, T. & Helgo, T. (2008). From change management to change leadership: embracing chaotic change in public service organizations.* Journal of Organizational Change Management 8(1), 82-96.

commitments, and to do so consistently, in a way, and at a standard prescribed for application in a specific context e.g., a workplace, in a way that is deemed effective for that context.

A competency is more than just knowledge and skills. It involves the ability to meet complex demands, by drawing on and mobilizing psychosocial resources (including skills and attitudes) in a particular context.[3]

The specific knowledge, skills, abilities, and commitments that a person competent in civility can exhibit are outlined in the Civility Competency Matrix® (See Chapter 7). For our purposes, a "skill" is defined as:

- Behaviors and/or knowledge that are learned through experience, including both technical and soft skills

- Something you exhibit, what you do, or carry out for a specific purpose, e.g., to achieve a pre-determined result on the job

With the skills related to civility, "how" you use the behavior or knowledge is extremely important and this awareness is often what identifies degrees of competency related to civility.

---

3   http://onlinelearninginsights.wordpress.com

## THE CIVILITY CULTURE COMPASS®

## USING THE CIVILITY CULTURE COMPASS®

The *Civility Culture Compass*® is used to assess four organizational conditions, which when "ideal" as described below, increase the success of civility initiatives. These conditions are:

» Change

» Alignment

» Engagement

» Readiness

The extent to which you can identify that the "ideal" conditions for each of the four compass settings are met will:

a) predict how effective a civility change initiative will be if implemented in your organization at the current time

b) identify where conditions need to be addressed to increase the success and sustainability of your civility initiative

c) help pinpoint contextual and conditional aspects that may contribute to incivility in your workplace

d) enable your team to plan a cohesive and comprehensive civility initiative

e) provide a starting point for building skills in 4 key competency areas that support ability to be civil, e.g., by devising a training plan

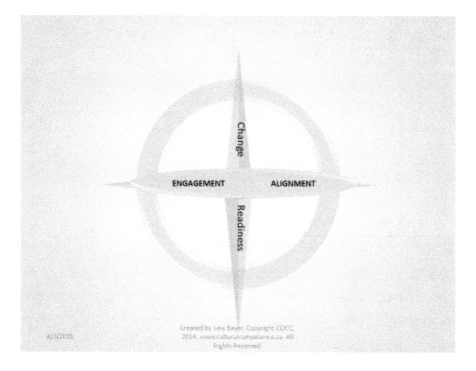

4/3/2015

## FOUR "CONDITIONS" ON THE COMPASS

Change – references the current context relative to change. What has happened in the organization in the last 6-12 months, what is currently happening or changing, and what changes are anticipated for the near and distant future?

» **Change** – Before implementing a civility initiative, ASK:

- ▶ What is the current situation?
- ▶ Have there been recent changes in the organization?
- ▶ Are there changes pending?
- ▶ Any change ongoing?
- ▶ Any changes anticipated in the community, sector, industry, or globally that could be impacting the organization now or in the near future?
- ▶ Do we understand the current need for change? E.g., Why do we think we need change?
- ▶ How receptive are we to change? E.g., Are our employees resistant?

We ask these questions as a means of understanding if this is the right time for implementing a civility initiative. We want to know if there will be distractions that we can't control. Are we anticipating personnel, logistic or economic changes that could derail or influence our efforts? As an example, if the change-makers spearheading the civility initiative are retiring within 12 months, it's not that we need to completely postpone the initiative, but we may need to consider how we will transition leadership of the initiative 8-10 months in. Or, let's say we are in the process of implementing LEAN, maybe we need to consider whether the volume of training required to transition to LEAN might result in our employees being too training-fatigued to take on civility skills training concurrently.

IDEAL conditions related to change would be:

- » No recent (e.g., in the past 60-90 days) significant changes that employees may still be recovering from
- » No significant changes planned (e.g., mergers, downsizing, relocation) planned for 3-6 months
- » Employees' overall attitude about change has been assessed;

hopefully a receptivity to change has been identified

» Awareness of untenable status quo

Enabling factors: clear goals, full communication of background and rationale for change

Hindering factors: lack of engagement, fear, low trust, unclear goals, uncertainty, unclear rationale

Skills that support a Condition of Change: Continuous Learning, Thinking Skills- specifically systems thinking and problem solving ability. Employees need to be able to adapt to change, to be resilient and to seek to understand context and consequences ongoing- these are outcomes of continuous learning ability.

**Alignment** – references the extent to which the organizations policies, procedures, values, mission etc., are currently aligned with, or positioned to support, a culture of civility.

» **Alignment** – Before implementing a civility initiative, ASK:

▶ Do our organizational values include civility? If not, why not?

▶ To what extent are day to day activities, behaviors, policies and processes currently aligned with the overriding goal, which in the case of most civility initiatives relates to building a better workplace?

▶ Is anything we are currently doing contrary to a culture of civility? (This is where we highly recommend even a short consult with a civility expert who may be able to pinpoint activities, policies, behaviors, and even processes that you do not immediately recognize as contributing to incivility in the workplace.) As examples:

▶ Are we telling people we want them to behave civilly, but then actually rewarding and/or encouraging uncivil behavior, e.g., Is it our practice to holding off starting meetings until the managers/employees who are consistently late arrive- thus rewarding them and essentially punishing those who were on time?

- ▶ Do we tell employees that we support and encourage diversity but then post notices that employees may not speak, write, or even sing in their first languages on the job?

- ▶ Do we expect employees to stay overtime or change shift times when we need them e.g., due to unexpected production schedule changes, but at the same time do not expect to occasionally accommodate those employees arriving or leaving early due to unexpected changes in their personal schedules?

- ▶ Do we tell employees that we want collaboration and teamwork but then create an environment where we pit them against each other and require them to compete for attention, accolades, assignments or rewards?

- ▶ Do we ask employees to be respectful of company property and safety regulations but then not follow through on our responsibility to keep those same employees safe at work?

- ▶ Do we expect front-line employees to adhere to respectful workplace policy, e.g., disallow profanity on the job, but then also expect employees to tolerate inappropriate language from their managers?

- ▶ And so on....

IDEAL conditions related to Alignment would be:

- » Agreement, and buy-in by leadership, that it's time for positive change (even if they don't know yet what that will look like) e.g., this relates to leadership having determined a goal such as Jim Collins' (author Good to Great) "Hedgehog Principal."

- » Managers and leaders have knowledge of desired goals and objectives of the initiative.

» Review (and update if necessary) of organizational values and their definitions.

» Review of workplace policies and procedures and identification of what is and what's not working from a leadership point of view.

» Willingness and ability to update policies and procedures as may be required.

» Awareness, (general) by leadership, of general Human Rights, Labor Laws, Bullying Legislation, Accommodation, etc.,

» Respectful workplace policy in place.

» Aligning the organization to the external environment requires forethought and taking proactive actions. Aligning employees' performance to the strategic direction requires leadership and monitoring. The strategic plan must be created against the backdrop of the organization's values; its moral compass. These values need to lay the foundation for the accepted behaviors in the organization.[4]

» Communication plan in place, e.g., to help communicate company vision and goals to all employees.

» Polling of employees to identify characteristics and/or issues of the current workplace culture from their perspective, e.g., ask them via survey or online poll, "What are the three things you would change about your workplace culture?" Or, "What are the top three stressors in your job?" Or, "What policies, behaviors, or activities in the workplace, if not changed or corrected, could potentially lead to you quitting your job?"

» Review and tracking (you can use this data as a starting point for evaluating impact of training down the road) of any/all of the following:

▸ Requests for stress leave and/or interoffice transfers

---

4   http://www.sergaygroup.com/Smart-Talk/Strategic-Alignment.html

- Retention rates
- Sick days
- Participation in workplace events identified as optional or social
- Harassment or bullying claims

Enabling factors: sufficient systems and processes in place to support initiative, direct activities (by setting and rationalizing priorities)

Hindering factors: poor/unclear communication, ineffective communication system.

Skills that Support a Condition of Alignment: Strategic Thinking and Systems Thinking – specifically, employees need to be able to take on a big picture perspective on problems, situations and events. They need to view information from different perspectives and points of view, to interpret implications and make appropriate recommendations. Social Intelligence and Cultural Competence for Leadership- they need to be able to understand employees' perspective, read verbal and nonverbal cues and assess contextual elements appropriately.

Some suggestions for additional alignment assessments are included in Chapter 9. Tools You Can Use.

Engagement- When we talk about engagement, we are talking about how consistently, and to what extent, employees are choosing to contribute to the organization in a meaningful way (beyond the basic requirements of their job descriptions). By this definition, attendance is not necessarily an indication of engagement. Simply doing one's job at the minimum standard required is participation, but participation doesn't necessitate engagement. Engagement requires "buy-in." Engaged employees believe that the work they do, and that they as individuals, have value. Fully engaged employees choose to self-motivate, to be accountable, to work well with others, to find solutions and to be positive. Engagement requires trust- this is key. We'll discuss this more in Chapter 6- Assessing Civility. Basically, if engagement is low, the likelihood that employees are ready for change is also low, and the effectiveness of any change initiative – no matter how effective the individual tools are, will be significantly reduced.

**Engagement** – Before implementing a civility initiative, ASK:

» To what extent do employees "choose" to participate in non-required workplace activities, e.g., social events, team sports, volunteer opportunities etc.?

» Do employees trust us? And do we trust them?

» Do employees show confidence in our decision-making? Or, is there frequent push-back and resistance?

» Do employees seem happy at work?

» If we could not offer wage increases, how many employees would stay with us, e.g., weather the storm and be loyal?

» When provided with opportunities for growth and training, do employees invest, e.g., give their own time or pay part of the cost?

» To what extent do employees support each other, e.g., be accountable to each other, have each other's back, and/or engage personally/socially as well as at work?

» Overall, how would we rate collaboration in our workplace?

» Have we seen increases in sick days? Turnover? Grievances?

» How do our employees respond to change? E.g., Are they resilient? Adaptive? Resistant?

IDEAL conditions related to Engagement in the workplace:

» High engagement, e.g., as indicated by high trust, and/or high "happy at work" scores. Engagement should be high:

▶ At the leadership level – this is important

▶ At all other levels

Enabling Factors: safety (physical and mental), trust across work teams, effective communication, appropriate rewards and incentives

Hindering Factors: fearfulness about job security, tyrannical management style, lack of training opportunities, low or few opportunities for questioning and open communication

Skills that Support a Condition of Engagement: Continuous Learning as it builds self-efficacy and confidence. Systems-thinking which supports adaptive capacity and problem-solving. Cultural Competence and Social Intelligence which both support empathy, team-orientation and shared perspective among and across work teams.

**Readiness** – There are 2 types of "readiness":

TYPE 1: Organizational "readiness" – here we are talking about a readiness and ability for an organization to expend resources such as managements' and/or employees' time, and a budget for training. The extent to which we are "ready" resource wise, will determine the timing, scope and approach of the Civility Initiative. Additionally, the organization has to actively create a performance and culture management focus that leaders identify, understand, and agree upon during a time of strategic change.[5]

**Readiness -** Before implementing a civility initiative, ASK:

» Are we prepared to commit our time, money, and energy to this initiative?

» Do all stakeholders understand that this is an ongoing, and long term investment?

---

5  http://smallbusiness.chron.com/approaches-organizational-strategic-alignment-14151.html

» What specifically do we want to achieve?

» IDEAL conditions for organizational readiness:

» Availability of resources e.g., personnel, time, budget for an initiative

» Identification of a specific goal related to civility, e.g., improve retention, eliminate bullying, improve innovation by embracing diversity, reduce stress by increasing respectful interactions

» Existence of plans and structures in place to support the new goals and outcomes – to trace path between mandate - engagement efforts - goals/outcomes

» All employees see the connection between the work they do every day to the company mission/strategic focus regarding the initiative

» Employees' individual goals and work performance measures are connected to the organization's vision re; the initiative

TYPE 2: Skills readiness – related to how competent employees (and/or leaders) are in the 4 key civility skill areas (below). We are going to employ a range of assessment approaches and methodologies to determine this readiness. And, the level of readiness will inform our training goals and individual learning plans. The 4 key skill areas are:

» Social Intelligence

» Cultural Competence

» Continuous Learning

» Systems Thinking

NOTE: These four key skill areas make are outlined on the Civility Culture Compass®

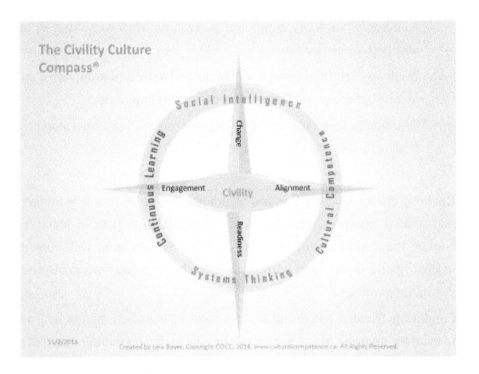

ASK:

» Have we identified where our leaders and teams are "competency-wise" in the 4 key competency areas that support the ability to be civil and build a culture of civility at work?

- ▶ Social Intelligence

- ▶ Cultural Competence

- ▶ Continuous Learning

- ▶ Systems Thinking

» Have we either trained someone in-house, or recruited or retained a qualified civility trainer to deliver the competency training we need to address the identified civility skills gaps?

IDEAL conditions for skills readiness

» Completion of skills assessments by all employees (including leadership) in 4 key competency areas understood to underpin ability to be civil at work.

» Analysis of the assessment outcomes and determination, based on ideal Alignment conditions, of where skills gaps exist.

» Training in some or all of 4 key competency areas understood to underpin ability to be civil at work.

Enabling Factors: Clear goals and communication plan, training budget and related resources available, and communication plan in place to convey the rationale and benefits of training. Trainers well-versed in civility and in the loop with respect to the organizations goals and evaluation strategy.

Hindering Factors:  Training for the sake of training, incomplete or inaccurate analysis of assessments, training fatigue, training only part of the team, training in only one or some of the competency areas but not all, fear.

Skills that Support a Condition of Readiness: Continuous Learning in that individuals can self-direct some of the learning. Social Intelligence as a means of ensuring communication of the plan and the training approach is appropriate, and Systems Thinking as a way of devising training plans that support the overriding goals and also support collaboration.

---

█ CHAPTER SNAPSHOT

» Learning to be civil is at first an experiential exercise, that is, our attitudes about kindness, and respect, and compassion, and graciousness, and generosity etc., develop as a result of our childhood experiences and upbringing.

» In many workplaces, the pull towards incivility gets stronger because:

- ► Choosing incivility is easier than choosing civility.

- ► There are more rewards than consequences for being uncivil.

- ► We aren't learning to be civil through our experiences and interactions at work, and without experiencing civility, it's difficult to understand the benefits of it.

- ► The written and unwritten rules have changed so much, and are changing ongoing, and so many of us just aren't sure of the current expectations so we mirror the behavior of whomever seems to be leading at a specific time, in a specific context.

- ► Civility in the workplace has been dismissed for a very long time as something "nice to have" and so civility is rarely strategically or formally taught.

- ► Even when they know what civility is, many people simply don't have the skills they need to exhibit civility in an ever-changing workplace.

» In a workplace context, where incivility can be attributed to a lack of experiential education, the plan for fostering a culture civility in the workplace is to change their experience. We do this by:

- ► creating an environment where positive change (learning) is required and supported- this to replace an environment where bad habits and negativity have been endorsed over positive change/learning

- ► encouraging (and in fact requiring by way of policy and procedure) this positive change in the form of behavior in four key skill areas that underpin an ability to be civil

» The Civility Culture Compass® offers a model for a creating a culture of civility in your workplace. The Compass outlines a proactive, competency-based approach to shifting organizational culture from toxic and negative to respectful and positive. The Civility Culture Compass® is used to assess four organizational conditions, which when "ideal" as described below, increase the success of civility initiatives. These conditions are:

- ▶ Change
- ▶ Alignment
- ▶ Engagement
- ▶ Readiness

» Civility as a core competency requires that an individual can exhibit certain measurable, and related knowledge, skills, abilities, and commitments, and to do so consistently, in a way, and at a standard prescribed for application in a specific context e.g., a workplace, in a way that is deemed effective for that context.

# CHAPTER 6

# ASSESSING CIVILITY IN YOUR WORKPLACE

*"Learning without thought is labor lost. Thought without learning is intellectual death."*

- Confucius

If you are following the 3-step process for starting a civility initiative, you will have already set an "end in mind" goal (likely related to building a better workplace). Identifying this goal would have required completing some type of general organizational assessment e.g., based on the 4 conditions outlined in the *Civility Culture Compass*®. (See Chapter 8 for a sample).

Hopefully, you've also defined civility, including detailing indicators of what civility looks like in the context of your workplace (these indicators will be used to measure success), so the next step will be to assess civility in your workplace.

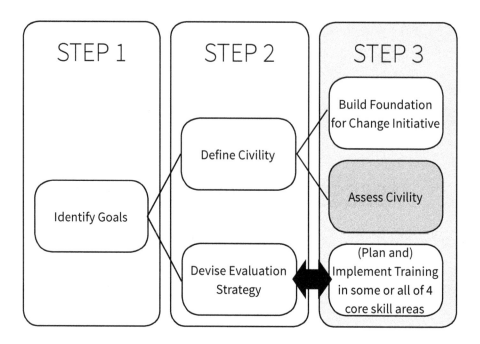

## WHAT IS A NEEDS ASSESSMENT?

A Needs Assessment is a systematic exploration of the way things are and the way they should be. These "things" are usually associated with organizational and/or individual performance.[1]

The purpose of conducting a needs assessment is to better understand the reason why things are the way they are- rather than the way they should be and how we want them to be. Analyzing the issues and factors that are creating the current situation, helps us know what the solution is to get us where we want to be, and where, when, and how we will apply that solution.

We often make assumptions about the reason for things being how they are and this can result in costly mistakes. For example, if we

---

1    http://alumnus.caltech.edu/~rouda/T1_HRD.html

automatically assume that low productivity in a manufacturing context is due to lack of employee competence, we might spend a lot of time and money delivering training, only to discover that the problem wasn't competence at all. Maybe the problem was in fact outdated equipment or internal systems. Given the speed of change and the cost of these mistakes, organizations simply cannot afford to make rash decisions-needs assessment is an effective way to control some of the investment costs of change.

Another key reason we recommend doing an assessment is that if you use the Compass and assess the four civility culture conditions, you may in fact find that addressing these conditions solves your problem, and you don't need training after all.

Assessment for workplace training may include assessing one or all of the organization (in its entirely or one or more departments, or divisions), the team(s), or the individual(s).

## ▌ SOME INTERESTING STATISTICS ABOUT TRAINING:

One in three workers thinks the time he/she spent in his/her last training session probably would have been better spent elsewhere, according to a survey by Hudson, a staffing and consulting services company.

Among these workers, 12% think the training was a complete waste of their time.

Self-improvement was the main reason for participation in training; 68%of respondents said they attended training because they thought it would provide useful, job-related information. Another 28% said they were told to go. The last 3% went to training to meet people or to get out of the office.[2]

Trainingindustry.com estimates that:

> » 2013 Corporate and government spend for training activities in N.A.

---

2    http://www.cio.com/article/2447352/training/time-in-training-often-wasted.html

(North America) was approximately $141.7B. We believe the average spend for all corporate training activities (employee and customer) to be about .7 percent of annual revenues (or $7 for every $1000 in company revenues). Generally speaking, the larger the company the more they spend on training as a percent of revenue. Companies that are more technology oriented tend to spend more, while companies who are more service oriented tend to spend much less. *Note: ASTD estimates the 2012 market to have been $164.2B, down from $171.5B which they reported for 2011, or 1.1 percent of revenues.*

» Spend for training services has increased by about 5.2 percent from 2012, much better than what was originally anticipated (original expectations were that the market would grow at a modest 2.5 percent. Spend levels have now exceeded the industry's high market in 2007 of about a $136B. Our best estimates find the ten year industry low mark to be in 2002 with spend at about $109B, and again dropping to $110B in 2009 (revised from earlier estimates).

» The global market for training expenditures in 2013 was about $306.9B, an increase from $291.7B in 2012. We believe N.A. represents about 46% of the global market ($141.7B) and Europe to be about 29%, or $89B of the global market. Asia comes in at $31B (10 percent), India $21.5B (seven percent), Australia $9.2B (3 percent), South America $6.3B (2 percent), Africa $3.6B (1 percent), and the rest of the world $4.6B (1.1 percent).

» Approximately 75 percent of the global spend for training is in North America and Europe. Asia and India, the two most populated regions in the world, combined make up about 17 percent of the global market.

» Companies spend about 44 percent of their training related dollars on employees, compared to 49 percent on customers, and seven percent on suppliers and channel partners.

» Companies in North America spend approximately 58 percent of their training budget on insourced activities (people, facilities, etc.), and about 42 percent of their budget on outsourced services. This translates into a supplier market for outsourced services of $59.5B and an insourced spend of $82.2B. *Note: ASTD estimates companies spend 60 percent of their training budgets on internal resources and 40 percent with external suppliers.*

»   The top 5 non-BPO market segments for outsourced training are IT ($2.9B; 4.9 percent), Leadership ($2.6B; 4.4 percent), Learning Technologies ($4.0B; 6.7 percent), Sales Training ($2.2B; 3.8 percent), and Content Development ($3.5B; 5.9 percent). All other segments account for about $44.2B. The market is so highly fragmented that the top five segments represent only 12 percent of the total market spend.

»   Training BPO (business process outsourcing) services in N.A. was about $5.76B, or 9.7 percent of the external spend for training services. This includes both comprehensive and selective outsourcing deals. We estimate the out-tasked market for training services was about 90 percent of the sourcing market, or $53.7B. Respectively, licensing of content and training technologies was about $34.1B (58 percent), and contracting for training resources to be about $19.6B (32.3 percent).[3]

Deloitte Consulting LLP, a leading research and advisory firm empowering Human Resource (HR) organizations to drive bottom-line impact has completed research showing that overall spending on training rose 15 percent to $1,169 per learner on average in 2013. The rise in training spending is a signal that businesses are responding to a growing skills gap as the economy recovers by investing more in employee development.[4]

Average training expenditures for large companies have increased from

---

3    http://www.trainingindustry.com/blog/blog-entries/how-big-is-the-training-market.aspx

4    The Corporate Learning Factbook 2014: Benchmarks, Trends, and Analysis of the U.S. Training Market

$11.3 million in 2012 to $17.6 million in 2013, while small companies remained basically flat ($301,082 in 2013 vs. $294,532 in 2012), and midsize companies saw a decrease from $2 million to $1.2 million.[5]

Training is an important part of efforts to reduce workplace injury, illness, and death. In the United States, the total cost of workplace health and training alone is over $100 billion per year.[6]

So after reviewing the above statistics, here are some important questions to think about.

1. Would your organization benefit by spending less on training that one in three workers will likely perceive as a waste of time?

2. If planning strategic training in just one to four key competency areas could potentially increase your profitability by 30%, wouldn't you want to do that training?

3. If you knew that 67% of employees would actively engage in the training indicated in #2, wouldn't you be further inclined to do that training?

4. If you knew you could save time and money by administering one or more quick assessments to identify exactly which of four key competency areas your team needed training in- with little expenditure of time and resources, would you conduct these assessments?

5. If there was evidence that training in one or more of these four key areas could resolve issues related to retention, engagement, and profitability, would you want to engage in this training?

If you answered yes to one or more of the questions above, civility training offers a solution to better managing the costs, time requirements, and employee buy-in aspects of workplace training. The next step is completing a needs assessment to identify your training needs.

_____

5   https://trainingmag.com/2013-training-industry-report
6   http://blogs.cdc.gov/niosh-science-blog/2010/01/29/training/

_____

## BENEFITS OF COMPLETING A NEEDS ASSESSMENT?

One of the key reasons a needs assessment is completed prior to launching a training plan is to manage resources. Training takes time and money and so it just makes sense to have an idea what you are training, why you are training, and who needs the training *before* you train.

There are many additional benefits to completing a needs assessment, these include increased ability to:

» focus the training on what's important at a specific time for a specific learner

» identify strengths and weaknesses of learners

» identify continuous improvements to current structure

» fit learning to learner

» identify a future learning path

» fit trainer to the need of the leaner

» identify metrics by which to measure success

» align gaps in goals

» build a framework for a training communication plan

» establish expectations for return on investment

» asses engagement

» identify risks

» build a frame of reference

» enable priorities for action to be established

» plan the most effective development of limited resources, for instance, to ensure cost effectiveness and value for money

» justify investment in training by showing how it will contribute to achieving corporate objectives

» provide a basis for integrating training into the business by getting line management involvement and commitment

## APPROACH TO WORKPLACE CIVILITY ASSESSMENT

There are two typical approaches to completing a workplace civility assessment:

1. Helping people identify performance issues and consider what skills gaps are causing the issues as well as how planned training can help to solve them.

2. Taking a big picture view of the whole organization. Consider current, present, and future activities and goals, and then develop training plans to meet the identified current and anticipated training needs.

Depending on the outcomes you are looking for, you will choose either #1 or #2. For example, if your primary issue is attrition and your goal is retention, you might consider starting with #2. If your issue is a specific employee or group of employees who are not working well together, you might start with #1.

With civility initiatives, because we can often identify elements of overall workplace culture as causing incivility at work, we typically recommend starting with an Organizational Culture Assessment. **Primarily, we are assessing the current situation relative to the four conditions identified as strong influences of successful civility training. These are outlined in the Civility Culture Compass®.**

» Change

» Alignment

» Readiness

» Engagement

At Civility Experts Worldwide, we customize these civility condition assessments, and much of this process is proprietary. However, there are some general assessments (mostly paper-based) you can use to get started. Details about the sample assessments listed below are included in Chapter 9, Tools You Can Use. There is also additional detail in Sources and Resources. It is always recommended that you use a combination of several needs assessment methods including:

- » direct observation
- » questionnaires
- » consultation with persons in key positions, and/or with specific knowledge
- » review of relevant literature
- » interviews
- » focus groups
- » tests
- » records & report studies
- » work samples

## RECOMMENDED ASSESSMENT PROCESS:

While it is understood that identifying a key issue or problem (or more than one) that the organization is looking to address with a civility solution is in fact part of assessment, we consider it to be more of an awareness raising exercise for the organization. However, the data collected in completing this pre-work is used to inform the next steps which we consider to be the "formal" assessment.

Assessment Process Phase 1: Complete a general organizational culture assessment – start by asking the questions outlined for each of the four conditions of the Compass as outlined in Chapter 5. And then if you don't have enough information to move forward, do additional organizational culture assessment.

■ SAMPLE GENERAL WORKPLACE CULTURE ASSESSMENTS:

» Civility Culture Compass® General Assessment [7]

» The Denison Organizational Culture Survey[8]

» Organizational Health Index[9]

» Organizational Culture Assessment Instrument[10]

Assessment Process Phase 2: After you are able to establish how ideal the current situation is for each of the four conditions, try to identify aspects of any less than ideal conditions that you can adjust. This is achieved through administering additional, targeted assessments- specific to one or more of those four conditions: Readiness, Change, Alignment, and Engagement.

■ ALIGNMENT

Some strong indicators of potential misalignment between current organizational processes, workplace culture etc., a culture of civility include: team conflict, quantity of miscommunications, bullying claims, low morale, low retention, and accountability issues.

■ SAMPLE ALIGNMENT ASSESSMENTS:

» Organizational Values Assessment Tool[11]

» Civility Symptoms Survey® Civility Experts Worldwide[12]

» Clark & Landrum Civility Scale® Cindy Clark/Eric Landrum Boise

---

7   Owned by Civility Experts Worldwide, www.civilitexperts.com

8   http://former.denisonconsulting.com/diagnostics/organizational-culture

9   http://www.mckinseysolutions.com/

10  http://www.ocai-online.com/

11  http://www.careleaders.com/assessment/valuesAssessment.html

12  www.civilityexperts.com/assessments

State University[13]

» Ranson Civility Quotient[14]

» Civility Norms Questionnaire[15]

» Positive Culture Assessment[16]

Please see additional information in Chapter 9- Tools You Can Use.

## ENGAGEMENT

There are many indicators of low engagement. Sometimes it is true that attendance and number of sick days or stress-leave requests seem like obvious signs that people are not engaged. But these are not always accurate, for example there may be legitimate physical or psychological reasons a person isn't coming to work. Because we understand engagement to mean employees are actively choosing to contribute in a positive way beyond their basic job requirements, we find a stronger indicator of engagement is the overall level of trust. This is because high levels of trust typically correlate with employees stating that:

» They feel valued as individuals

» They feel their contribution has value

» They feel empowered

» They feel that they are treated fairly

» They feel they are compensated fairly

» They feel empowered to self-direct and/or make decisions

» They have a sense of shared purpose

» They feel they can overcome workplace challenges

» They feel supported

13  http://hs.boisestate.edu/civilitymatters/research-instr.htm

14  http://stopbullyingtoolkit.org/Civility-Quotient-Assessment.pdf

15  http://stopbullyingtoolkit.org/Civility-Quotient-Assessment.pdf

16  http://www.iedex.com.au/index.php/organisational-assessments/positive-culture-surveys.html

>> They are happy at work

When the above are perceived, people are more likely to perform well and to exhibit positive, respectful behaviors.

## SAMPLE ENGAGEMENT ASSESSMENTS:

>> Happiness at Work Survey[17]

>> Franklin Covey Trust Quotient[18]

>> Organizational Trust and Engagement Index [19]

>> Gallup Q12 Engagement Survey[20]

## CHANGE

One strong indicator of that change in a workplace that could be inhibiting respectful behavior is the degree of hardiness- hardiness references the physical and/or "bounce-back" from stress and change. Hardiness fosters resilience and resilience of individuals collectively contributes to an organization's overall adaptive capacity.

## SAMPLE CHANGE ASSESSMENTS:

>> Change Management Readiness Assessment[21]

>> Organizational Capacity Assessment Tool[22]

>> Resilience Assessment[23]

---

17  https://www.happinessatworksurvey.com/info/scores

18  http://www.franklincoveyme.com/trust-quotient-tq-assessment

19  http://www.speedoftrust.com/How-The-Speed-of-Trust-works/speed-of-trust-measurement

20  https://q12.gallup.com/public/en-us/Features

21  http://www.change-management.com/tutorial-change-management-assessments.htm

22  http://www.peecworks.org/peec/peec_inst/01795CC4-001D0211.52/M.%20Casey%20Org.%20Capacity%20Assessment%20Tool%20%28paper%20version%29.pdf

23  http://www.wmich.edu/emrl/resilienceassessment.htm

---

» Change Resistance Assessment[24]

## READINESS

One strong indicator of readiness is understanding whether Learners (employees) are physiologically hardy and whether they feel psychologically safe. When employees do not feel their basic needs are being met, it is not likely they will actively participate in learning, and/or the learning will not transfer to the workplace. As an example, if an employee does not feel safe at work, or if he/she feels underpaid or taken for granted, if he/she is unhealthy because of overwork or lack of breaks, he/she may be consciously or subconsciously focused on figuring out how to get these basic needs met. And, if this basic need is not met, learning – no matter how good training is, will not be a priority. (Please see Maslow's Hierarchy of Needs Chart and assessment in Chapter 9- Tools You Can Use)

## SAMPLE READINESS ASSESSMENTS:

» Hierarchy of Needs Self-Test[25]

» Hardiness Test[26]

» Workplace Stress Assessment[27]

» Learning Culture Assessment[28]

## USING ASSESSMENT OUTCOMES

Once we have the outcomes of our assessment, we are going to set a

24  http://www.wmich.edu/emrl/resilienceassessment.htm

25  www.businessballs.com. © alan chapman 2003. Disclaimer: Sole risk with user. Neither alan chapman nor businessballs.com accepts liability for any issues or damages arising from the use of this tool.

26  http://www.queendom.com/tests/access_page/index.htm?idRegTest=700

27  http://www.stress.org/self-assessment/

28  http://www.ashpfoundation.org/selfassessment/selfassessmenthelix11151211.html

training plan goal and outline some learning objectives. We use a version of SMARTER approach to this goal-setting, specifically we consider:

**S** – specific; what *exactly* do you want to be different after the training?

**M** – measurable; How will you know there has been behavior change? What will you compare the "after" to?

**A** – applicable; are you sure these are skills the employees needs to exhibit on the job? e.g., don't train just for the sake of training.

**R-** realistic - can we really teach/train what we need to with the resources available?

**T** – teachable - are we sure, e.g., via assessment, that the identified gaps are based on "skill versus will"? e.g., not so easy to change attitude and attitude is a big part of civility.

**E** – evaluated; Do we have an evaluation plan in place? How will we know we have met our goals? How will we know which aspects worked and which didn't?

**R** – rewarded; What are the benefits to the employee when he/she exhibits this positive behavior? How can you ensure the benefits will be experienced? What are the benefits to the organization? e.g., goes to return on investment.

Assessment Process Phase 3: If conditions were not ideal for any of the four factors, we would conduct further assessment in the identified foundational area. We do this to better understand the factors influencing civility in the organization and we want to have a clearer view of where we can address any or all of these four conditions. In this way, we lay a foundation for success – and then we can start our civility training in one or more of four civility competency areas- this is our discussion in Chapter 7. However, it must be stated that sometimes, once you address the condition- and/or restore one or more of the influencing conditions to "ideal" status, you could find that the behaviors or issues you set out to address have been resolved. If the symptoms of incivility have been alleviated, it may be that no civility training is actually required.

## CHAPTER SNAPSHOT

» A Needs Assessment is a systematic exploration of the way things are and the way they should be. These "things" are usually associated with organizational and/or individual performance.[29]

» The purpose of conducting a needs assessment is to better understand the reason why things are the way they are- rather than the way they should be and how we want them to be. Analyzing the issues and factors that are creating the current situation, helps us know what the solution is to get us where we want to be, and where, when, and how we will apply that solution.

» One of the key reasons a needs assessment is completed prior to launching a training plan is to manage resources.

» There are two typical approaches to completing a workplace civility assessment:

» Help people identify performance issues and consider what skills gaps are causing the issues as well as how planned training can help to solve them.

» Taking a big picture view of the whole organization. Consider current, present, and future activities and goals, and then develop training plans to meet the identified current and anticipated training needs.

» The recommended assessment process is:

▶ Phase 1: Complete a general organizational culture assessment.

▶ Phase 2: If general organizational culture assessment identifies issues related to incivility, administer assessments to identify which one or more of the four civility culture conditions:

---

29  http://alumnus.caltech.edu/~rouda/T1_HRD.html

Readiness, Change, Alignment, and Engagement, is not ideal.

- ▶ Phase 3: When one or more of the four civility culture conditions has been identified as not ideal, conduct further targeted assessments in that specific foundational area.

» One of the ways the Compass can save organizations time and money is because sometimes once the influencing conditions are restored to "ideal," the incivility symptom is resolved and no training is necessary.

## CHAPTER 7

# THE CIVILITY COMPETENCY MATRIX

*"You can't talk yourself out of a problem you've behaved yourself into."*
Stephen R. Covey

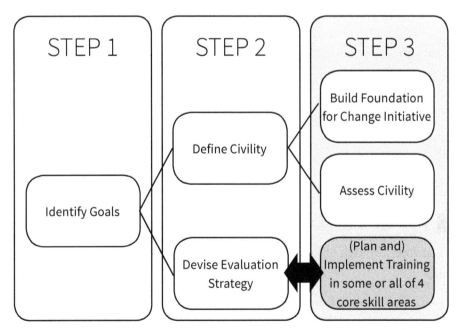

As per Covey's words of wisdom above, if civility is a problem in your workplace, just talking about it isn't likely going to resolve your issues. Discourse certainly has its place, but when habits are ingrained, expectations not clearly defined, and/or when people don't know what they don't know, training is how to solve the problem.

The Civility Culture Compass® outlines four conditions, which when met, increase the likelihood that efforts to build a culture of civility will be successful. The Compass also depicts four key skills that collectively make up overall competency in civility. These are the skill areas in which training is planned and implemented.

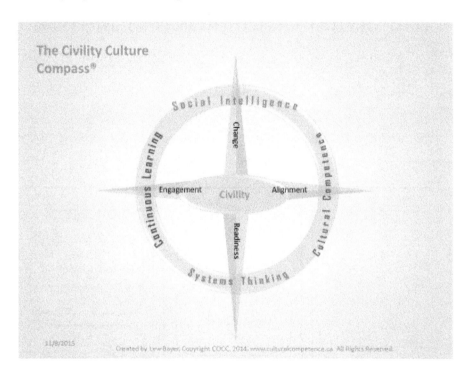

The Civility Culture Compass®

## FOUR KEY SKILLS AREAS FOR COMPETENCY IN CIVILITY

The four key skill areas identified as required for competency in civility are:

- » Continuous Learning
- » Social Intelligence
- » Systems Thinking
- » Cultural Competence

The identification of these four skills as key to an individual's ability to exhibit civility at work was based on the review of projects we've completed at Civility Experts Worldwide over the past 18 years. After analyzing outcomes – we use the Kirkpatrick Evaluation Model (See Chapter 9 for information on this), we started to see patterns emerge. And, we were able to identify clusters of skills that seemed to correlate with exhibition of civility as defined by Civility Experts Worldwide. We offer more detail on this process in the Civility Competency Matrix® Train the Trainer Program.

> » A **conscious awareness** of the impact of one's thoughts, actions, words and intentions on others; combined with,
>
> » A **continuous acknowledgement** of one's responsibility to ease the experience of others (e.g., through restraint, kindness, non-judgment, respect, and courtesy); and,
>
> » A **consistent effort** to adopt and exhibit civil behaviour as a non-negotiable point of one's character.

As outlined in Chapter 2, the definition is important as it describes *exactly* what success will look like. As a result, we are able to identify behavior that results in this success and we can measure the extent to which the behaviors are exhibited, and how and when, and by whom. And if we can measure the skill, we can then measure it prior and post training. And when the learning is transferred to the workplace, we can determine the impact on the workplace.

### PATTERNS OF IMPACT- CIVILITY TRAINING AT WORK

In reviewing projects where we saw a transfer of learning to the workplace after civility training, some of the patterns that emerged were:

| Civility-Related Training; Skill Area | Measurable Impact to the Organization |
|---|---|
| Continuous Learning | - Culture of learning indicators increased e.g., quicker transition to roles, "stickiness" of training, more participation in non-assigned learning<br>- Change readiness indicators increased, e.g., less resistance to change, fewer stress and sick days taken<br>- Employees self-assessed as more resilient, e.g., better able to cope independently<br>- Employees self-assessed as self-identifying skill gaps, e.g., understood value of ongoing learning, actively sought out training<br>- Decreased dependency by employees for organization to manage all learning, e.g., individuals self-directed more often including off-site learning, engaged in mentorship activities<br>- Post-evaluation showed reduced overall fear of change, e.g., fewer negative comments, increased trust (verified by survey) and self-increased confidence to overcome barriers,(managers reported less coaching required) |
| Social Intelligence | - Increased abilities (individually assessed) to interpret verbal, tonal, contextual and nonverbal cues correctly, e.g., ability to predict and/or identify when context created conflict versus individuals choosing it<br>- Employees self-identified social style and were able to adapt same if/as required, e.g., choose to adopt style favored by another<br>- Increased understanding of the written and the unwritten rules of the workplace, e.g., recognize when expectations were not being met based on what was not said or written |
| Cultural Competence | - Increased understanding of influencing contextual factors, e.g., shift work results in certain workplace culture nuances, male-dominated work group results in certain workplace culture nuances<br>- Decreased fearfulness related to diversity, gender, and generations at work, e.g., self-identifying bias, stereotypes, prejudices that were perceptions versus reality<br>- Increased recognition of shared vision, e.g., that each individual has value |
| Systems Thinking | - Increased productivity, less wasted resources due to increased alignment, e.g., individuals and teams showed greater accountability to each other and organization; increased recognition of interdependencies |

## CIVILITY COMPETENCY MATRIX- OVERVIEW

The Civility Competency Matrix® is a training tool that details the knowledge, skills, and abilities for each of the four key skill areas that build competency in civility. Training supports and curriculum are customized for organizations. These solutions are based on the Matrix and on the organizational assessment outcomes.

| Competencies that Support a Culture of Civility | |
|---|---|
| Core Competencies | Indicators of Competence |
| Continuous Learning | Embraces change, engages in self-analysis, is resilient, anticipates challenges, seeks purpose, seeks opportunities for discourse, welcomes debate and interaction. |
| Thinking Skills | Engages in problem-solving, can make effective decisions, practices systems-thinking, sets goals understands interconnectedness, is accountable. |
| Social Intelligence | Shows respect, works well with others, uses social radar, self-identifies and adapts social style, understands rationale for and follows, written and unwritten rules. Trusts others and seeks to be trusted, exhibits restraint, takes responsibility, sets and practices personal standards for decorum, exhibits common courtesy, understands generosity. |
| Contextual Cultural Competence | Is aware of values, recognizes shared needs and vision, engages in collaboration activities, shows team-orientation, considers perspective of others, shows empathy, recognizes bias, appreciates differences, adapts to context, monitors tone can define "appropriate" based on workplace culture |

The Matrix also outlines four competence-based roles – because as you may recall in Chapter 4, building a culture of civility is best managed as a change initiative. And best practice for change initiatives includes assigning a change management team.

Level 1 – Ambassador

Ambassadors are learning; about themselves, their team-mates, about the organization, about civility generally and about the initiative. The

GOAL- ENGAGEMENT, LEARNING and TRUST

Level 2 – Coach

Coaches are supporting and guiding the Ambassadors. Supports may include providing civility-oriented information, tools, opportunities, and activities to leverage engagement etc. GOAL- EMPOWERMENT, SKILLBUILDING and CHANGE READINGESS. You have to be an Ambassador before you can coach.

Level 3 – Change-Maker

Change-makers are directing and managing the initiative/change; Only Coaches can become Change-makers. GOAL- STRATEGIC PLAN, STANDARDS and DIRECTION towards desired outcome.

Level 4 – Exemplar

Exemplars are envisioning and leading. GOAL – INSPIRATION, ALIGNMENT, and COLLECTIVE CHANGE

In this chapter we are just providing an overview of the four key skills. If you are interested in learning more, or you'd like a Site License, Trainer's Kits or curriculum so that you can deliver training in one or more of the four skill areas, please see Sources and Resources.

## ABOUT CONTINUOUS LEARNING

Continuous learning is learning how to learn. Every day presents new opportunities to learn from our experiences, but to take advantage of these opportunities we need to develop our continuous learning skills, including being able to:

- » think in different ways
- » self-reflect
- » inquire and ask questions
- » seek feedback from others
- » draw conclusions

- » gather insights
- » conceptualize the learning process
- » organize our learning
- » participate in training
- » set goals
- » actively engage in gathering knowledge
- » understand our learning style
- » practice applying what we learn
- » adapt and change
- » mprove ourselves on an ongoing basis

Blogger Charles Jennings says that *"...continuous learning is the only sustainable asset in a world of constant change."*[1] I would agree with this statement. If you are not willing to learn ongoing, you simply will not thrive in the new world of work. Continuous learning benefits individuals by building confidence, increasing competency, improving performance, and enabling future opportunities.

Continuous Learning also brings measurable benefits to organizations. For example, in organizations that support a culture of continuous learning, there are often higher levels of engagement, greater accountability, increased co-operation, high productivity, and reduced turnover- this due in part to increased trust and a mutual understanding by both the employer and the employee that continuous learning increases employability.

There is also a bottom line benefit of Continuous Learning in that organizations with skilled workers have a competitive advantage and usually manage change, as well as the costs often associated with managing change, more effectively than organizations that do not

---

1   Source: http://charles-jennings.blogspot.com/2011/10/in-complex-world-continuous-learning.html

support a culture of Continuous Learning. One of the key outcomes of continuous learning is that individuals become "knowledge workers."

Knowledge worker – definition: An individual who "thinks for a living" – that is, he/she values and develops thinking skills and continuous learning habits that enable him/her to be creative, innovative and forward thinking. Knowledge workers are effective problem solvers who recognize challenges as opportunities. Knowledge workers analyze the situation at hand and question when appropriate, are constantly learning and growing and are confident they have, or can acquire knowledge needed to be successful. Knowledge workers forge ahead in a positive, open-minded, information seeking and gathering way that enables them to be resilient, adaptive and ready for change. They embody excellent continuous learning skills, the foundation of a change management mindset.[2]

The specific aspects of Continuous Learning that help an individual exhibit civility are:

» Self-identifying their own learning styles, the learning style of their immediate supervisor and other colleagues.

» Recognizing the components of learning culture that exist in the workplace.

» Considering the nature of change and how change can/will impact their ability to do their job ongoing.

» Becoming aware of the overall organizational adaptive capacity, e.g., what does the big picture look like? Is the individual, team, leadership, etc., able and willing to adapt as necessary?

---

2    Howell, Wright, Bayer, Workplace Education Manitoba, The Change Imperative, 2011.

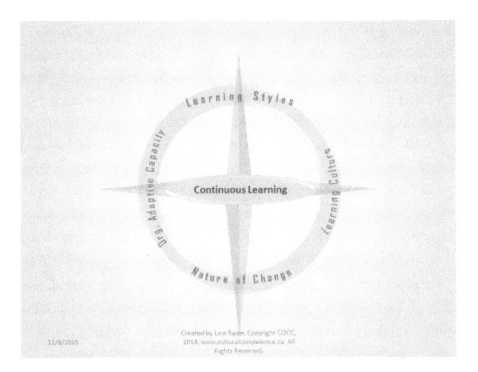

How specifically does continuous learning relate to civility?

In organizations where incivility is assessed as high, we frequently find low adaptive capacity overall. We also see that the organizational culture (e.g., hierarchy, policies) may actually inhibit an individual's ability to self-direct, to develop, and/or to learn on the job. Some workplaces actually discourage thinking and learning is not rewarded. Under these conditions, people tend to develop poor habits, they can become complacent, they don't adapt to change well, and this causes resentment, boredom, closed-mindedness, and fearfulness that can manifest as uncivil behavior. If employees are unhappy and disengaged, if they don't feel valued and there is no incentive to grow, they are frequently not welcoming of new employees or other workplace changes.

## ABOUT SYSTEMS THINKING

Systems Thinking is the ability to see the big picture, and to distinguish patterns instead of conceptualizing change as isolated events. Systems Thinking requires a paradigm shift - from being unconnected to interconnected to the whole, and from blaming our problems on something external to a realization that how we operate, our actions, can create problems.[3] (Senge 1990,10). While it might seem obvious to think about the systems, research indicates that we simply aren't thinking like we used to. Many experts attribute this decline to an overdependence on technology, others blame lifestyle shifts, heightened competitiveness due to a widening world market, the pace of change, or increased stress.

An unprecedented study that followed several thousand undergraduates through four years of college found that large numbers didn't learn the critical thinking, complex reasoning and written communication skills that are widely assumed to be at the core of a college education.

Many of the students graduated without knowing how to sift fact from opinion, make a clear written argument or objectively review conflicting reports of a situation or event, according to New York University sociologist Richard Arum, lead author of the study. The students, for example, couldn't determine the cause of an increase in neighborhood crime or how best to respond without being swayed by emotional testimony and political spin.

Arum, whose book *Academically Adrift: Limited Learning on College Campuses* (University of Chicago Press) comes out very soon, followed 2,322 traditional-age students from the fall of 2005 to the spring of 2009 and examined testing data and student surveys at a broad range of 24 U.S. colleges and universities, from the highly selective to the less selective.

Forty-five percent of students made no significant improvement in their critical thinking, reasoning or writing skills during the first two years of college, according to the study. After four years, 36 percent showed no

---

3    The Fifth Discipline: The Art and Practice of the Learning Organization, and The Fifth Discipline Fieldbook: Strategies and Tools for Building a Learning Organization, Peter Senge, 1990, 10

significant gains in these so-called "higher order" thinking skills.

Systems thinking requires:

» A clear understanding of the organizational goals

» An understanding of the internal and external systems that are impacting the organization (At a macro level, the systems impacting the community, and the sector, and the world economy etc., and at a micro level, the systems impacting the department, the team, and the individual)

» An understanding of the networks- the connections, interrelationships and interdependencies influencing the systems

» Ongoing understanding of the specific workplace environment and related conditions

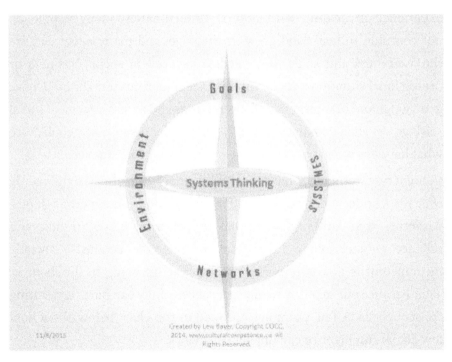

How specifically does Systems Thinking relate to civility?

When people are not able to see how they fit into the big picture they tend to become confused, disillusioned, and disengaged. When they don't see interconnectedness, they feel separate and tend to blame and make assumptions about how and why things are happening. This can result in learned helplessness, victim-syndromes, passive (and overt) aggression, and most damaging of all- mistrust. When trust goes, respect follows close behind and all sorts of incivility happens.

## ABOUT SOCIAL INTELLIGENCE

According to Karl Albrecht, researcher and author of *Social Intelligence-The New Science of Success*, Social Intelligence (SI) is in the simplest terms, "The ability to get along with people." It is assumed that people acquire this skill experientially as they grow up, mature, and gain experience in dealing with others. Unfortunately, many people do not continue to learn and grow as they age, and many never acquire the awareness and skills they need to succeed in social, business or professional situations. Social Intelligence underpins our ability to have good judgment in interpersonal interactions and across a range of social settings. As such "common sense" and "having a sense of people," are what happens when you actually use your Social Intelligence.

Current research shows that social intelligence has declined significantly over the last decade. The reasons for this include, among other things: parenting style shifts, generational and cultural issues, trends, and reliance on technology. At present, how we've become so socially incompetent is not as important as what we're going to do about it. This, because our inability to interact success-fully can have devastating consequences. A few examples outlined in the chart below show how low Social Intelligence can impact us at work.

| | Indicators of low Social Intelligence | Impact (degree of impact varies with context) |
|---|---|---|
| Individual | » Inability to read verbal and tonal cues<br>» Inability to exercise restraint<br>» Communication faux pa. e.g., Interrupting, ignoring | » Low confidence<br>» High stress<br>» Incivility |
| Team | » Failure to see value in<br>» contribution of others<br>» Inability to adapt to change<br>» -Increased miscommunication and/ or lack of communication | » Ineffective teamwork<br>» Low resilience<br>» Poor performance<br>» Lack of service orientation |
| Organization | » Failure to identify demographic Shifts both internal and external<br>» Inability to create an empowering environment<br>» Difficulty fostering "fit" | » - Difficulty recruiting and/or low retention<br>» Poor engagement<br>» Lowered productivity |

The good news is that psychologists have identified that Social Intelligence can be improved- we can actually teach it. And our ability to teach it effectively enables us to meet the demands of increasingly diverse, ever-changing workplaces. In the new world of work – where collaboration may well be considered currency- Social Intelligence, is absolutely essential to success.

In terms of ability to exhibit civility, there are four elements of Social Intelligence that are important:

» Social Radar; ability to correctly interpret nonverbal and contextual cues

» Social Style, and specifically the ability to adapt one's style

» Social Knowledge- of the written and the unwritten rules

» Understanding of the social expectations specific to the workplace; the nuances of the organizational cultural context

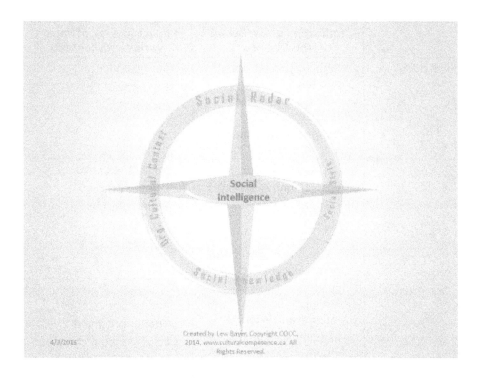

How specifically does social intelligence relate to civility?

There is a cluster of behaviors that collectively make up social intelligence, they are:

- » paying attention
- » focusing on someone or something other than oneself
- » connecting with others in a meaningful way
- » being aware of our surroundings
- » thinking about what might be appropriate in a certain context
- » consciously adapting behavior to show consideration and respect for others
- » considering the impact of our words and actions
- » seeking to understand expectations for social behavior in different contexts
- » exhibiting common courtesies; meeting general social expectations

This cluster of behaviors represents habits that socially successful people engage in. When a person does not engage in these behaviors, he/she may be perceived as rude. Frequently people with low Social Intelligence are not even aware that they are being perceived as rude, and often they have developed inappropriate social habits. Related to the workplace specifically, Albrecht, (*Social IQ-The New Science of Success*) suggests that low social radar combined with poor social knowledge can result in persistent rude behaviors he calls "toxic." Toxic and disrespectful behaviors are often contagious. When allowed to do so, rudeness spreads like a virus and wreaks havoc on health, productivity, self-esteem and relationships. Left unattended, the incivility virus quickly becomes a social epidemic, at which point treating the behavioral symptoms is barely manageable. Given that recent public opinion polls showed that 69 percent of respondents agreed that people are getting ruder, it is safe to say we are facing incivility in epidemic proportions. (See Chapter 9 Tools You Can Use for a Toxicity Survey)

## ABOUT CULTURAL COMPETENCE

A geographically dispersed, culturally diverse workforce and marketplace is the new reality. Global businesses and organizations need people who can work effectively in cultural diversity, and to create an environment that promotes mutual respect and creative collaboration.

Exposure to new cultures and to multicultural social networks and teams in a workplace is more likely to have positive consequences if those involved have been properly trained to understand and appreciate fundamental cultural differences and values that impact workplace relationships. Factors such as communication style, management style, and approaches to diversity and inclusion are as varied as cultures.

The way forward is cultural competence, this includes:

» learning about our own culture, our own biases and attitudes

- » recognizing and understanding differences (real and perceived) in behaviors, beliefs, styles of work, and styles of communicating
- » being sensitive to identified differences
- » communicating effectively, and working together with people who are different than we are

Cultural Competence is not easy to achieve. By way of a Cultural Continuum[4], Cross et al suggest there are 6 stages. The first of these is "cultural destructiveness" (See Chapter 9) And this is the level where we see heightened incivility in workplaces.

Steven Covey states, *"Strength lies in differences, not similarities."* And we find this to be true in organizations. When we can capitalize on what makes us different – we each bring our own unique strengths and perspectives to the table at work – and with enough skills and knowledge, we can harness these differences to create something even better. A better team, a better product, a better company, a better world. The goal of cultural competence in the workplace is to create a sense of community such that we can build "citizenship." In his book *Community*, Peter Block describes citizenship as follows:

Citizenship- is a state of being. It's a choice for activism and care. A citizen is one who is willing to do the following:

- » Hold oneself accountable for the well-being of the larger collective of which we are a part.
- » Choose to own and exercise power rather than to defer or delegate it to others.
- » Enter into a collective possibility that gives a workplace community its own sense of being.
- » Acknowledge that the community grows out of the possibility of citizens. Community is built not by specialized expertise, or great

---

4    http://www.unc.edu/~wfarrell/SOWO%20874/Readings/cultcompetencecont.htm

leadership, or improved services; it is built by great citizens.

» Attend to the gifts and capacities of all others, and act to bring the gifts of those on the margin into the center.

Developing skills in cultural competence requires:

» Empathy- knowing what it is and how to recognize and exhibit it.

» Cultural knowledge, e.g., about the diverse groups that may be represented in your organization.

» Values- specifically that you understand your own values, the organizational values and the values of others. This because for most people, our values underpin our motivations and drive our decision-making.

» Organizational Culture- every organization has a culture of its own and you really have to experience it to understand it. Also, culture changes as the people in the culture change and so these elements of cultural competence is very difficult to achieve.

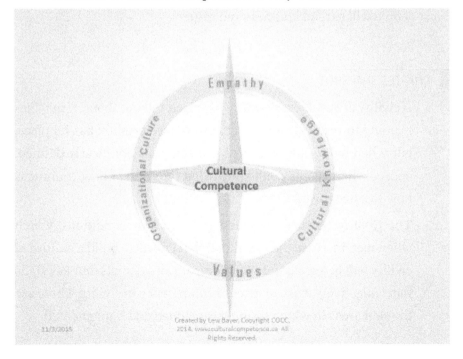

## HOW SPECIFICALLY DOES CULTURAL COMPETENCE RELATE TO CIVILITY?

When civility assessments show low tolerance for diversity, high mistrust, conflict, poor team orientation and high turnover, we often find that the causal factors relate to low cultural competence. There has been a lot of change in workplaces in terms of demographics; more people of culture, more women in leadership positions, up to four generations working together, etc., and when people are stressed or fearful due to change, they tend to default to their weaker selves. Biases, stereotypes and prejudices tend to come forward. People make assumptions and presume the worst of each other. Because we focus on differences, mistrust and self-preservation take over and we behave badly. Because communication is sometimes hindered, individuals don't have the opportunity to discover that we are more alike than we are different. Often we have the same values but different habits or traditions and so the outward behaviors are not reflective of the inner workings and motivations. If we can find a way to engage in a discussion about values, and if we can teach people to focus on the sameness, we remove the mistrust and fearfulness and most people will extend kindness and respect.

## CHAPTER SNAPSHOT

» If civility is a problem in your workplace, talking about it isn't likely going to resolve your issues. Discourse certainly has its place, but when habits are ingrained, expectations not clearly defined, and/or when people don't know what they don't know, training is how to solve the problem.

» The Civility Culture Compass® outlines four conditions, which when met, increase the likelihood that efforts to build a culture of civility will be successful. The Compass also depicts four key skills that collectively make up overall competency in civility. These are the skill areas in which training is planned and implemented.

» The Civility Competency Matrix® is a training tool that details the knowledge, skills, and abilities for each of the four key skill areas that build competency in civility. These skill areas are:

- ▶ Continuous Learning- learning strategies for learning ongoing

- ▶ Social Intelligence- is the ability to effectively identify and interpret nonverbal, verbal, and contextual cues, to adapt social style, and to apply written and unwritten social rules- this enables you to get along with others

- ▶ Systems Thinking- the ability to see the big picture, to distinguish patterns, to recognize interconnectedness of the systems, and to see your role within the systems

- ▶ Cultural Competence- is being able to appreciate fundamental cultural differences and values that impact workplace relationships, and doing so in a way that benefits the parties involved and leverages differences- real or imagined

- ▶ Training in one or more of these four key skills areas under "ideal" conditions, can result in measureable impact to the bottom line.

# CHAPTER 8

# PUTTING IT ALL TOGETHER

**HOW TO BUILD A CULTURE OF CIVILITY IN YOUR ORGANIZATION:**

1. Identify problems and issues in your workplace.

Recommend: Use the Symptoms of Incivility Survey- identify any of the symptoms you are experiencing in your workplace.

2. Choose your "Hedgehog Concept" e.g., Choose Civility.

3. Determine the "end in mind." Set a goal related to the specific change you want to see. Expand the goal using SMARTER formula. E.g., GOAL: Assess and address competency gaps in continuous learning skills of all employees (200) in xyz division by Dec. 31, 20XX. Transfer of learning will be measured by comparing pre and post training trust levels. If successful, we will see at least a 10% increase in employee retention in our xyz division.

S (Specific)

M (Measured)

A (Attainable/Attained by)

R (Realistic)

T (Timed/Timing)

E (Evaluated)

R (Return on investment or Reward)

4. Identify indicators of success and determine how you will measure these indicators.

5. Use the Civility Culture Compass to identify the extent to which each of four conditions that support a successful civility change initiative are "ideal." These conditions are:

    a. Change

    b. Alignment

    c. Engagement

    d. Readiness

6. Once you have ensured the conditions are right – begin to assess competency in the four key areas that support a culture of civility, these are:

    a. Social Intelligence

    b. Continuous Learning

    c. Systems Thinking

    d. Cultural Competence

7. Devise a training plan based on the outcomes of your assessment. The plan will include:

    a. Learning Objectives

    b. Evaluation Strategy

8. Assign a change initiative team to manage the change. There are four main roles on the team:

    a. Exemplar

    b. Change-maker

    c. Coach

    d. Ambassador

9. Roll out the change/learning plan.

10. Evaluate outcomes.

11. Revisit the four conditions on the Civility Culture Compass ongoing and adjust as necessary.

12. Adjust roles and goals ongoing.

13. Track successes and set-backs.

14. Reward civility- celebrate organizational culture change.

## ▌ EATING AN ELEPHANT

At a glance it can seem that building a culture of civility is a tremendous undertaking. However, it is well worth the effort to engage in this important endeavor. (In Chapter 1 we talked about all the possible positive outcomes of civility training). Once you've identified that there is a problem, (In Chapter 6 we talked about how to assess general civility in your workplace.) you just need to commit to start. And if you can't take on a comprehensive civility initiative, why not start with one bite?

I can tell you from 18 years of experience in the field, that civility training results in- or is at least a contributing factor in achieving each and every one of the following outcomes. So if you have limited time or resources, and/or if you cannot do a comprehensive assessment, it is recommended that you choose just one positive outcome from the list below. Choose something that is important in your specific workplace. Check the condition indicated in bold. (These are the conditions that our research and experience show to be most likely to impact the outcome indicated. And then once you have addressed that condition, IF the problem has not resolved itself, then you would build competency in the skill area(s) recommended (indicated by an arrow) for that outcome.) (While all four skills overlap, we have found some outcomes readily and consistently tied to one or two of the skills.) In this way, you can take a short cut and go directly to training in a key area and still experience the benefits of civility in your workplace.

» Increased retention     **ENGAGEMENT**

▶ Continuous Learning, Systems Thinking

» Greater individual and organizational adaptive capacity   **READINESS/CHANGE**

▶ Continuous Learning, Cultural Competence

» Employee autonomy   **ENGAGEMENT**

▶ Continuous Learning, Systems Thinking

» Individual skills mastery and increased confidence   **READINESS/CHANGE**

▶ Cultural Competence, Social Intelligence

» More effective goal setting **ALIGNMENT**

▶ Systems Thinking, Continuous Learning

» Better alignment of daily activity with organizational goals **ALIGNMENT**

▶ Cultural Competence, Systems Thinking

» More accountability   **ALIGNMENT**

▶ Social Intelligence, Cultural Competence

» Increased safety **ENGAGEMENT**

▶ Social Intelligence, Systems Thinking

» Greater consistency in service delivery   **CHANGE**

▶ Social Intelligence, Cultural Competence, Systems thinking

» Increased respect in the workplace **ENGAGEMENT**

▶ All skills contribute

» More frequent exhibition of common courtesies **ENGAGEMENT**

▶ Social Intelligence

» Generalized reciprocity   **ALIGNMENT**

- Cultural Competence,
  » More civil discourse **READINESS**
    - Cultural Competence, Systems Thinking
  » More efficient communication **ENGAGEMENT/ALIGNMENT**
    - Social Intelligence, Cultural Competence
  » Increased acceptance of diversity **READINESS/CHANGE**
    - Cultural Competence, Social Intelligence, Continuous Learning
  » Greater team-orientation **ENGAGEMENT**
    - Systems Thinking, Cultural Competence
  » More collaboration **ENGAGEMENT/ALIGNMENT**
    - Social Intelligence, Cultural Competence, Systems Thinking

## HIGHLIGHTS FROM THE CHAPTERS:

» Civility in the workplace is an issue all around the world.

» There is an increasing body of research suggesting that incivility in the workplace is systemic and epidemic and it's time for a change.

» To successfully imbed civility into your workplace culture, it is necessary to approach civility in the workplace as a change initiative.

» While a Respectful Workplace policy may be required, and can be useful, the policy in and of itself does not guarantee a respectful workplace.

» 70% of change initiatives fail.

» Engagement is essential to facilitating lasting, meaningful culture change and in order for a civility initiative to be successful, organizations must be "change-ready" skills-wise. This means employees must be competent in four skill areas that underpin the ability to exhibit civility at work.

» The first step in the 3-step civility plan is to have an end in mind. Goal setting is based on this desired outcome and your SMARTER goal will drive the civility initiative process.

» Civility Experts Worldwide defines civility as.....

  ▶ A **conscious awareness** *of the impact of one's thoughts, actions, words and intentions on others; combined with,*

  ▶ A **continuous acknowledgement** *of one's responsibility to ease the experience of others (e.g., through restraint, kindness, non-judgment, respect, and courtesy); and,*

  ▶ A **consistent effort** *to adopt and exhibit civil behaviour as a non-negotiable point of one's character.*

» There is growing evidence that civility can have tremendous positive and measurable impacts on organizations, including:

  ▶ Engagement, Morale, and Retention

  ▶ Confidence, Continuous Learning, and Competency

  ▶ Respect, Restraint, and Responsibility

  ▶ Psychological Safety, Stress Management, and Resilience

  ▶ Change Readiness, Adaptive Capacity and Profitability

» Step 2 in the process for creating a workplace civility initiative has 2 sub-steps: Sub-step 1 is to define civility. Your definition should support your "Hedgehog Concept" which is to Choose Civility so it will likely be an expanded SMARTER version of a basic goal to "build a better workplace." The definition must be specific to your workplace context, and you must include behavioral indicators-these are descriptions of what exactly civility looks like on the job.

» Sub-step 2 is to devise an evaluation strategy. You have to define civility – so you know exactly what behaviors you are looking for, before you can outline a strategy for evaluating whether or not, and how, those behaviors are being exhibited, and whether or not, and how, this is benefiting the organization.

» Civility is not the same as courtesy, or the same as manners, or etiquette; these are all related but different.

» A Civility Initiative is a change imperative for companies that want to thrive in the new world of work.

» Companies that openly promote civil communication among employees earn 30% more revenue than competitors, are four times more likely to have highly engaged employees, and are 20% more likely to report reduced turnover.[1]

» If an increase in revenue isn't incentive enough, there are two other issues to consider when you need to persuade your leadership or team to support your civility initiative, they are:

   i.   How to get over **the "civility = manners= soft skills, and soft skills are nice to have but not necessary skills" hurdle**, and...

   ii.   What will convince your team that civility training is worthwhile- will it be the costs, benefits, or consequences of civility/incivility in the workplace?

» Your ability to explain what civility is relative to skills and competencies at work, combined with your ability to identify which proven outcomes of civility will be most meaningful to your stakeholders, will impact the likelihood that your organization will choose civility. Some helpful information in this regard...

   ▶ There is increasing evidence that skills once presumed to be "soft" or nice to have are in fact critical to long term success.

   ▶ Soft skills can be described as a cluster of personal qualities related to willingness, attitude, personality, and social intelligence.

   ▶ Soft skills incorporate "Essential Skills"- these are the skills

---

1   http://www.webershandwick.com/uploads/news/files/Civility_in_America_2011.pdf

and abilities needed for work, learning, and life. Essential skills provide the foundation for learning all other skills and enable people to evolve with their jobs and adapt to workplace change.

▶ Exhibiting civility requires incorporating a range of soft and essential skills in different combinations.

▶ Research shows that the majority of one's financial success is due to skills in "human engineering." Human engineering includes elements of your personality and your ability to communicate, negotiate, and lead. Human engineering is less reliant on technical knowledge- as previously understood, and more reliant on soft skills.

» There is evidence that civility in the workplace results in:

▶ Increased revenue and engagement

▶ Increased Morale, Physical and Mental Health, and Happiness at Work

▶ Increased Team Orientation and Ability to Work Well with Others

▶ Increased Performance and Productivity

» To survive and to thrive in the new world, and the new world of work, we need to learn continuously and we need to learn at the pace of change.

» To be competent in the 4 skills (Social Intelligence, Continuous Learning, Cultural Competence and Systems Thinking) that build a culture of civility and/or enable an individual to exercise civility ongoing, you need to be able to adapt to change.

» When managed properly, the stress of change can be positive, e.g., cause the human brain to use more of its capabilities, improve memory, and intelligence and even increase productivity.

» Change can be frightening, but it's not so scary if you change your perspective and see it as an opportunity to learn.

» You don't need a grand launch or a catchy tag line for your civility initiative.

» The crises has already happened, incivility is likely already impacting your bottom line.

» Fear is not a good motivator- for a lot of things, but especially not when it comes to fostering civility.

» Building a culture of civility does not have to be an abrupt, painful process. When done properly, making the change from uncivil to civil is a continuous process where small, subtle, painless processes enable people to think and act differently.

» Take a page from Jim Collins book *Good to Great* – literally. Be a hedgehog not a fox. If your goal is to build a better workplace, CHOOSE CIVILITY- that's your Hedgehog Concept.

» Learning to be civil is at first an experiential exercise, that is, our attitudes about kindness, and respect, and compassion, and graciousness, and generosity etc., develop as a result of our childhood experiences and upbringing.

» In many workplaces, the pull towards incivility gets stronger because:

  ▸ Choosing incivility is easier than choosing civility.

  ▸ There are more rewards than consequences for being uncivil.

  ▸ We aren't learning to be civil through our experiences and interactions at work, and without experiencing civility, it's difficult to understand the benefits of it.

  ▸ The written and unwritten rules have changed so much, and are changing constantly, and so many of us just aren't sure of the current expectations so we mirror the behavior of whomever seems to be leading at a specific time, in a specific context.

  ▸ Civility in the workplace has been dismissed for a very long time as something "nice to have" and so civility is rarely strategically or formally taught.

- ▶ Even when they know what civility is, many people simply don't have the skills they need to exhibit civility in an ever-changing workplace.

» In a workplace context, where incivility can be attributed to a lack of experiential education, the plan for fostering a culture civility in the workplace is to change their experience. We do this by:

- ▶ creating an environment where positive change (learning) is required and supported- this is to replace an environment where bad habits and negativity have been endorsed over positive change/learning

- ▶ encouraging (and in fact requiring by way of policy and procedure) this positive change in the form of behavior in four key skill areas that underpin an ability to be civil

» The Civility Culture Compass® offers a model for a creating a culture of civility in your workplace. The Compass outlines a proactive, competency-based approach to shifting organizational culture from toxic and negative to respectful and positive. The Civility Culture Compass® is used to assess four organizational conditions, which when "ideal" as described below, increase the success of civility initiatives. These conditions are:

- ▶ Change

- ▶ Alignment

- ▶ Engagement

- ▶ Readiness

» Civility as a core competency requires that an individual can exhibit certain measurable, and related knowledge, skills, abilities, and commitments, and to do so consistently, in a way, and at a standard prescribed for application in a specific context e.g., a workplace, in a way that is deemed effective for that context.

» A Needs Assessment is a systematic exploration of the way things are and the way they should be. These "things" are usually associated with organizational and/or individual performance.[2]

» The purpose of conducting a needs assessment is to better understand the reason why things are the way they are- rather than the way they should be and how we want them to be. Analyzing the issues and factors that are creating the current situation, helps us know what the solution is to get us where we want to be, and where, when, and how we will apply that solution.

» One of the key reasons a needs assessment is completed prior to launching a training plan is to manage resources.

» There are two typical approaches to completing a workplace civility assessment:

» Help people identify performance issues and consider what skills gaps are causing the issues as well as how planned training can help to solve them.

» Taking a big picture view of the whole organization. Consider current, present, and future activities and goals, and then develop training plans to meet the identified current and anticipated training needs.

» The recommended assessment process is:

> ▶ Phase 1: Complete a general organizational culture assessment.

> ▶ Phase 2: If general organizational culture assessment identifies issues related to incivility, administer assessments to identify which one or more of the four civility culture conditions: Readiness, Change, Alignment, and Engagement, is not ideal.

> ▶ Phase 3: When one or more of the four civility culture conditions has been identified as not ideal, conduct further targeted assessments in that specific foundational area.

---

2    http://alumnus.caltech.edu/~rouda/T1_HRD.html

» One of the ways the Compass can save organizations time and money is because sometimes once the influencing conditions are restored to "ideal," the incivility symptom is resolved and no training is necessary.

» If civility is a problem in your workplace, talking about it isn't likely going to resolve your issues. Discourse certainly has its place, but when habits are ingrained, expectations not clearly defined, and/or people don't know what they don't know, training is how to solve the problem.

» The Civility Culture Compass® outlines four conditions, which when met, increase the likelihood that efforts to build a culture of civility will be successful. The Compass also depicts four key skills that collectively make up overall competency in civility. These are the skill areas in which training is planned and implemented.

» The Civility Competency Matrix® is a training tool that details the knowledge, skills, and abilities for each of the four key skill areas that build competency in civility. These skill areas are:

  ▶ Continuous Learning- learning strategies for learning ongoing

  ▶ Social Intelligence- is the ability to effectively identify and interpret nonverbal, verbal, and contextual cues, to adapt social style, and to apply written and unwritten social rules- this enables you to get along with others

  ▶ Systems Thinking- the ability to see the big picture, to distinguish patterns, to recognize interconnectedness of the systems, and to see your role within the systems

  ▶ Cultural Competence- is being able to appreciate fundamental cultural differences and values that impact workplace relationships, and doing so in a way that benefits the parties involved and leverages differences- real or imagined

» Training in one or more of these four key skills areas under "ideal" conditions, can result in measureable impact to the bottom line.

## ▌ SAMPLE WORKPLACE APPLICATION OF THE FOUR SKILLS

As a way of showing how the civility competencies overlap and tie into an individual's ability to be civil, provided below is an excerpt from Ms. Olen Juarez-Lim, Civility Experts Philippines, AICI FLC on professional presence.

According to Ms. Juarez-Lim, for most business professionals, "presence" relates to an ability to present oneself in a way that conveys credibility and to influence others through your leadership and communication skills. When people are perceived not to have "presence," it is frequently because they do not show high social intelligence, they do not follow expected social rules, they do not communicate respect, and they seem "me-focused" versus "other-focused."

Olen (Juarez-Lim recounts an experience.)

I was at a driveway in a client's office building waiting for my car and I noticed a tall, gray-haired man stepping down from his SUV. He was scanning the area with his smile and all of a sudden, people were drawn to him like a rock star. I too was caught in the rapture and all of a sudden I recognized the man as the CEO of the company! I said to myself, "Wow." In less than 15 seconds this man has drawn everyone to his presence.

In gatherings, meetings, and events or just simply out on the street, there is always this one individual people will notice. He/she has a commanding entrance, and an attractiveness that isn't overpowering. He/she engages with a smile and eye contact. When they speak, people listen. They have quiet confidence that suggests when they lead, people follow. They may stop traffic as they cross the street (extreme). There's an allure that is effortlessly echoed like metal being captivated in by a magnet. That is Personal Presence.

When people are asked to define Personal Presence, they may refer to it as "I'll know it when I see it," as un-definable, they will call it the "X" factor. According to *Merriam-Webster dictionary, Presence is the fact or condition of being present; the part of space within one's immediate vicinity the bearing, carriage, or air of a person; especially: stately or distinguished bearing or a noteworthy quality of poise and effectiveness (the actor's commanding presence). It is therefore attributed to appearance, behavior (appropriate for a context as its mostly positive behaviors we focus on), communication (timely, effective, and thoughtful), and authenticity of a person.

Personal Presence is difficult to define but is easily detected. (We use our social radar to detect it by way of social cues, tone of voice, nonverbal communication, etc.) It comes in instantaneously and the effect is powerful. There is something special about people with presence. The way they connect with their eyes as if you are the only person in the room. They speak with much enthusiasm yet not filling the air with noise. They look polished, with poise and confidence, but never arrogance. They have great personality and charm but never an exaggerated sense of self-importance. They act with a purpose and have grace under pressure. They are trusted and respected and have a natural, unforced quality. They are at ease and inspire the same genuine confidence to influence others positively. This is largely due to social intelligence.

Genuine and authentic, yes this is difficult to fake. Personal Presence is the belief we have in ourselves that everything is aligned with – from our non-verbal signals to the energy we put forth, it has to be closely synched that our credibility is built solid. The impact of Personal Presence helps us achieve our goals and ambitions.

## FIRST IMPRESSIONS

Recently I purchased a vehicle and went to several car dealerships around my city. Obviously if I'm purchasing something as expensive as a car, I needed to get my money's worth and I was a hawk when it came to first impressions from the salesperson and the car.

As I entered Car dealer A, the sales people didn't seem to be energetic or enthusiastic about someone buying from them. But because I was interested in this particular brand, I pursued and ask questions until I finally was assisted to check out the car I want. The sales person was a fairly decent looking young man, had cold hands and was not too quick in replying to my questions.

Car dealer B, I was welcomed upon entering, the young lady with quite short skirt and high pitched voice was enthusiastic to make her sale, always referring to the money value and every car I liked was not on stock.

Car dealer C was a stretch for me. I was met by a young lady in uniform. She spoke very well and was knowledgeable for the most part but she didn't strike me as particularly special in any way. But there was no question with the car; it was a dream for me.

Car dealers A and B failed my first impression test. The first impression one makes has something to do with how you made a person feel at the onset of the first chance meeting.

If there's anything I've learned in life, making a successful impression can come down to a blink of an eye after meeting someone. People will make assumptions based on their perception and will always believe that no matter how much you present them with facts, sadly they will always refer to the first impression they have of you. We are wired to make quick assumptions about people and more often we relate to others similar to us. The conclusions drawn from the observations are surprisingly accurate and lasting.

Malcolm Gladwell in his book *Blink*, describes the type of unconscious thinking called rapid cognition as something that moves quicker and acts mysteriously, gauging what is important from that quick encounter. It is referred to as thin slicing – "Thin-slicing harnesses this powerful adaptive unconsciousness, allowing us to make smart decisions based on minimal information and minimal deliberation.*" (Paul Marsden, Blink Summary: The Power of Thinking Without Thinking)

_____

This thin-slicing is influenced by our values and our cultural competence. Depending on our experiences we make judgments and assumptions as well as smart decisions- and it's our continuous learning that enables us to adjust our perceptions and hone our adaptive consciousness.

"Thin-slicing is not an exotic gift. It is a central part of what it means to be human. We thin-slice whenever we meet a new person or have to make sense of something quickly or encounter a novel situation. We thin-slice because we have to, and we come to rely on that ability because there are lots of situations where careful attention to the details of a very thin slice, even for no more than a second or two, can tell us an awful lot." Malcolm Gladwell, Blink.

Therefore paying attention to the details of how we project ourselves that constitute our first impression is vital. And it's all about details, details, details. It's the details that separate luxury from inferior, excellence from mediocrity.

What value can we derive from this knowing that snap judgments are made about us? First is awareness, it allows us to use this information to our advantage, letting us prepare for these interactions. When going for a job interview, it prepares you to project the image you want the employers to see and land that job. Second, it allows us to prepare and practice Excellence doesn't happen overnight. It takes practice to connect and use valuable details such as non-verbal communication that ultimately creates big impressions.

How a person presents him/herself at work (e.g., consider the three different car dealers) incorporates all four core skills related to civility:

## SOCIAL IQ

- » Knowing what is appropriate clothing
- » Being aware of how people respond to one's presence, e.g., are they bowled over? Interested? Approaching?

» Knowing what the expectations are for greeting and approaching people

» Knowing when and how to adjust personal style to accommodate needs of others

» Having ability to put focus on others' needs and wants versus one's own.

» Being appropriate, e.g., watching for cues that a listener may not want to talk about money, or apologizing when it's clear that a customer is distressed about the car she wants being out of stock

## CULTURAL COMPETENCE

» Recognizing that "appropriate" approach, clothes, tone of voice etc., varies depending on age, gender, ethnicity, etc.

» Choosing not to judge others unfairly based on their outward appearance or behavior

» Awareness of personal biases and perceptions

» Having the ability to assess when a difference makes a difference and then adjusting your behavior accordingly

» Recognizing that individuals, teams, families, communities, cities, countries, and certainly organizations are each cultures within a culture

» Understanding

## CONTINUOUS LEARNING

» Being able to learn from mistakes

» Building on existing skills

» Ability to ask questions e.g., when in uncomfortable settings

» Ability to recognize that change requires adjustments

## SYSTEMS THINKING

» Recognizing that we are all interconnected, e.g., someone knows someone who knows someone, so be careful what you say and do

» Understanding that every action on our part is going to impact someone or some system in some way

» Recognizing that we contribute to the current system and that in our contribution we are impacting other systems

Best Practices- Recommended by Olen Juarez-Lim; Ways to convey civility through your personal image:

## WATCH YOUR ATTITUDE

Attitude Is Everything and Self Perception Determines Direction, that's according to Nick Vujicic, author and inspirational speaker, born with no arms and no legs. His story simply puts things in perspective, the message of faith and hope, displays how our attitude can ultimately lead us to failure or success.

What we declare is what we attract. Our attitude is everything about how we see life, deal with it and manage it. We can't control what life brings – the hurdles, trials - but we can control our own attitude towards it. A positive attitude, optimism and enthusiasm work like a magnet for success and change. One of the earlier books of inspiration I read was Dr. Cherie Carter Scott's book, *If Life is a Game, These are the Rules,* and rule number 4 always resonates with me: "Lessons are repeated until they are learned;" it clearly defines that each hurdle may be treated as opportunities to learn from. Once we get what the present situation is teaching us we evolve and change and consciously make decisions not to repeat them.

This process is important for Personal Success in that knowing that we are not perfect and have room for improvement we can make conscious decisions to take care of our brand to get ahead in life. Lessons present us with teachers who will teach us the valuable lesson until we get it right. We may dodge the issue facing us but rest assured it will always come back until we face it and learn from it. By shifting your perspective to what value the situation presents, it alters your view of approaching things. It equips you to evaluate things differently, makes you look into the positive sides of things and ultimately, you grow wiser.

Mirjam Stoffels, founder of sevent2success, said "Positive thinking changes the brain. Positive thinking really does change your brain. In a real physical way. The science is called neuroplasticity. Scientists are proving the brain is endlessly adaptable and dynamic. It means that our thoughts can change the structure and function of our brains. Repetitive positive thought and positive activity can rewire your brain and strengthen brain areas that stimulate positive feelings. The brain can form new neural pathways — if we do the work. Just like exercise, the work requires repetition and activity to reinforce new learning." Therefore, you can tell success by the way you think it. If you tell your mind to feel confident, your body moves confidently.

## BE A PERSON OF CHARACTER AND AUTHENTICITY

Personal Presence is work from the inside out. No matter how well dressed we are, maneuver the table with precision or speak well, people can tell if we are sincere or not. Everyone nowadays is sophisticated enough to tell the difference from a sincere smile to a nervous one. Having strong personal values and beliefs that are non-negotiable in developing character and Authenticity. It is ingrained from your core and ultimately is the barometer from which people gauge your worth. When you know who you are and what you stand for, people believe in you. It acts as a foundation to guide you in making decisions that are true to your beliefs. You act, work, speak your worth. Clients, office mates, employers would always remember how you made them feel.

## HONE YOUR CONVERSATIONAL SKILLS

The way you communicate, tone of voice and the energy you put into communicating speaks about your charisma. Speak with certainty and conviction so it gives you confidence to sell almost anything. Manage your body language, facial expression and tone of voice as these contribute greatly to the message being conveyed.

## DRESS APPROPRIATELY

The visual impact we make speaks volumes and comprises about 55% of the way we are perceived. Clothes do make an impact - from the fit, to the style, color choice, to the appropriateness of occasion and how we pay attention to details – it all matters! Our clothes communicate a message and to get ahead in business we project that image of trust and confidence. It helps form a mental picture of our first impression, which we know by now, is lasting. Part of the overall visual grade is grooming. Be neat and clean and be impeccable. From the details of unwanted hair in the nose, or upper lip, to your scent or smell and the minding the personal details is just pure common sense. Knowing the impact that we create when we meet people, we need to make a conscious effort in taking care of our brand. The way we will be perceived is entirely up to us. The way we are accorded respect is entirely up to us. It may take effort but I guarantee the rewards are great.

# CHAPTER 9

# TOOLS YOU CAN USE

**NOTE: If you are a workplace trainer or human resources professional who plans to deliver civility training, please visit** www.civilityexperts.com **where you can use the free Civility Culture Compass® Assessment, enroll in a Civility Train the Trainer program, and/or download at low cost the Civility Matrix® Workbook which includes all of the tools included in this Chapter.**

**Symptoms of Viral Incivility© in the Workplace** ASSESSMENT

Created by Lew Bayer, President Civility Experts Worldwide.

If world-scale incivilities—such as war and crime, political leaders' public temper tantrums, professional athletes' very unsportsmanlike conduct, over-the-top celebrity self-indulgence, rampant bigotry and racism—do not have you convinced, consider how many of the following symptoms of viral incivility you have experienced in your own home, workplace or community in the past two weeks:

» Persistent miscommunication, such as non-responsiveness, misunderstandings, arguments, withholding of information, diminished morale and/or mood, negative attitudes, lack of energy, poor engagement, lowered confidence, and measurable lack of accountability

» Decreased productivity, increased tardiness and laziness, reduced quality and quantity of output, diminished collaborative effort

» Increased customer service complaints, visible decrease in product and/or service standards

» Growing gap in alignment between personal or corporate goals and leadership's abilities, lack of integrity and ethics

» Inability to adapt effectively to change

» Inability to navigate cultural and communication barriers

» Increased difficulty recruiting and hiring competent personnel

» Difficulty identifying and practicing core values

» Lowered common sense, failure to attend to social cues and follow social conventions

» Increased disengagement, difficulty maintaining relationships, less involvement in social, civic and community events

Research shows that typically social capital, self-worth, productivity, health, and certainly profitability in business settings all increase when you choose civility.

» Better stress management

» Increased exercising of restraint

» Improved morale

» More efficient communication

**Take Action**

## SAMPLE TEMPLATE FOR A RESPECTFUL WORKPLACE POLICY

Created by Petroleum Human Resources Council of Canada http://www.petrohrsc.ca/media/15025/Respectful%20Workplace%20Policy%20Template.pdf

## RESPECTFUL WORKPLACE POLICY TEMPLATE

*This template on respectful workplace policy can be used by any company operating within Canada to prevent and deal with discrimination and harassment in the workplace. Aside from adopting this policy, companies are encouraged to provide education and training for their employees and contractors, whenever applicable, on the following key topics: human rights in the workplace; managing diversity; and the company's respectful workplace policy and procedures.*

## POLICY OVERVIEW:

(**Company name**) is committed to creating an inclusive and healthy workplace where employees are valued and treated with dignity and respect. It is intended that this policy will prevent discrimination and harassment of any type and provides guidelines on addressing workplace discrimination/harassment as quickly and efficiently as possible.

Petroleum Human Resources Council of Canada | Conseil canadien des ressources humaines de l'industrie du pétrole

## COVERAGE:

This policy applies to all employees and independent contractors of (**company name**) while engaged in any activity related to their employment or contract with (**company name**), whether on company property or elsewhere (e.g. business trip, conferences, social gatherings, etc.).

## DEFINITION OF TERMS:

**Discrimination** is any act or omission that results in unjust or prejudicial treatment of different categories of people. Differences may be based on race, marital status, religious beliefs, family status, colour, age, gender, ancestry, physical disability, place of origin, mental disability, source of income, sexual orientation, or any other ground covered by (**reference provincial human rights legislation**).

**Workplace discrimination**, as defined by the Canadian Human Rights Commission, means putting an employee at a disadvantage based on prohibited grounds. Discrimination may happen intentionally or inadvertently and results in barriers to workplace equity because it blocks access to equal opportunities.

**Harassment** is a form of discrimination and means any unwanted physical or verbal conduct directed to one or more individuals and causes offence or humiliation. As a guideline, an example of a discriminatory or harassing behavior is making derogatory remarks or compromising invitations that result in a negative or hostile work environment.

Petroleum Human Resources Council of Canada    Conseil canadien des ressources humaines de l'industrie du pétrole

Recruitment

**Sexual Harassment** means any offensive or humiliating behavior on the grounds of gender. This includes demands for sexual favors in exchange for rewards or favorable consequences. Generally, sexual harassment is deliberate, unsolicited, and one sided. Anyone can be a victim or a perpetrator of sexual harassment.

## RESPONSIBILITIES:

In general, individuals covered in this policy have a responsibility to ensure that the working environment is free from harassment. Key responsibilities include refraining from actions and behaviors that might constitute discrimination/harassment as well as any other reasonable involvement to achieve the objectives of this policy (e.g. reportingincidents).

Employers, managers, and supervisors are responsible to immediately act upon any situation involving discrimination/harassment. They should also ensure that employees are oriented on human rights in the workplace as well as this policy.

## CONFIDENTIALITY:

To protect the interest of all individuals involved in any process involving reported incidents or formal written complaints of discrimination/ harassment, confidentiality will be maintained throughout the process to the extent practicable and appropriate under the circumstances, and as permitted by law.

Petroleum Human Resources Council of Canada — Conseil canadien des ressources humaines de l'industrie du pétrole

Copyright © 2008 Petroleum Human Resources Council of Canada

## ▪ REPORTING DISCRIMINATION/HARASSMENT:

Any individual covered by this policy who has experienced discrimination/harassment at (***company name***) or at any work-related event outside the company should be proactive and encouraged to act before the behavior becomes repetitive by informing the harasser his/her behavior is inappropriate and ask him/her to stop. If the harassment continues or if the petitioner does not wish to bring the matter directly to the alleged harasser, the person should report the problem to one of the following individuals:

(***List the positions/titles who the individual can report to. Examples include his/her Manager, Vice President and/or the CEO***). These individuals have been appointed by the company as "Advisors" under this policy.

Note: During the orientation process, individuals should be advised to take notes, as much as possible, about incident(s) constituting discrimination/harassment. Records of events are not necessary to file a complaint. However, records provide specific details and strengthen any case. Ideally, records should describe the incident and include the dates, times, locations, possible witnesses, and the individual's response.

The Advisor shall inform the petitioner of his/her right to keep the matter at the report stage or make a formal written complaint under this policy as well as other rights including:

» Any counseling or other support services provided within and outside of the organization; and

» Other avenues of recourse such as filing a discrimination/harass-

Petroleum Human Resources Council of Canada | Conseil canadien des ressources humaines de l'industrie du pétrole

Recruitment

ment complaint with the (**reference provincial human rights commission/tribunal**). Complaints must be e-filed within (**period of time specified within the provincial legislation**) after the alleged incident.

## AT THE MEETING STAGE

After discussing the matter the petitioner and the Advisor agree that no discrimination/harassment occurred at the incident(s) in question, the Advisor will take no further action and will make no record in any file.

If it was determined that discrimination/harassment has occurred, but the petitioner does not wish to make a formal written complaint, the Advisor should still engage in proactive measures to resolve the incident (e.g. informal discussions with the harasser). No formal investigation will be undertaken nor will written records be kept.

The Advisor may still make a written complaint if there have been previous complaints against the alleged harasser. Written complaints by an Advisor should be signed and provided to the petitioner, alleged harasser and management.

If the petitioner decides to make a formal written complaint, the Advisor should assist the petitioner in drafting a complaint and provide copies to the petitioner, alleged harasser and management.

## INVESTIGATING THE COMPLAINT

Upon review of the formal written complaint, an investigation should

Recruitment

be conducted immediately. Possible investigators include another designated individual within the company, or an outside investigator, for as long as the appointed person can conduct a thorough and unbiased investigation.

At a minimum, an investigation should include individual interviews with the petitioner, the alleged harasser(s) and witnesses to the incident, if any. The alleged harasser(s) should be given enough information about the allegations against them to allow them to respond appropriately.

On completion of the investigation, the investigator will inform the petitioner, alleged harasser, and management, as to his/her findings and recommendations.

## DISCIPLINARY ACTION AND CLOSURE

If the investigation substantiates the complaint of discrimination/harassment, the harasser will be disciplined appropriately. Depending on the nature and severity of the harassment, disciplinary actions may include: a verbal and/or written apology; letter of reprimand from the organization; referral to counseling; removal of certain employment privileges; temporary suspension with or without pay; and/or termination of employment or contract. No documentation will be placed on the petitioner's file where the complaint is filed in good faith, whether the complaint is upheld or not.

If the investigation fails to find evidence to support the complaint, no documentation will be placed on the alleged harasser(s)' file(s).

Petroleum    Conseil canadien des
Human Resources    ressources humaines
Council of Canada    de l'industrie du pétrole

Copyright © 2008 Petroleum Human Resources Council of Canada

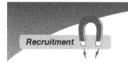

Important note: Regardless of the outcome of a harassment complaint made in good faith, petitioners, advisors, as well as anyone who supported or was involved in the petition and/or investigation will be protected from any form of retaliation by the rest of the employees of (*company name*).

Petroleum | Consell canadien des
Human Resources | ressources humaines
Council of Canada | de l'industrie du pétrole
Copyright © 2008 Petroleum Human Resources Council of Canada

## THE CIVILITY-CHANGE INITIATIVE PLAN AT A GLANCE

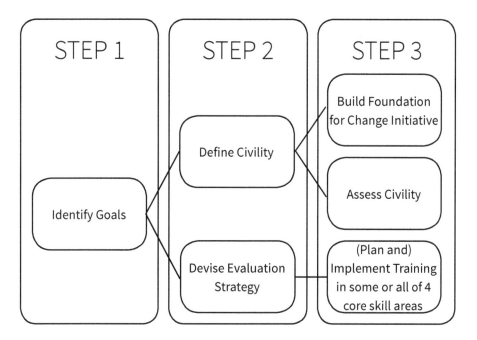

**END IN MIND- Step 1 in the 3-Step Process for Devising a Civility Initiative.**

QUESTIONS TO ASK

1. What exactly do you want to happen as a result of the initiative? Stated differently, what is the purpose of building a culture of civility?

NOTE: Using Civility Experts *Symptoms of Viral Incivility* checklist can help you identify what you don't want. And/or, review the list of 32 possible positive outcomes of civility training included at the beginning of Chapter 2 in the Civility at Work: A Civility Initiative Toolkit can help you identify what you do want.

2. Why do you want whatever it is that you want?

3. What specifically is the benefit or impact to the employee(s), and/ or to the organization, if you get what you want?

4. Are there any drawbacks or unfavorable consequences to you, the team, or the organization if you get what you want?

5. What evidence do you have that the outcome you want could, or would, in fact result from the initiative? And are you prepared if the outcomes are different than you expected?

6. Are your goals realistic, e.g., SMARTER; specific, measurable, attainable, realistic, time-set and/or timely, evaluated, and rewarding/rewarded?

Practice writing a SMARTER goal here:

**DEFINING CIVILITY - CHAPTER 2**

## Outcomes of Civility Training - Checklist

Created by Lew Bayer, President Civility Experts Worldwide.

### Outcomes of Civility Training

- » Increased retention
- » Greater individual and organizational adaptive capacity
- » Employee autonomy
- » Individual skills mastery and increased confidence
- » More effective goal setting
- » Better alignment of daily activity with organizational goals
- » More accountability
- » Greater consistency in service delivery
- » Increased respect in the workplace
- » More frequent exhibition of common courtesies
- » Generalized reciprocity
- » More civil discourse
- » Increased acceptance of diversity
- » Greater team-orientation
- » More collaboration
- » Increased innovation
- » Improved thinking skills
- » Improved self-respect
- » More self-directed learning
- » Improved culture of learning
- » Greater change readiness
- » Improved engagement
- » Higher understanding of shared purpose

- » Increased trust
- » More responsibility-taking
- » Higher self-rated happy at work scores
- » Employee hardiness
- » Increased psychological safety

## THE POWER OF PAYING ATTENTION- EXAMPLE

Paying attention is one of the 25 best practices for exhibiting civility as outlined by Dr. P. Forni in *Choose Civility*.

Here is an example of how powerful a few minutes of paying attention can be, a short excerpt that captures the humanity and gratitude aspects of civility. It was written by my friend and colleague, Anjali Handa, Author *of I Choose Blissful.*[1]

He's sitting in a food court. By himself. Eating. Quietly, intentionally. A salad with beans in a container from home. Chopsticks. His head is down, concentration on his meal.

He looks my age.

Wedding ring.

Occasionally he lifts his head to watch the crowd as he chews. Two or three quick scans around the room, then back to his meal.

Bags under his eyes. What's kept him up?

No cell phone, no book.

Casual boots, corduroy pants, a dress shirt under his fleece sweater.

Where does he work? What does he do?

Does he eat by himself often?

He looks sad. He looks like he's travelled far.

Salad is done. He drinks up the sauce and slowly closes his container. One deep sigh before he stands up and walks away. Not down the stairs, but across the room.

---

1   http://www.ichooseblissful.com/people-watching-i-thank-him-for-being-him/

Where is he going?

Slow, heavy strides. He seems sleepy.

Maybe he feels unnoticed.

I noticed him.

I thank him for being my calm in the middle of corporate chaos.

I thank him for reminding me about being alone.

I thank him for being there.

I thank him for being him.

## DEFINITION OF CIVILITY

**CIVILITY IS:**

» A conscious awareness of the impact of one's thoughts, actions, words and intentions on others; combined with,

» A continuous acknowledgement of one's responsibility to ease the experience of others (e.g., through restraint, kindness, non-judgment, respect, and courtesy); and,

» A consistent effort to adopt and exhibit civil behaviour as a non-negotiable point of one's character.

## DRAW A HOUSE- TRAINING ACTIVITY

**Purpose-** To help others understand why it is important to define civility.

**Application-** Suggested that you can use this activity at the early stages of a workplace civility initiative. The goal is to get the participants to start thinking about how they define civility and what civility should look like in their workplace. It's best to do the activity at the very beginning of class, before any discussion of civility.

**Outcome-** A common frame of reference and a workplace definition of civility.

FRAME OF REFERENCE: a set of ideas, conditions, or assumptions that determine how something will be approached, perceived, or understood.

This activity is a modified version of an exercise drawn from Withers and Lewis, *The Conflict and Communication Activity Workbook*. It was adapted by Lew Bayer, Civility Experts. Here's how it works:

» Trainer asks participants to work in pairs, one pen and one blank piece of paper between them.

» Participants are asked to work together to draw "house"; they must hold the pen together and they cannot speak while they complete the activity. Instruct the participants that they cannot just write the word and when they are finished they should just wait quietly for the other groups to finish.

» Allow 2-3 minutes for the participants to draw a "home."

» Then, ask the groups to turn over the paper. This time ask them to draw "Civility."

**Debrief-** After the participants have completed the activity, ask them to describe their experience. Responses may include:

» One of us had to lead; the other followed.

» I had trust that the other person knew what I was thinking because we couldn't talk each other.

» For "house", participants might have found it easy, e.g., they just drew a house but it was harder to draw "civility."

» What did people draw? Frequently, if you have a participant group that has worked together for a long time, who have all lived in North America for example, or if many in the group share a cultural background, they might have interpreted "house" as a "box with a triangle roof"- a typical "house" as understood by most North Americans. And for "civility" you might see blank pages, you might see handshakes, you might see smiley faces, or table settings, you might see peace signs. etc.

Trainer should explain:

» This exercise is to illustrate how important a common frame of reference is- give definition of frame of reference. Explain that when we don't have the benefit of oral communication, we have to use our nonverbal cues, our experiences, our perceptions and try to work well with others (e.g., 2 people, 1 pen working together) If English is a second language for someone, or he/she is from a different country or background, he/she might interpret "house" as "home" and think of something other than a house- which is what most North Americans will draw. (Maybe he/she draws a flag, a map with his/her country shown, a hearth, a family, a heart etc.) Ask participants to consider the types of houses they drew. Any condos? Any cottages? Houseboats? That most of participants drew a box frame house with a pointed roof suggests a common frame of reference.

» When we start to think about less concrete things such as values and concepts like "civility" it is very difficult to know that people are thinking without communication. (You can see how this activity could be uses as an ice-breaker or opening activity to start a communication course.) We can't make assumptions – words matter and they have power. How can we expect to achieve civility in a workplace if we've never had a conversation about what civility is? We need to do this to ensure that we are all on the same page. It is at this point that you could introduce your organization's definition of civility, or, if you haven't yet devised a definition, start the conversation about how to define it.

**Take-away-** Participants should have a starting point for discussing civility and/or working together to devise a definition that could apply to their workplace.

This activity, created by Civility Experts Worldwide, is adapted from an activity in Withers and Lewis, *The Conflict and Communication Activity Workbook.*

## ▎ REFERENCED IN CHAPTER 2 – CHECKLIST FOR PERSONAL VALUES

Adapted from Charlotte Roberts, Fifth Discipline Field Book. This exercise is designed to help you reach a better understanding of your most significant values.

**What I Value Most...**From this list of values (both work and personal), select the ten that are most important to you-as guides for how to behave, or as components of a valued way of life. Feel free to add any values of your own to this list. Be prepared to explain to your tablemates why you chose these values.

| | | | |
|---|---|---|---|
| Achievement | Friendships | Physical challenge | Excitement |
| Civility | Growth | Pleasure | Fast Living |
| Adventure | Having a family | Power and authority | Fame |
| Affection (love and caring) | Helping other people | Privacy | Financial Gain |
| Arts | Helping society | Public service | Wisdom |
| Challenging problems | Honesty | Purity | Purity |
| Change and variety | Independence | Quality of what I take part in | |
| Close relationships | Influencing others | Quality relationships | |
| Community | Inner harmony | Recognition (respect from others, status) | |
| Competence | Integrity | Religion | Work with Others |
| Competition | Intellectual status | Reputation | Work Alone |
| Cooperation | Involvement | Responsibility and accountability | |
| Country | Job tranquility | Security | Freedom |
| Creativity | Knowledge | Self-respect | Order |
| Decisiveness | Leadership | Serenity | Personal Growth |
| Democracy | Location | Sophistication | Stability |
| Ecological awareness | Loyalty | Stability | Conformity |
| Economic security | Market position | Status | _____ |
| Effectiveness | Meaningful work | Supervising others | _____ |
| Efficiency | Merit | Time freedom | _____ |
| Ethical practice | Money | Truth | |
| Excellence | Nature | Wealth | |

## CHAPTER 3

### *I Choose Civility: Steps to Adopting Civility as a Core Personal Value*
- WORKSHEET

I personally define civility as:

I can explain to others in my workplace that "Civility" incorporates other personal values that they may have adopted in the following ways:

a) Civility includes honesty in that....

b) Civility includes accountability in that....

c) Civility includes integrity in that ....

d) Civility includes teamwork in that .....

e) Other: _____


f) I believe the outcomes/benefits of civility are:

g) To me:

h) To others:

i) To the workplace:

j) To the community:


I believe some behaviors that show I am civil include:


I believe that barriers to exhibiting civility include:


### REFERENCED IN CHAPTER 3 - SOFT SKILLS AND CIVILITY CHECKLIST

This checklist based on work by Lei Han, Stanford engineer, Wharton MBA [2] and the Civility Experts Worldwide definition of civility.[3] And the Civility Competency Matrix[4]

---

2    https://bemycareercoach.com/soft-skills/list-soft-skills.html#comment-79983

3    https://civilityexperts.com

4    Lew Bayer, Civility Experts Worldwide, 2014

## IF WE DEFINE CIVILITY AS:

> » A **conscious awareness** of the impact of one's thoughts, actions, words and intentions on others; combined with,

> » A **continuous acknowledgement** of one's responsibility to ease the experience of others (e.g., through restraint, kindness, non-judgment, respect, and courtesy); and,

> » A **consistent effort** to adopt and exhibit civil behaviour as a non-negotiable point of one's character.

You can see how each of the soft skills identified by Lei Han includes an element of civility. How many of these soft skills are you competent in? The extent to which you can exhibit these skills could be an indication of your overall ability to exhibit civility.

| I have this skill (Check for Yes) | Self-regulated Skills<br>Han's Skill Definition | Civility Element<br>& Link to CEW definition |
|---|---|---|
| | Growth mindset – Looking at any situation, especially difficult ones, as an opportunity for you to learn, grow, and change for the better. Focusing your attention on improving yourself instead of changing others or blaming anyone. | Continuous Learning<br><br>Conscious Awareness of Impact on Others |
| | Self-awareness – Knowing and understanding what drives, angers, motivates, embarrasses, frustrates, and inspires you. Being able to observe yourself objectively in a difficult situation and understand how your perceptions of yourself, others, and the situation are driving your actions. | Continuous Learning, Social Intelligence with elements of Emotional Intelligence<br><br>Conscious Awareness of Impact on Others |
| | Emotion regulation – Being able to manage your emotions, especially negative ones, at work (e.g. anger, frustration, embarrassment) so you can think clearly and objectively, and act accordingly. | Thinking Skills, Personal Management Basics<br><br>Conscious Awareness of Impact on Others<br><br>Continuous Acknowledgement of Responsibility<br><br>Consistent Effort to Exhibit Civil Behavior |

| | | |
|---|---|---|
| | Self-confidence - Believing in yourself and your ability to accomplish anything. Knowing that all you need is within you now. | Thinking Skills<br><br>Continuous Acknowledgement of Responsibility |
| | Stress management- Being able to stay healthy, calm, and balanced in any challenging situations. Knowing how to reduce your stress level will increase your productivity, prepare you for new challenges and supports your physical and emotional health, all of which you need for a fulfilling, successful career. | Social Intelligence, Thinking Skills, Personal Management Basics<br><br>Conscious Awareness of Impact on Others<br><br>Consistent Effort to Exhibit Civil Behavior |
| | Resilience – Being able to bounce back after a disappointment or set back, big or small, and continue to move onward and upward. | Continuous Learning, Thinking Skills<br><br>Conscious Awareness of Impact on Others |
| | Skills to forgive and forget- Being able to forgive yourself for making a mistake, forgive others that have wronged you, and move on without "mental or emotional baggage." Freeing your mind from the past so you can focus 100% of your mental energy on your near and long-term career goals. | Continuous learning<br><br>Conscious Awareness of Impact on Others<br><br>Continuous Acknowledgement of Responsibility |
| | Persistence and perseverance – Being able to maintain the same energy and dedication in your effort to learn, do, and achieve in your career despite difficulties, failures, and oppositions. | Thinking Skills<br><br>Consistent Effort to Exhibit Civil Behavior |
| | Patience – Being able to step back in a seemingly rushed or crisis situation, so you can think clearly and take action that fulfills your long term goals. | Social IQ, Thinking Skills, Personal Management Basics<br><br>Conscious Awareness of Impact on Others<br><br>Consistent Effort to Exhibit Civil Behavior |
| | Perceptiveness – Giving attention and understanding to the unspoken cues and underlying nuance of other people's communication and actions. Often times, we are too busy thinking about ourselves and what we are saying, we leave little room to watch and understand others' action and intentions. If you misinterpret others' intentions, you can easily encounter difficulties dealing with people and not even know why. | Social IQ<br><br>Conscious Awareness of Impact on Others<br><br>Continuous Acknowledgement of Responsibility |

## SOFT SKILLS LIST – PEOPLE SKILLS

People Skills address how to best interact and work with others so you can build meaningful work relationships, influence others' perception of you and your work, and motivate their actions. I have split them into two sections – Conventional and Tribal

**Conventional** – List of people skills you can find in most job descriptions and you will be assessed on some or all of these in your performance reviews depending on your level.

| I have this skill (Check for Yes) | Self-regulated Skills<br>Han's Skill Definition | Civility Element<br>& Link to CEW definition |
|---|---|---|
| | Communication skills – Being able to actively listen to others and articulate your ideas in writing and verbally to any audience in a way where you are heard and you achieve the goals you intended with that communication. | Communication Skills<br>Conscious Awareness of Impact on Others<br>Consistent Effort to Exhibit Civil Behavior |
| | Teamwork skills – Being able to work effectively with anyone with different skill sets, personalities, work styles, or motivation level to achieve a better team result. | Communication Skills, Social IQ<br>Conscious Awareness of Impact on Others<br>Continuous Acknowledgement of Responsibility |
| | Interpersonal relationship skills – Effective at building trust, finding common ground, having empathy, and ultimately building good relationships with people at work and in your network. | Social IQ, Communication Skills<br>Conscious Awareness of Impact on Others<br>Continuous Acknowledgement of Responsibility |
| | Presentation skills – Effectively presenting your work results and ideas formally to an audience that captivates their attention, engages their input, and motivates them to act in accordance to your desired outcome. | Communication Skills<br>Consistent Effort to Exhibit Civil Behavior |
| | Meeting management skills – Leading a meeting to efficiently and effectively reach productive results. At least 50% of meetings today are a waste of time. | Thinking Skills<br>Consistent Effort to Exhibit Civil Behavior |

| | Facilitating skills – Being able to coordinate and solicit well represented opinions and feedback from a group with diverse perspectives to reach a common, best solution. | Organizational Cultural Competence, Communication Skills<br><br>Consistent Effort to Exhibit Civil Behavior |
|---|---|---|
| | Selling skills - Building buy-in to an idea, a decision, an action, a product, or a service. This is not just for people in sales. | Communication Skills, Thinking Skills<br><br>Consistent Effort to Exhibit Civil Behavior |
| | Management skills – Creating and motivating a high performing team with people of varied skills, personalities, motivations, and work styles. | Social IQ, Communication Skills, Organizational Cultural Competence<br><br>Conscious Awareness of Impact on Others<br><br>Continuous Acknowledgement of Responsibility |
| | Leadership skills – Defining and communicating vision and ideas that inspire others to follow with commitment and dedication. | Social IQ, Communication Skills, Organizational Cultural Competence<br><br>Conscious Awareness of Impact on Others<br><br>Continuous Acknowledgement of Responsibility |
| | Mentoring / coaching skills - Providing constructive wisdom, guidance, and/or feedback that can help others further their career development.[1] | Social IQ, Communication Skills, Organizational Cultural Competence<br><br>Conscious Awareness of Impact on Others<br><br>Continuous Acknowledgement of Responsibility |

## PEOPLE SKILLS "TRIBAL"

List of people skills that you will not typically find in job descriptions. They are also essential to your career success. I call it tribal because they are more "insider knowledge" that you gain from work experience or from mentors. Some people can go through their entire career and not be aware of some of these skills.

| I have this skill (Check for Yes) | Self-regulated Skills<br>Han's Skill Definition | Civility Element<br>& Link to CEW definition |
|---|---|---|
| | Managing upwards – Proactively managing your relationship with your boss, his/her expectations of your work, and his/her perception of your performance. Whether you are challenged, given opportunities, or recognized at work heavily depends on your ability to communicate, manage expectations, and build a good relationship with your boss. | Social IQ, Communication Skills, Organizational Cultural Competence<br><br>Continuous Acknowledgement of Responsibility |
| | Self-promotion skills – Proactively and subtly promoting your skills and work results to people of power or influence in your organization and network. It is not enough that your boss knows you do great work. You need to subtly build your reputation with all key people that can influence your performance review. This is because hard work alone does not guarantee success. | Social IQ, Communication Skills, Organizational Cultural Competence<br><br>Conscious Awareness of Impact on Others<br><br>Consistent Effort to Exhibit Civil Behavior |
| | Skills in dealing with difficult personalities – Being able to still achieve the work result needed while working with someone whom you find difficult. | Social IQ, Communication Skills<br><br>Conscious Awareness of Impact on Others |
| | Skills in dealing with difficult/unexpected situations – Being able to stay calm and still are effective when faced with an unexpected or difficult situation. This includes being able to think on your feet and articulate thoughts in an organized manner even when you are not prepared for the discussion or situation you are in. | Social IQ, Communication Skills, Organizational Cultural Competence, Continuous Learning<br><br>Conscious Awareness of Impact on Others |
| | Savvy in handling office politics – Being able to understand and proactively deal with the unspoken nuances of office and people dynamics so you can protect yourself from unfairness as well as further your career. Office politics is a fact of life. If you don't choose to play, it can play you. | Social IQ, Communication Skills, Organizational Cultural Competence, Continuous Learning<br><br>Conscious Awareness of Impact on Others |
| | Influence / persuasion skills - Being able to influence perspectives or decision making but still have the people you influence think they made up their own minds. | Communication Skills<br><br>Conscious Awareness of Impact on Others |

| | | |
|---|---|---|
| | Negotiation skills - Being able to understand the other side's motivations and leverage and reach a win-win resolution that you find favorably, satisfies both sides, and maintains relationships for future interactions. | Social IQ, Communication Skills, Organizational Cultural Competence, Continuous Learning<br><br>Continuous Acknowledgement of Responsibility |

■ REFERENCED IN CHAPTER 3- POWER OF ESSENTIAL SKILLS CASE STUDY

**Essential Skills Solutions @ Kleysen Transport**

*A Workplace Education Manitoba Partnership Profile www.wem.mb.ca*

*When WEM clarified the ways Essential Skills levels can affect workplace performance, management at Kleysen Transport realized that previously-unattributed issues might be Essential Skills-based. After a WEM needs assessments confirmed the need for specific gap training – which was delivered – the company then enjoyed a second revelation: workers performing with appropriate ES levels require a whole different style of supervision, management and leadership. That's when management decided it was time to develop a whole new vision.*

Winnipeg's Kleysen Transport has come a long way since it first hit the road in 1935 as a family-owned cartage company at the height of the Depression. Now employing 500 people across Canada, the company is a diversified national carrier and logistics firm that specializes in bulk, flatdeck, multi-commodity trans load and intermodal services. From 2000 to 2006, the company that bills itself "The Transportation Solutions Company" more than doubled its revenue -- from $45 million to over $100 million – before eventually being sold to the Mullen Group.

As Kleysen's exceptional growth began leveling off and divisional mergers, expansions and stream-lining occurred, the impact of years of continuous change began taking their toll on workforce cohesion and productivity. Explains Human Resources Manager Christiane

Devlin: "It's not enough to come in and just process paper. People need to understand their contribution and the impact their decisions have on the greater good. And sometimes there's a gap in terms of skills and abilities, knowledge, decision-making ability, problem-solving, etc., and then you have to say, well how do we bridge that gap?"

It was at that same time that Devlin received an awareness-raising call from WEM that piqued her curiosity. At the subsequent meeting, she remembers, the impact and clarity that came to her as she began to think of the Kleysen workforce in terms of their Essential Skills was near-instantaneous. Thinking skills, problem-solving, document use, computer use, oral communication, working with others: she could see them all as being critical building blocks in comprehending and participating in the Kleysen big picture.

"When I met with WEM the first time," remembers Devlin, "what I realized is that if you look at the nine Essential Skills it's possible to say 'Well, how do we know that everybody knows, for example, exactly all of what a document *means*?' Sure, maybe everybody can process it, but do they understand what it means as far as what we do or how we do it or *why* we do it? If you're a Dispatcher and you're looking at a document on your screen - how does it fit into the bigger picture and what's the impact? Essential Skills broke it down for us into its most basic components: they broke it down into bite-sized, manageable pieces." And so the partnership began.

The business case for training got swift and positive approval from executives when they heard it would be customized to the Kleysen culture, held on-site for an hour or two at a time and be created entirely from Kleysen-specific processes, materials and objectives. "We developed it so that people in Accounting or a Dispatcher or Customer Service or somebody in Recruitment or Administration: they could all participate," says Devlin. "We said let's start off small, make sure it's relevant and valuable, create success, get as many people through as we can, get the feedback and build from there. And we did."

Over the next few months the training moved ahead as the partners planned, with Devlin calling it an overall success for both the intended AND unintended outcomes. With a smile she explains that there have been less errors in scheduling observed and managers are reporting a notable increase in teamwork, with dispatchers offering more help to drivers and vice versa. Managers also say they're having to spend less time refereeing problems, and a decline in customer service complaints suggests issues are being resolved at the appropriate levels.

And as the Kleysen employees became more knowledgeable about Essential Skills, as well as their tasks and how to perform them, they began providing feedback.

"We're very fortunate in this operation to have a very large and loyal and long-serving group," says Devlin thoughtfully. "And one of the things we got out of the training was people told us 'you can give us communication skills and thinking skills and problem-solving skills, etc., but what we're missing is: we know where we came from but we don't know where we're going next.' That feedback was *very* important to us."

In fact, the extraordinary nature of that response prompted another call for clarity – this time from the executive group itself. To develop that new and forward-thinking vision, they wisely reasoned, the first order of business would be to get an up-to-date picture of the now-enhanced skills and capabilities of the employees. "We thought we would start with the employees and move up," notes Devlin, "but we've changed the strategy a bit. We're going to develop executive training first and then have that content filter down."

And while Kleysen executives acquire the knowledge and skills needed to better-focus employees' efforts, Devlin wants to maintain the positive energy and momentum for the employees themselves. "The training was a good refresher but it wasn't enough, so at the same time as we do the Leadership piece we'd like to do some Essential Skills-based computer training to support better customer care."

Devlin says she can't over-emphasize the value of Essential Skills and Kleysen's partnership with WEM. "We very much see this as a continuum of education, with Essential Skills, where we'll continue to build. Really, it's been the kind of experience where it's almost been too good to be true. The Essential Skills language is helping create a foundation for training. They're part of every job and they're how we can talk about the skill requirements of the job. Without WEM," she declares, "we'd never have been able to pull it off."

## CHAPTER 4

**Sample short surveys to use in your workplace to start the conversations related to change initiatives- these created by Civility Experts Worldwide:**

## PERSPECTIVES ON CHANGE

| I Believe that.... | YES | Somewhat | NO |
|---|---|---|---|
| 1. Change is inevitable | | | |
| 2. Change is ongoing | | | |
| 3. Change is mostly good | | | |
| 4. Change is something I have no control over | | | |
| 5. Change is something that happens to me | | | |
| 6. Change is something I choose to actively participate in | | | |
| 7. Change is always hard | | | |
| 8. Change must be managed to be effective | | | |
| 9. A person can never prepare enough for change. | | | |
| 10. Change always presents opportunities | | | |

Copyright Civility Experts Worldwide, 2013.

## PERSPECTIVES ON CIVILITY

| I Believe that…. | YES | Somewhat | NO |
|---|---|---|---|
| 1. Civility is important | | | |
| 2. Civility is something you have to work at every day | | | |
| 3. Civility is hard work for little reward | | | |
| 4. Civility (exhibited by others) is something I have no control over | | | |
| 5. Incivility at work is something I just have to accept | | | |
| 6. Civility is something I choose to actively participate in | | | |
| 7. Choosing civility is always hard | | | |
| 8. Civility requires changing and I am afraid of change | | | |
| 9. A person can never be too kind or too polite | | | |
| 10. There are lots of benefits to choosing civility | | | |

## PERSPECTIVES ON LEARNING

| I Believe that…. | YES | Somewhat | NO |
|---|---|---|---|
| 1. Learning is necessary | | | |
| 2. Learning is ongoing | | | |
| 3. Learning is good for me | | | |
| 4. Learning is something I have no control over | | | |
| 5. Learning is something the employer is responsible for | | | |
| 6. Learning is something I choose to actively participate in | | | |
| 7. Learning new things is always hard | | | |
| 8. Learning doesn't just happen, you have to have plan | | | |
| 9. A person can never learn enough | | | |
| 10. Learning always presents beneficial opportunities | | | |

**CHAPTER 5**

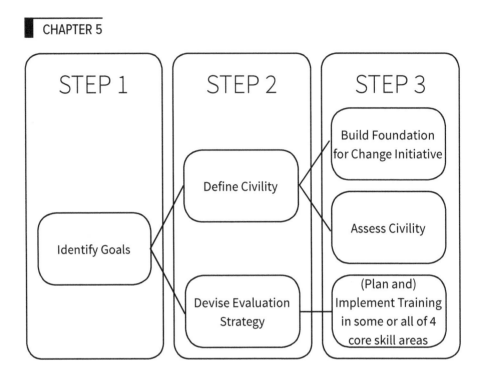

A Civility Change Initiative is a 3-step process (chart above), that utilizes the *Civility Culture Compass®* Model to build a foundation – that is, create conditions- that support a culture of civility.

» Once the foundation is in place – you will have identified, assessed, and addressed:

▶ Change- the past, current, and future situation

▶ Alignment- the clarity and cohesiveness of your goals and understanding of the same across the leadership team

▶ Engagement of work team

▶ Readiness- "competency-wise"

» Building on the foundation, you will devise a training plan to build civility competencies. The civility competency training plan is based on the *Civility Competency Matrix®* which details skills required in 4 key areas related to competency in civility.

» In implementing the civility initiative, you will use a range of tools such as assessments, evaluation strategies, training plans, etc. and you will engage in various activities including assigning tasks to various stakeholders.

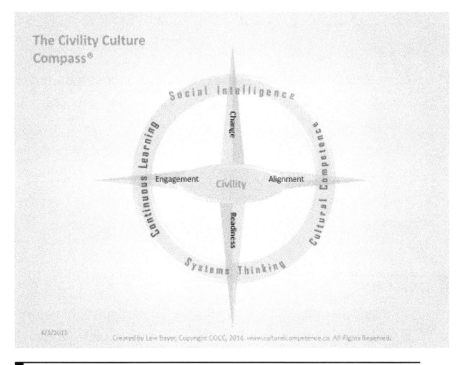

## CIVILITY CULTURE COMPASS – 4 CONDITIONS ASSESSMENT QUESTIONS:

### ALIGNMENT

» Do our organizational values include civility? If not, why not?

» To what extent are day to day activities, behaviors, policies and processes currently aligned with the overriding goal, which in the case of most civility initiatives relates to building a better workplace?

» Is anything we are currently doing contrary to a culture of civility? (This is where we highly recommend even a short consult with a civility expert who may be able to pinpoint activities, policies, behaviors, and even processes that you do not immediately recognize as contributing to incivility in the workplace.)

## ▌CHANGE

- » What is the current situation?

- » Have there been recent changes in the organization?

- » Are there changes pending?

- » Any change ongoing?

- » Any changes anticipated in the community, sector, industry, or globally that could be impacting the organization now or in the near future?

- » Do we understand the current need for change? E.g., Why do we think we need change?

- » How receptive are we to change? E.g., Are our employees resistant?


## ▌ENGAGEMENT

- » To what extent do employees "choose" to participate in non-required workplace activities, e.g., social events, work team sports, volunteer opportunities etc.?

- » Do employees trust us? And do we trust them?

- » Do employees show confidence in our decision-making? Or, is there frequent push-back and resistance?

- » Do employees seem happy at work?

- » If we could not offer wage increases, how many employees would stay with us, e.g., weather the storm and be loyal?

- » When provided with opportunities for growth and training, do employees invest, e.g., give of their own time or pay part of the cost?

- » To what extent do employees support each other, e.g., be accountable to each other, have each other's back, and/or engage personally/socially as well as at work?

» Overall, how would we rate collaboration in our workplace?

» Have we seen increases in sick days? Turnover? Grievances?

» How do our employees respond to change? E.g., Are they resilient? Adaptive? Resistant?

## READINESS

**Organizational**

» Are we prepared to commit our time, money, and energy to this initiative?

» Do all stakeholders understand that this is an ongoing, and long term investment?

» What specifically do we want to achieve?

**Individual(s)**

» Have we identified where our leaders and teams are "competency-wise" in the 4 key competency areas that support ability to be civil and build a culture of civility at work?

▶ Social Intelligence

▶ Cultural Competence

▶ Continuous Learning

▶ Systems Thinking

Have we either trained someone in-house, or recruited or retained a qualified civility trainer to deliver the competency training we need to address the identified civility skills gaps?

## CHAPTER 6

## ORGANIZATIONAL CULTURE ASSESSMENT INSTRUMENT – OCAI ONLINE

The Organizational Culture Assessment Instrument (OCAI) is a hassle-free tool for diagnosing organizational culture, developed by professors Robert Quinn and Kim Cameron. OCAI is a validated instrument, based on the Competing Values Framework, and used by thousands of companies worldwide. It takes about seventeen minutes to measure the current as well as the preferred culture. By rating six key aspects of organizational culture that were found to determine success, the respondent assesses the current and preferred organizational culture. The outcome is based on the Competing Values Framework and consists of four culture types: Clan Culture, Adhocracy Culture, Market Culture, and/or Hierarchy Culture. OCAI Online is owned by Marcel Lamers Msc and Marcella Bremer MscBA they started using the OCAI nationwide in 2008, when they researched the overall culture in the Dutch health care sector.   For more information: **Organizational Culture Assessment Instrument**

### ORGANIZATIONAL CULTURE INVENTORY – HUMAN SYNERGISTICS INTERNATIONAL

The OCI® provides organizations with a visual profile of their operating cultures (Current Culture) in terms of the behaviors that members believe are required to "fit in and meet expectations." Such expectations guide the way they approach their work and interact with each other. In turn, these behavioral norms have a significant impact on the organization's ability to solve problems, adapt to change and perform effectively. For more information: **Organizational Culture Inventory**

### ORGANIZATIONAL HEALTH INDEX – MCKINSEY

McKinsey's Organizational Health Index is a comprehensive, survey-based assessment of an organization's effectiveness and management practices. Worldwide, more than 600 major companies have used the tool to gauge their organizational health, diagnose organizational culture, and identify paths to performance improvement. Results are benchmarked against industry leaders and regional trends. For more information: **Organizational Health Index**

---

**▌ THE DENISON ORGANIZATIONAL CULTURE SURVEY – DENISON CONSULTING**

The Denison Organizational Culture Survey (DOCS) has been used by more than 5,000 companies worldwide since first becoming available over 20 years ago. Using the Denison Organizational Culture Survey, organizations are able to benchmark their organizational culture scores against a global database and develop action plans to improve their current practices. The DOCS is designed to assess an organization's strengths and weaknesses as they apply to organizational performance. The survey has 60 items that measure specific aspects of an organization's culture in each of the four traits and twelve management practices outlined in the Denison Model. For more information: **The Denison Organizational Culture Survey**[5]

The **Organizational Civility Scale** was created by Dr. Cindy Clark and Dr. Eric Landrum. The scale has been approved by the    Institutional Review Board at Boise State University.

The Scale is an effective tool for measuring:

»  • civility

»  • incivility

»  • job satisfaction,

»  • stress

»  • and coping

It takes about 20 minutes to complete and it can be used for any number of employees in any organization. [6]

---

5    https://www.thechangesource.com/8-tools-to-assess-and-accelerate-organizational-culture-change/

6    http://hs.boisestate.edu/civilitymatters/research-instr.htm

## Additional Resources:

### ASSESSING INDIVIDUAL CIVILITY COMPETENCY

### CIVILITY SELF-ASSESSMENT

| | Never | Sometimes | Frequently | Always | Totals |
|---|---|---|---|---|---|
| Pay Attention | | | | | |
| Acknowledge Others | | | | | |
| Think the Best | | | | | |
| Listen | | | | | |
| Be Inclusive | | | | | |
| Speak Kindly | | | | | |
| Don't Speak Ill | | | | | |
| Accept and Give Praise | | | | | |
| Respect even a subtle 'No.' | | | | | |
| Respect Others' Opinions | | | | | |
| Mind your Body | | | | | |
| Be Agreeable | | | | | |
| Keep it down! Rediscover silence | | | | | |
| Respect other people's Time | | | | | |
| Respect other people's Space | | | | | |
| Apologize earnestly | | | | | |
| Assert Yourself | | | | | |
| Avoid personal questions | | | | | |
| Care for your guests | | | | | |
| Be a considerate guest | | | | | |
| Think twice before asking for favors | | | | | |
| Refrain from idle complaints | | | | | |
| Accept and give constructive criticism | | | | | |
| Respect the environment and be gentle to animals | | | | | |
| Don't shift responsibility and blame | | | | | |

*The 25 Rules for Civility from
Choosing Civility by P.M. Forni

## Maslow's Hierarchy of Needs

▌QUICK SELF-TEST BASED ON THE 'HIERARCHY OF NEEDS'[7].

Self-actualization personal growth and fulfilment

Esteem needs achievement, status, responsibility, reputation

Belongingness and Love needs family, affection, relationships, work group, etc.

Safety needs protection, security, order, law, limits, stability, etc.

Biological and Physiological needs basic life needs - air, food, drink, shelter, warmth, sex, sleep, etc.

Read the following eight statements and tick below those that apply to you. There are no right or wrong answers. Interpretation guide below.

**A** I am successful in life and/or work, and I'm recognized by my peers for being so. I'm satisfied with the responsibility and role that I have in life and/or work, my status and reputation, and my level of self-esteem.

---

7    www.businessballs.com. © alan chapman 2003. Disclaimer: Sole risk with user.  Neither alan chapman nor businessballs.com  accepts liability for any issues or damages arising from the use of this tool.

**"B" (the 'B' is smaller than the other letters)**  I am part of, and loved by, my family.  I have good relationships with my friends and colleagues - they accept me for who I am.

**C**  My aim is self-knowledge and enlightenment.  The most important thing to me is realizing my ultimate personal potential.  I seek and welcome 'peak' experiences.

**D**  Aside from dieting and personal choice, I never starve through lack of food, nor lack of money to buy food.  Aside from the usual trauma of moving house, I have no worry at all about having somewhere to live - I have 'a roof over my head.'

**E**  I generally feel safe and secure - job, home, etc. - and protected from harm.  My life generally has routine and structure - long periods of uncontrollable chaos are rare or non-existent.

| Interpretation: | | Maslow said that needs 1-4 are deficiency motivators and are generally satisfied in order when the previous need is fully or partially satisfied. If ticked above they are probably satisfied. If a need ceases to be satisfied there is less or no motivation to strive to maintain or satisfy higher level needs.  Need 5 is a growth motivator and if ticked this is likely to be a focus of motivation. This test is based on Maslow's Hierarchy of Needs. |
|---|---|---|
| circle | | |
| 1  Biological Needs | D | |
| 2  Safety Needs | E | |
| 3  Belongingness and Love Needs | B | |
| 4  Esteem Needs | A | |
| ------------------------------------------------ | | |
| 5  Self-Actualization Needs | C | |

## ▋ ADDITIONAL TOOLS AND SUPPORTS RELATED TO CHAPTER 6

According to three separate research projects by Harvard University, the Carnegie Foundation, and the Stanford Research Institute, success in getting, keeping, and advancing in a job depends 85% on "people skills," or soft skills, and only 15% on technical skills.[8]

A study conducted on CEOs, by Stanford Research Institute & Carnegie Mellon in the USA: Long term job success depends 75% on people skills and only 25% on technical knowledge.[9]

Study done by Harvard University: 85% of jobs & promotions are because of the candidate's attitude & soft skills and only 15% due to facts and figures engineers have.[10]

## ▋ SUGGESTED GROUP "TEMPERATURE" DISCUSSION GROUP ACTIVITY- DUTIES CIVILITY IMPOSES

1. Our duty to be civil toward others does not depend on whether we like them or not.

2. Civility creates not merely a negative duty not to do harm, but an affirmative duty to do good.

3. We must come to the presence of our fellow human beings with a sense of awe and gratitude.

4. Civility assumes that we will disagree; it requires us not to mask our differences but to resolve them respectfully.

5. Civility requires that we listen to others with the knowledge of the possibility that they are right and we are wrong.

6. Civility requires that we express ourselves in ways that demonstrate our respect for others.

7. Civility allows criticism of others, and sometimes even requires it, but the criticism should always be civil.

---

8   http://www.greenbookee.com/soft-skills/

9   https://learnskills.org/wordpress/tag/stanford-research-institute

10  http://www.ccl.org/leadership/pdf/community/harvardbusinesswhitepaper.pdf

8. Civility discourages the use of legislation rather than conversation to settle disputes, except as a last, carefully considered resort.

Source: Taken from *Civility: Manners, Morals, and the Etiquette of Democracy*, by Stephen L. Carter

## CHAPTER 7 [11]

## SELF-ASSESSMENT CONTINUOUS LEARNING[12]

Continuous learning is about expanding your ability to learn by regularly upgrading your skills and increasing your knowledge. Strong continuous learning skills are required to successfully adapt to changing work and life demands. Complete this self-assessment to help you understand your continuous learning strengths and areas for improvement.

---

11  http://www.gosignmeup.com/kirkpatrick-phillips-model/

12  http://gov.mb.gc.ca

Instructions:

1.  Read each statement in Section 1 and place a check mark in the column that best describes how well you can complete that task. Tip: Think about your work and life experiences as you consider each task.

2.  Review your response for each task. If you have checked seven or more in the "Somewhat" and/or "No" columns, you may want to consider upgrading your continuous learning skills.

3.  Complete Section 2 to identify your continuous learning strengths and areas for improvement.

Section 1: Self-Assessment

I can... Yes     Somewhat     No

Learn new things.

Ask questions when I do not understand something.

Ask for feedback and/or advice from more experienced co-workers.

Identify learning or training programs that are available to me at work and in my community.

Learn by observing more experienced co-workers.

Find and use learning materials and/or resources (e.g. searching the Internet, reading articles).

Seek out and participate in training courses.

Identify and understand my skill strengths and the areas where I need improvement.

Develop my own learning goals at work and in my personal life.

Apply the lessons I have learned from past experiences to new situations.

Try new ways of doing things.

Use newly learned skills and knowledge to improve my work.

Recognize my preferred learning style (e.g. learning by seeing, hearing or doing).

Be responsible for my own learning.

Maintain my skill levels by practicing what I have learned.

TOTAL

Section 2: Personal Development

Completing this section will help you identify your continuous learning strengths and areas that may require improvement.

> » Look at the "Yes" column in Section 1 to identify your continuous learning strengths, and record them below.
>
> » Look at the "Somewhat" and/or "No" columns in Section 1 to identify the areas that you need to develop or strengthen, and record them below.

CONTINUOUS LEARNING STRENGTHS:

I am confident that I can...

E.g. ask for feedback and advice from more experienced co-workers.

1.

2.

3.

Tip: Consider using your strengths to help a colleague, friend or family member improve their continuous learning skills.

AREAS FOR IMPROVEMENT:

I would like to improve my ability to...

E.g. try new ways of doing things.

1.

2.

3.

## ABOUT SYSTEMS THINKING

Excerpt: Peter Singe – Navigating Webs of Interdependence

Points to ponder

1. We all live in webs of interdependence.

2. "It is not to understand systems.....it is to understand how it is that the problems that are most vexing......come about. To get a perspective on those problems that gives us some leverage and insight as to what we might do differently."

3. What does it take? A real and persistent commitment to learning.

4. Intelligence is always about systems. Balancing short and long term – forgoing short-term benefits for long-term gains.

5. We spend too much time talking about smart individuals. That is not the type of smartness we need. The smartness we need is collective. It's not about the smartest guy in the room.

6. We need value chains and supply chains that are managed from the beginning to the end.

7. If it was obvious what needed to be done, we would be doing it.

Systems Thinking – A way to optimize everything you do- An overview

Systems:

» Deterministic system – determine the outcome knowing the process

» Systems have boundaries and multiple layers of context

» Systems have inputs and outputs

» Inputs are turned into outputs through processes

» We optimize systems by economizing resources, rearranging (removing barriers) or providing tools

» Every system has structures (stable parameters – may also pose limitations on the process – e.g.- the counters or cabinets in your kitchen.) Structures of the system limit its capacity.

» Barriers – hold the process back[13]

---

13  https://www.youtube.com/watch?v=HOPfVVMCwYg

## ABOUT CULTURAL COMPETENCE

## THE CULTURAL COMPETENCE CONTINUUM- BY TERRY L. CROSS, M.S.W.

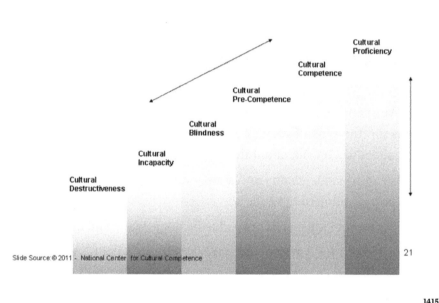

# Cultural Competence Continuum

(Cross, Bazron, Dennis and Isaacs, 1989)

Slide Source: © 2011 - National Center for Cultural Competence
21

1415

## SAMPLES- INDIVIDUAL ASSESSMENT TO ASSESS GENERAL SOCIAL AWARENESS

### Self-Assessment Quiz-Toxic or Nourishing?-Leaner Handout

Are You "Toxic?" or "Nourishing?" Karl Albrecht. www.karlabrecht. com, Used with permission.

This brief quiz comes from the *Social Intelligence Profile*, which is a comprehensive self-assessment questionnaire based on Karl Albrecht's

14  http://www.unc.edu/~wfarrell/SOWO%20874/Readings/cultcompetencecont.htm

15  http://nccc.georgetown.edu/

concepts, as presented in his book *Social Intelligence: the New Science of Success* (Jossey-Bass/Wiley, 2005).

Between each of the pairs of behaviors on the list, write a number from 0 through 4, to show how often you exhibit one or the other. Use 0 for very "toxic" behavior, 1 for mostly toxic behavior, 2 for a combination of both toxic and "nourishing" behaviors, 3 for mostly nourishing behavior, and 4 for very nourishing behavior. Add the scores to get your total score for "nourishing" behavior. The maximum possible score is 100. The higher the score, the less toxic you – as an individual are. The higher the collective score, e.g., of a work team, the less toxic the team, department or workplace is.

## WORKPLACE TOXICITY EXERCISE

| "Toxic" Behavior: | Score | "Nourishing" Behavior: |
|---|---|---|
| Scowling, "stay-away" signals | | Keeping a positive, |
| Throwing verbal barbs, "zingers" | | Kidding positively |
| Patronizing or "parenting" people | | Communicating "adult to adult" |
| Putting others down non-verbally | | Affirming others with positive "strokes" |
| Seeking approval excessively | | Speaking & acting assertively |
| Flattering others insincerely | | Giving honest compliments |
| Losing your temper frequently | | Pausing to listen and think |
| Playing "head games" with people | | Communicating openly and honestly |
| Disagreeing aggressively | | Dialoguing, exchanging views |
| Speaking dogmatically, inflexibly | | Expressing respect for others' ideas |
| Bragging, scoring "status points" | | Acknowledging the successes of others |
| Gossiping, violating confidences | | Keeping confidences |
| Breaking promises & agreements | | Making only promises you will keep |
| Joking at inappropriate times | | Using humor constructively |

| Monopolizing the conversation | | Sharing "air time" with others |
|---|---|---|
| Interrupting others frequently | | Hearing others out |
| Changing the subject capriciously | | Letting the topic "play out" |
| Complaining excessively | | Giving constructive suggestions |
| Giving someone the "hard sell" | | Suggesting, advising, negotiating |
| Insisting on getting one's way | | Compromising, helping others |
| Attacking or criticizing others | | Confronting constructively |
| Shooting down others' ideas | | Deferring judgement, listening, reflecting |
| Inducing guilt in others | | Persuading honestly; negotiating |
| Ridiculing others | | Supporting others; sympathizing |
| Giving unwanted advice | | Offering information, ideas, and options |

Total Score: _____

Howard Gardner's theory of multiple intelligences suggests that there are many different kinds of intelligence. In which area do you perform the highest? Take this 10-question quiz to discover your which of the multiple intelligences is your greatest strength. [16]

## ▌ AN EXERCISE IN COMMONALITY- FOR CULTURAL COMPETENCE TRAINING

Try this simple but effective exercise. Take two people who appear to be different (in terms of ethnicity, gender, age, etc.) and have them face each other. Ask them to use what they see and believe to list all the differences between them. Have them develop the list jointly. When they are finished, have them list all the things that they perceive having in common. Ask them to discuss what they have learned from the exercise.

---

16  http://psychology.about.com/library/quiz/bl-mi-quiz.htm

___

Without a doubt, the list of qualities the people share will be longer and more revealing. And when people realize how much they have in common, there is a greater chance that their differences will seem less important. Skin color doesn't matter when people share the same hopes, dreams, and fears. Families are families; we all care for our young and love our parents. We breathe the same air and share the same space on this planet.

The dialogue following this exercise is especially important. The people who participated in the exercise now have something in common. Even if they don't admit it at first, they have begun to understand the foundation of their shared humanity and discovered something about themselves. This knowledge is a great building block for a more complex discussion; it is a reference point to which you can return.

The exercise works especially well with young people, who quickly give up preconceived concepts and accept people as individuals. It also helps diverse groups, coming together for the first time, create the trusting relationships needed to address other topics.[17]

## CIVILITY CULTURE COMPASS® GENERAL ASSESSMENT

**Ability to be Socially Intelligent**

*3 Questions:*

-Able to perceive others' messages and interpret appropriately given social context?

-Able to adjust communication/social style in light of others' cultural and personal styles and social context?

- Knowledge of and ability to recognize what behaviors –written and unwritten - are expected and understood in certain cultures, and in workplace generally?

---

17   Community Weaving, Roberts & Newman

## ABILITY TO EXHIBIT CULTURAL COMPETENCE

*3 Questions*:

-Show sensitivity to others by striving to understand their perspective, and value and respect differences?

-Are self-directed and appropriate in situations where personal or moral judgement required?

-Are sensitive to and able to reflect on his/her own cultural heritage, values and biases and how they may affect others?

## ABILITY TO ENGAGE IN CONTINUOUS LEARNING

3 Questions:

-Seek chances to acquire knowledge and skills to improve work performance?

-Willingness to incorporate new concepts, methods or modalities in learning?

-Open to learning about other cultural groups and strategies to communicate across cultural barriers?

## ABILITY TO EMPLOY SYSTEMS THINKING

3 Questions:

-Able to operate effectively within and across systems within the organization?

-Able to recognize and adapt to needs of interconnected systems?

-Understand and accept personal role in the context of various systems?

## CHANGE

*3 Questions*:

-Is the organization experiencing cultural change (either influx of individuals from different countries, nationalities and/or cultures, or change in "org" (is this short for 'organization's?) focus/growth to international markets resulting in cross-border/cross cultural business relationships, or change in org marketing focus to include immigrant population as target customers?)

-Have the goals and background and rationale related to the change been fully communicated so all employees at every level have knowledge of them?

-Is there a feeling of receptivity to/agreement with the need for organizational change?

## ALIGNMENT

*3 Questions:*

-Is there an effective communication plan in place to relay all relevant information related to the change?

-Have the goals and desired outcomes related to the initiative been fully communicated so all employees at every level have knowledge of them?

-Are there structures AND incentives in place to support goals and outcomes?

-Do all employees of your organization see the connection of the work they do every day to the company mission/strategic focus regarding the initiative?

## READINESS

*3 Questions:*

-Do you think it's true in your company that people would be willing to make the effort and accept the risks involved in doing something new if: they were sufficiently dissatisfied with the status quo and if information about a proposed change was communicated thoroughly?

-Do people in your company resist change even if there is a clear vision and objectives, and the change could have a good result?

-Do individuals and teams within your organization collaborate very well?

## ENGAGEMENT

*3 Questions:*

-Is there high absenteeism, turnover, negativity, lack of motivation at your company, either generally or within a specific department?

-Do your departments share/model the vision and values that have been established for your organization?

-Do company meetings include an open forum, where employees are free to, and feel safe to, openly share ideas, thoughts, questions and concerns, and are encouraged to contribute to organizational processes?

## EXCERPT ABOUT STRESS AT WORK

**Stressed bank employee wins *Wallace* and mental distress damages**

A recent decision by the Ontario Superior Court of Justice once again demonstrates the increased willingness of courts to grant large awards to employees whom the court believes have been unfairly treated in relation to their terminations. Readers of our *FOCUS* e-mail alerts will recall that under the principles established by the decision of the Supreme Court of Canada in *Wallace v. United Grain Growers* (see "Fairly, reasonably and decently": Employers obliged to deal in good faith with dismissed employees, Supreme Court rules" on our Publications page, and "Appeal Court denies "*Wallace*" damages to unsuccessful candidate of "sloppy" hiring process" on our What's New page) the notice period of a wrongfully dismissed employee may be lengthened if their termination is accompanied by bad faith acts by the employer that cause the employee some form of harm. (again, text size inconsistency)

Moreover, when certain preconditions are met, the court may decide that the employer's conduct is serious enough to constitute a separate cause of action - the tort of intentional infliction of mental distress or nervous shock. This was the case in *Prinzo v. Baycrest Centre for Geriatric Care*, (see "Bullying at work: another form of workplace violence" on our Publications page) a case in which the Ontario Court of Appeal upheld damages of $15,000 for nervous shock suffered by the employee.

In *Zorn-Smith v. Bank of Montreal* (December 2, 2003) the Court awarded both *Wallace* and mental distress damages to an Ottawa-area bank employee who had been terminated without notice after 21 years of service, holding that the Bank's "callous disregard" of the employee had been "flagrant and outrageous."

## UNDERQUALIFIED AND OVERWORKED

The employee, Susanne Zorn-Smith, had been considered for the position of Financial Services Manager, but told that she was not sufficiently qualified. She had also been told that, if she were placed in the position, the Bank would expect her to take many courses, both on the job and on her own time, and that, because she was the mother of two young children and expecting a third, she would likely be unable to meet the Bank's expectations.

Nonetheless, after returning from maternity leave in 1999, Zorn-Smith was asked to take the position of Financial Services Manager. Although she had none of the educational qualifications or credentials specified in the job profile, she accepted the position. The trial judge found that she took the position during a "very busy and chaotic" time for Financial Services Managers in the Bank, that she had to work long hours without lunch breaks, and that she had to return to work in the evenings from 9:00 p.m. to 1:00 a.m. in order to keep up with her work load. The judge also found that, during this time, Zorn-Smith was being pressured to upgrade her qualifications or face losing her job.

Work pressures led to problems in her home life, and Zorn-Smith went on short-term disability leave. Upon her return, she assumed a lower paying and less stressful position. However, she was soon back in the Financial Services Manager position, working long hours in circumstances of what the trial judge found to be chronic understaffing. By the beginning of 2001, Zorn-Smith was the only employee in her branch with significant Financial Services Manager experience and knowledge. In addition to working some nights during the week, she was also going to the branch on Sunday nights to get ready for the week. At home, her marriage was in significant trouble. In the trial judge's words, on February 20, 2001, Zorn-Smith "simply stopped functioning." Again, Zorn-Smith took short-term disability leave.

### GRADUAL RETURN TO WORK A "DISASTER"

In May 2001, Zorn-Smith's physician filled out a report in which he indicated that her symptoms were severe and included reduced sleep, poor concentration, increased fatigue and increased obsessive thinking. Her degree of impairment was described as total. The report focused on the need for changes in the workplace, and described the idea of Zorn-Smith returning to work on a part-time basis as a "disaster" that would result in her "being paid one half as much to do three times as much." When asked to provide additional comments, the physician responded: "Managers including this patient will continue to burnout until the deficiencies of staff are addressed."

Despite this assessment, the employer took the position that Zorn-Smith was capable of returning to work part-time. It offered her either a part-time or full-time position as a Financial Services Manager or Customer

Service Representative, and advised her that she should return to work at the end of May or file an appeal of the Bank's decision. Zorn-Smith did not return to work, did not appeal and did not resign her position. On June 29, 2001, the Bank advised her that her position had been terminated.

## DISABILITY CAUSED BY "UNREASONABLE WORK DEMANDS"

At trial, the judge held that Zorn-Smith continued to be disabled on May 28, 2001 and was, therefore, entitled to receive disability benefits beyond that date. Zorn-Smith's refusal to accept one of the positions offered to her did not constitute cause for dismissal. Rather, the trial judge found that at the time of her dismissal, Zorn-Smith had been incapable of performing any bank job requiring a high level of responsibility or the exercise of significant decision-making authority. The judge held that, when the Bank cut off Zorn-Smith's benefits, it had incorrectly applied a test of "total disability" as the threshold for eligibility for benefits, whereas the appropriate test provided in the benefits plan was inability to perform one's regular job.

The judge also faulted the Bank for blaming Zorn-Smith's problems on her allegedly poor time-management skills and marital problems. In the judge's view, the problem lay with the workplace environment itself:

"[T]here was nothing in the evidence to suggest that Ms. Zorn-Smith could not cope with everything, had her work demands been within some reasonable parameters. They simply were not. Expectations were placed on her that required her availability for banking business well beyond normal working hours. Those demands quite understandably butted up against the legitimate demands on the home front that Ms. Zorn-Smith have some time and energy in the evenings and on the weekends for her children and husband. Having a spouse and children, and needing or wanting to spend non-working hours with them is a normal part of life. Although occasional long hours to cover special circumstances can arise in most jobs, long-term understaffing resulting in chronic, unreasonable demands being placed on employees, especially those not in the higher-income earning echelons, is unreasonable. I find that Ms. Zorn-Smith's adjustment disorder with depressed and anxious mood was caused predominantly by unreasonable work demands, and not by family stresses."

The judge also disagreed that Zorn-Smith's failure to avail herself of the Bank's appeal process invalidated her wrongful dismissal claim. The Bank had not provided her with any specific information about the appeal process, or offered her any assistance in pursuing an appeal, which would have been reasonable given that the Bank was aware of Zorn-Smith's poor concentration and inability to think clearly.

## WALLACE DAMAGES

The judge awarded Zorn-Smith 16 months of damages in lieu of notice, an award extended by the addition of *Wallace* damages for the Bank's bad faith and unfair treatment of the terminated employee. The judge gave the following examples of this conduct:

» The Bank had allowed the workplace to become damaging to Zorn-Smith's health and, instead of taking responsibility for this state of affairs, blamed the employee.

» It applied a higher standard for "disability" than the one in the policy itself.

» The Bank did not contact Zorn-Smith's physician, despite his request that he be contacted for further information.

» The Bank failed to advise Zorn-Smith about how to appeal its termination decision, or what further medical information it required of her.

Concluding her findings on this factor in the notice period, the trial judge stated:

"I consider the Bank's treatment of Ms. Zorn-Smith at the time of her dismissal to be conduct amounting to bad faith and unfair dealing that justifies a longer notice period. I have no doubt that the way in which Ms. Zorn-Smith was treated at the time of her dismissal worsened her psychological state and lengthened the time it took for her to get back on her feet and to be able to consider other employment. That must be compensated through a lengthening of the notice period."

## DAMAGES FOR MENTAL SHOCK

The trial judge also held that the preconditions for an award of damages for the intentional infliction of mental suffering were present in this case. Those preconditions are:

- » flagrant or outrageous conduct
- » that is calculated to produce harm, and
- » that results in a visible and provable illness.

According to the judge, the Bank knew that Zorn-Smith was exhausted as a result of chronic under-staffing yet, rather than taking action to alleviate the situation, took advantage of her commitment to the Bank in total disregard of the toll this was taking on her health and family life. In awarding Zorn-Smith $15,000 damages as compensation for mental suffering, the judge concluded:

"This callous disregard for the health of an employee was flagrant and outrageous. That Susanne Zorn-Smith would suffer a further burnout was predictable - the only question was when it would come. It was foreseeable that such a burnout would cause her mental suffering. I find that the Bank's conduct was the primary cause of Susanne Zorn-Smith's adjustment disorder with depressed and anxious mood."

## ▌ IN OUR VIEW

This decision suggests that, if an employer knowingly maintains work conditions marked by chronic understaffing and an employee suffers stress-related illnesses as a result, the employer could be liable for damages for infliction of mental distress. Particularly damaging to the employer's case was the fact that Zorn-Smith's supervisor, in correspondence with the Bank's Occupational Health Services, acknowledged that Zorn-Smith's branch was short-staffed by five persons, and that Zorn-Smith had been doing the work of three employees. In these circumstances, and without a concrete plan to address the short-staffing, the Bank's offer to accommodate Zorn-Smith with a part-time job in a less stressful position or face dismissal was seen as insufficient.

It should be emphasized that the second part of the test for intentional infliction of mental distress - conduct that is calculated to produce harm - will be met even though the wrongdoer does not have the actual malicious purpose of causing harm. All that is required is that the consequences of the conduct are known to be substantially certain to follow.

For further information, please contact Jennifer Birrell
at (613) 940-2740.

# SOURCES, RESOURCES AND RECOMMENDED READING

# CIVILITY AT WORK - A CHANGE IMPERATIVE

*(Items are listed in the order the books are referenced in the chapters)*

## INTRODUCTION

1. https://hbr.org/2013/01/the-price-of-incivility/

2. http://www.webershandwick.com/news/article/civility-in-america-2013-incivility-has-reached-crisis-levels

3. http://www.gov.mb.ca/labour/labmgt/emp_standards/submissions/lee.pdf (Lee & Brotheridge, 2005)

4. http://www.businessinsider.com/disturbing-facts-about-your-job-2011-2?op=1#ixzz3XCZH6nbq

5. *Quality of Working Life' report from Chartered Management Institute and Workplace Health Connect*

6. UK HSE stress statistics

7. http://www.economist.com/node/10329261

8. http://usgovinfo.about.com/od/censusandstatistics/a/commute-times.htm

9. http://www.businessinsider.com/64-canceled-vacation-this-year-2010-9

10. http://www.grahamlowe.ca/documents/182/Under%20Pressure%2010-06.pdf

11. https://hbr.org/2013/01/the-price-of-incivility/

12. http://www.businessinsider.com/disturbing-facts-about-your-job-2011-2?op=1#ixzz3XCZfQwgq

13. https://hbr.org/2013/01/the-price-of-incivility/

14. http://www.forbes.com/sites/tykiisel/2012/10/16/65-of-americans-choose-a-better-boss-over-a-raise-heres-why/

15. http://www.edelman.com/insights/intellectual-property/trust-2013/

16. Handbook of Work Stress, Barling, Kelloway and Frone, eds., 2005.

17. J. Samra, M. Gilbert, M. Shain & D. Bilsker. Centre for Applied Research in Mental Health and Addiction (CARMHA).

18. https://www.ubalt.edu/jfi/jfi/reports/civility.PDF

19. https://www.ubalt.edu/jfi/jfi/reports/civility.PDF

20. http://www.grahamlowe.ca/documents/182/Under%20Pressure%2010-06.pdf

21. Roberts & Newman, Community Weaving, published by National Civility Center, 2003

22. Http://www.webershandwick.com/uploads/news/files/Civility_in_America_2011.pdf.\

## RECOMMENDED READING

Henry David Thoreau, *Walden,*

Dr. Pier Forni, *Choose Civility,*

Human Solutions Report, *Under Pressure,*

Pearson and Porath, *The Cost of Bad Behavior*, Penguin Publishers, 2009

*Edelmans Trust Barometer*

Dr. Pier Forni, *The Thinking Life,*

*Baltimore Workplace Study,*

Kent Roberts and Jay Newman, *Community Weaving,* Published by the National Civility Center, 2003.

## CHAPTER 1

1. https://hbr.org/2013/01/the-price-of-incivility/

2. http://www.bbc.com/capital/story/20140401-how-rude-why-polite-pays

3. http://www.sciencewa.net.au/topics/social-science/item/2174-reactions-to-workplace-incivility-explored/2174-reactions-to-workplace-incivility-explored

4. 2011 survey on workplace incivility by Bar-David Consulting and Canadian HR Reporter, http://www.benefitscanada.com/benefits/health-wellness/benefits-column-the-impact-of-workplace-incivility-62273

5. http://www.ncbi.nlm.nih.gov/pubmed/21280947

6. http://library.iated.org/view/SHIM2011REL

7. http://www.businessinsider.com/disturbing-facts-about-your-job-2011-2?op=1

8. *https://www.baylor.edu/mediacommunications/news.php?action=story&story=98313;* published online in the Journal of Organizational Behavior.

9. Research by Weber Shandwick and public affairs firm Powell

Tate with KRC Research, Civility in America Study 2014.

10. http://www.insightswest.com/; http://www.insightswest.com/?s=+civility

11. Jana Raver is an Associate Professor and E. Marie Shantz Faculty Fellow in Organizational Behaviour at Queen's School of Business; http://business.queensu.ca/executiveeducation/webinars/workplace_bullying.php

12. Jana Raver is an Associate Professor and E. Marie Shantz Faculty Fellow in Organizational Behaviour at Queen's School of Business, http://business.queensu.ca/executiveeducation/webinars/workplace_bullying.php

13. https://antibullyingsoftware.com/anti-bullying-laws/

14. https://www.fwc.gov.au/resolving-issues-disputes-and-dismissals/workplace-issues-disputes/anti-bullying

15. Compiled and written by Misty Harris, published online. http://o.canada.com/life/rudeness

16. http://www.japantoday.com/category/lifestyle/view/switching-to-manner-mode-the-importance-of-social-etiquette-in-urban-japan

17. http://beijingcream.com/2013/01/shenzhen-rolls-out-legislation-to-enforce-civilized-behavior/

18. http://www.gov.ph/2013/09/12/republic-act-no-10627/

19. http://proactive-resolutions.com/about/respectful-workplace-policies-facts-statistics/

20. http://www.findmehere.com/search/dictionary/c/change_process.htm

21. As many as 70 percent of corporate and other organizational change efforts fail, according to research conducted by MC Associates, the change management and leadership development unit of Manchester Partners International.

## RECOMMENDED READING

*2014 Civility in America Poll*

*ProActive ReSolutions Workplace Survey*

Richard Barrett, *Building a Values Driven Organization*, Routledge, 2011.

## CHAPTER 2

1. The Cost of Bad Behavior: How Incivility Is Damaging Your Business and What You Can do About It, By Christine Pearson, Christine Porath,

2. http://www.oxforddictionaries.com/us/?gclid=CjwKEAjwuc-moBRDmysGsgbDr5j0SJAAxL9abywMob-33GgbdmeuL_MrB-GvySpPo7dN4WNsJUK_6wGhoC4tvw_wcB

3. http://www.merriam-webster.com/

4. http://dictionary.reference.com/

5. http://dictionary.cambridge.org/us/

6. http://dictionary. http://www.colorado.edu/conflict/civility.htm

7. http://www.instituteforcivility.org/who-we-are/what-is-civility/

8. http://webs.purduecal.edu/deanofstudents/toward-a-model-of-community-civility-student-guide-12006/cambridge.org/us/

9. http://www.dallasnews.com/opinion/sunday-commentary/20100723-p.m.-forni-why-civility-is-necessary-for-society_s-survival.ece

10. Civility: Manners, Morals and the Etiquette of Democracy, Stephen Carter, 1998

11. http://hs.boisestate.edu/civilitymatters/

12. Community Weaving, published in 2003 by the National Civility Center, authors Kent Roberts and Jay Newman.

13. The Thinking Life, Dr. P. Forni, St. Martens Press, 2011, page 150.

14. http://www.ichooseblissful.com/people-watching-i-thank-him-for-being-him/

15. Return on Character; The Real Reason Leaders and Their Companies Win, Fred Kiel, Harvard Business Review Press, 2015, page 17.

16. The Platinum Rule http://www.platinumrule.com/whatisthe-platinumrule.html

17. https://books.google.ca/books?id=_xYSXM-kDp4C&printsec=-frontcover&dq=choose+civility,+forni&hl=en&sa=X&ei=LMk-WVYDbJNDTgwSlkIGoBw&ved=0CCsQ6AEwAA#v=onep-age&q=choose%20civility%2C%20forni&f=false

18. http://www.dallasnews.com/opinion/sunday-commen-tary/20100723-p.m.-forni-why-civility-is-necessary-for-soci-ety_s-survival.ece

19. Daniel Goleman, *Emotional Intelligence, 10th Anniversary Edition*, Bantam, 2005

20. http://psychology.about.com/od/branchesofpsycholog1/a/positive-psychology.htm

21. Peterson, C. (2006). A Primer in Positive Psychology. New York: Oxford University Press.

22. http://positiveintelligence.com/overview/science/

23. http://positiveintelligence.com/overview/science/

24. Saving Civility: 52 Ways to Tame Rude, Crude, & Attitude for a Polite Planet, Sara Hacala

## RECOMMENDED READING:

Stephen L. Carter, *Civility: Manners, Morals, and the Etiquette of Democracy*

Karl Albrecht, Social IQ; *The New Science of Success*

Benet Davetian, *The History of Civility*

Withers and Lewis, *The Conflict and Communication Activity Workbook.*

*Charlotte Roberts, Fifth Discipline Fieldbook*

Fred Kiel, *Return on Character,*

Bruce Weinstein, *Ethical Intelligence*

Daniel Goleman, *Emotional Intelligence*

Martin Seligma, *Authentic Happiness,* Atria Book Publishers, 2004

Shirzad Chamine, *Positive Intelligence*

Sarah Hacala, *Saving Civility; 52 Ways to Tame Rude, Crude and Attitude for a Polite Planet*

## CHAPTER 3

1. http://www.webershandwick.com/uploads/news/files/Civility_in_America_2011.pdf

2. http://www.webershandwick.com/uploads/news/files/Civility_in_America_2011.pdf

3. https://bemycareercoach.com/soft-skills/list-soft-skills.html#comment-79983

4. http://web.mit.edu/~jwk/www/docs/Mann%201918%20Study_of_Engineering_Educ.pdf

5. http://www.ccl.org/leadership/news/2002/softskillssurvey.aspx?pageId=694

6. http://under30ceo.com/acquire-soft-skills-fast-track-career-success/

7. Thinking, Fast and Slow, Daniel Kahneman

8. http://www.llsc.on.ca/literacy-essential-skills/what-are-essential-skills

9. http://en.careers.essentialskillsgroup.com/?p=important

10. Workplace Education Manitoba, WPG.KT.1-6, 2015 www.wem.mb.ca

11. http://www.towerswatson.com/

12. http://www.srdc.org/news/new-study-shows-net-benefits-of-essential-skills-training-in-the-workplace.aspx

13. http://www.apaexcellence.org/assets/general/2015-phwa-oea-magazine.pdf

14. Leiter, M. P., Day, A., Oore, D. G., & Laschinger, H. K. S. (2012). Getting better and staying better: Assessing civility, incivility, distress, and job attitudes one year after a civility intervention. *Journal of Occupational Health Psychology, 17*(4), 425-434.

15. http://positiveintelligence.com/overview/science/

16. https://www.academia.edu/1293046/The_Business_Case_for_Emotional_Intelligence

17. https://www.questia.com/read/1G1-397579873/taking-the-good-with-the-bad-measuring-civility-and (Motowidlo, Borman, & Schmit, 1997; Podsakoff & MacKenzie, 1997)

## RECOMMENDED READING:

Daniel Kahneman, *Thinking, Fast and Slow*

## CHAPTER 4

1. Source: American Management Association; A Global Study of Current Trends and Human Possibilities, 2006-2010. Introduction.

2. The Conference Board (2005) found that Eos around the globe identify "speed, flexibility, adaptability to change" as among their greatest concerns.

3. http://www.stress.org/americas-1-health-problem/

4. http://www.webmd.com/balance/stress-management/effects-of-stress-on-your-body

5. http://psychcentral.com/lib/how-does-stress-affect-us/0001130

6. http://blogs.hbr.org/cs/2011/02/make_stress_work_for_you.html

7. Source: http://blogs.hbr.org/cs/2011/02/make_stress_work_for_you.html

8. "How Work shifting is Changing the Way We Work" by Rieva Lesonsky (Sept 2011) (article)

9. "10 Trends: A Study of Senior Executives' Views on the Future" by Corey Criswell and Andre Martin for Center for Creative Leadership (CCL) (2007)

10. "The Future of Workplace Relations" by Sarah Podoro for ACAS Policy Discussion Papers (2011)

11. "The New Digital Economy: How It Will Transform Business" by Oxford Economics (June 2011)

12. "10 Trends: A Study of Senior Executives' Views on the Future" by Corey Criswell and Andre Martin for Center for Creative Leadership (CCL) (2007)

13. InfoWorld (website): "Cloud Computing" (article)

14. "Workplace of the Future: How Technology Will Change the Way We Work" by Erika Chickowski (Nov 16 2011)

15. U.S. Dept of Labour "Futureworks" study (1999)

16. "Impact of Social Media in the Workplace" by Marci Paino

17. Oxford Economics "New Digital Economy"

18. "The New Digital Economy: How It Will Transform Business" by Oxford Economics (June 2011)

19. "The New Digital Economy: How It Will Transform Business" by Oxford Economics (June 2011)

20. "10 Trends: A Study of Senior Executives` Views on the Future" by Corey Criswell and Andre Martin for Center for Creative Leadership (CCL) (2007)

21. "The Future of Workplace Relations" by Sarah Podoro for ACAS Policy Discussion Papers (2011)

22. Gov`t of Canada: Report of the Standing Committee on Banking, Trade and Commerce, "The Demographic Time Bomb: Mitigating the Effects of Demographic Change in Canada" (June 2006)

23. "10 Trends: A Study of Senior Executives` Views on the Future" by Corey Criswell and Andre Martin for Center for Creative Leadership (CCL) (2007)

24. "How Leadership Must Change to Meet the Future" p. 23 by PriceWaterhouseCooper (March 2008) (research paper)

25. "10 Trends: A Study of Senior Executives` Views on the Future" by Corey Criswell and Andre Martin for Center for Creative Leadership (CCL) (2007)

26. "Leadership Development: Past, Present and Future" by Hernez-Broome, Hughes for Center for Creative Leadership

27. "Leadership Development: Past, Present and Future" by Hernez-Broome, Hughes for Center for Creative Leadership

28. "Leadership Development: Past, Present and Future" by Hernez-Broome, Hughes for Center for Creative Leadership

29. "Why You Need a Resilient Workforce in Today`s Economy" by David Lee (2008) (article

30. "The Changing Nature of Organizations, Work, and Workplace" by Judith Heerwagen Ph.D. (Dec 2010) (article)

31. "The New Digital Economy: How It Will Transform Business" by Oxford Economics (June 2011)

32. Good to Great, Jim Collins, Harper Business 2001

33. "The Changing Nature of Organizations, Work, and Workplace" by Judith Heerwagen Ph.D. (Dec 2010) (article)

## RECOMMENDED READING:

Jim Collins, *Good to Great*, Harper Business 2001

## CHAPTER 5

1. From HumanNext LLC www.humannext.com Cultural Competence Profile
2. Karp, T. & Helgo, T. (2008). From change management to change leadership: embracing chaotic change in public service organizations. Journal of Organizational Change Management 8(1), 82-96.
3. http://onlinelearninginsights.wordpress.com
4. http://www.sergaygroup.com/Smart-Talk/Strategic-Alignment. html
5. http://smallbusiness.chron.com/approaches-organizational-strategic-alignment-14151.html

## RECOMMENDED READING:

Steven Covey Jr. *The Speed of Trust*

Robert Gagne, *The Conditions of Learning*

## CHAPTER 6

1. http://alumnus.caltech.edu/~rouda/T1_HRD.html
2. http://www.cio.com/article/2447352/training/time-in-training-often-wasted.html
3. http://www.trainingindustry.com/blog/blog-entries/how-big-is-the-training-market.aspx
4. The Corporate Learning Factbook 2014: Benchmarks, Trends, and Analysis of the U.S. Training Market

5. https://trainingmag.com/2013-training-industry-report

6. http://blogs.cdc.gov/niosh-science-blog/2010/01/29/training/

7. Owned by Civility Experts Worldwide, www.civilitexperts.com

8. http://former.denisonconsulting.com/diagnostics/organization-al-culture

9. http://www.mckinseysolutions.com/

10. http://www.ocai-online.com/

11. http://www.careleaders.com/assessment/valuesAssessment.html

12. www.civilityexperts.com/assessments

13. http://hs.boisestate.edu/civilitymatters/research-instr.htm

14. http://stopbullyingtoolkit.org/Civility-Quotient-Assessment.pdf

15. http://stopbullyingtoolkit.org/Civility-Quotient-Assessment.pdf

16. http://www.iedex.com.au/index.php/organisational-assess-ments/positive-culture-surveys.html

17. https://www.happinessatworksurvey.com/info/scores

18. http://www.franklincoveyme.com/trust-quotient-tq-assessment

19. http://www.speedoftrust.com/How-The-Speed-of-Trust-works/speed-of-trust-measurement

20. https://q12.gallup.com/public/en-us/Features

21. http://www.change-management.com/tutorial-change-man-agement-assessments.htm

22. http://www.peecworks.org/peec/peec_in-st/01795CC4-001D0211.52/M.%20Casey%20Org.%20Capaci-ty%20Assessment%20Tool%20%28paper%20version%29.pdf

23. http://www.wmich.edu/emrl/resilienceassessment.htm

24. http://www.wmich.edu/emrl/resilienceassessment.htm

25. www.businessballs.com. © alan chapman 2003. Disclaimer: Sole risk with user.  Neither Alan chapman nor businessballs.com ac-

cepts liability for any issues or damages arising from the use of this tool.

26. http://www.queendom.com/tests/access_page/index.htm?idRegTest=700

27. http://www.stress.org/self-assessment/

28. http://www.ashpfoundation.org/selfassessment/selfassessmenthelix11151211.html

29. http://alumnus.caltech.edu/~rouda/T1_HRD.html

## RECOMMENDED READING:

Stephen Covey; Speed of Trust

Stephen L. Carter, Civility: Manners, Morals, and the Etiquette of Democracy

## CHAPTER 7

For information about site licenses, Train the Trainer, curriculum and related supports for the Civility Culture Compass® and/ or the Civility Competency Matrix® please contact pr@civilityexperts.com. www.civilityexperts.com

1. Source: http://charles-jennings.blogspot.com/2011/10/in-complex-world-continuous-learning.html

2. Howell, Wright, Bayer, Workplace Education Manitoba, The Change Imperative, 2011.

3. The Fifth Discipline: The Art and Practice of the Learning Organization, and The Fifth Discipline Fieldbook: Strategies and Tools for Building a Learning Organization, Peter Senge, 1990, 10

4. http://www.unc.edu/~wfarrell/SOWO%20874/Readings/cultcompetencecont.htm

## RECOMMENDED READING:

Peter Block, *Community*

Peter Senge, *he Fifth Discipline: The Art and Practice of the Learning Organization, and The Fifth Discipline Fieldbook: Strategies and Tools for Building a Learning Organization*

Richard Arum, *Academically Adrift: Limited Learning on College Campuses*

## CHAPTER 8

1. http://www.webershandwick.com/uploads/news/files/Civility_in_America_2011.pdf
2. http://alumnus.caltech.edu/~rouda/T1_HRD.html

## RECOMMENDED READING:

Malcolm Gladwell, *Blink*

Dr. Cherie Carter Scott's book, *If Life is a Game, These are the Rules,*

## CHAPTER 9

1. http://www.ichooseblissful.com/people-watching-i-thank-him-for-being-him/
2. https://bemycareercoach.com/soft-skills/list-soft-skills.html#comment-79983
1. https://civilityexperts.com
2. Lew Bayer, Civility Experts Worldwide, 2014
3. http://www.ichooseblissful.com/people-watching-i-thank-him-for-being-him/
4. https://bemycareercoach.com/soft-skills/list-soft-skills.html#comment-79983

5. https://civilityexperts.com

6. Lew Bayer, Civility Experts Worldwide, 2014

7. https://bemycareercoach.com/soft-skills/list-soft-skills.html#comment-79983

8. https://www.thechangesource.com/8-tools-to-assess-and-accelerate-organizational-culture-change/

9. http://hs.boisestate.edu/civilitymatters/research-instr.htm

10. www.businessballs.com. © alan chapman 2003. Disclaimer: Sole risk with user. Neither Alan chapman nor businessballs.com accepts liability for any issues or damages arising from the use of this tool.

11. www.businessballs.com. © alan chapman 2003. Disclaimer: Sole risk with user. Neither Alan chapman nor businessballs.com accepts liability for any issues or damages arising from the use of this tool.

12. http://www.greenbookee.com/soft-skills/

13. https://learnskills.org/wordpress/tag/stanford-research-institute

14. http://www.ccl.org/leadership/pdf/community/harvardbusinesswhitepaper.pdf

15. http://www.gosignmeup.com/kirkpatrick-phillips-model/

16. http://gov.mb.gc.ca

17. https://www.youtube.com/watch?v=HOPfVVMCwYg

18. http://www.unc.edu/~wfarrell/SOWO%20874/Readings/cultcompetencecont.htm

19. http://nccc.georgetown.edu/

20. Community Weaving, Roberts and Newman

21. SOURCE: http://www.ehlaw.ca/publications/jan04/Zorn-Smith.shtml

## RECOMMENDED READING:

Withers and Lewis, *The Conflict and Communication Activity Workbook.*

Terry L. Cross M.S.W. *The Cultural Competence Continuum*

Roberts and Newman, *Community Weaving*

## ADDITIONAL RESOURCES AND INFORMATION

Optional clip on Organizational Change.

**http://www.youtube.com/watch?v=iuGjYfJ0HSY&playnext=1&list=PL7255D6305D0318AA.**

## SUPPORT EXCERPTS RELATED TO LEARNING AT WORK.

The flow of work, and the relentless demand for producing results, represents key drivers of the continuous learning environment. "... learners increasingly find the need to learn in the same environment where they work – their work context. In fact, the bulk of our learning environment continues to shift away from the classroom, away from formal training, and closer to the actual work performed." In a 2004 interview, Jonathon Levy, an e-Learning visionary, predicted: "Over the next 12-18 months, the end game will finally begin to come into view as traditional learning structures give way to more powerful performance support integration." Integration into what? Into the work context!

Mr. Levy's prediction implied we would not always be in the classroom when we learn. Instead, learning moments will increasingly confront our learners within workflows and processes. The need to learn becomes immediate, more urgent, and often encountered in a largely unstructured and uncontrolled context. This is a direct opposite to the stable realm of the formal classroom. *Source: Dawn-Marie Turner, PhD, CMC*

"...expanded discovery as essential to defining critical, design-influencing attributes of a continuous learning environment. Forget defining knowledge and skill requirements, at least for now. The starting point, and the primary focus of this expanded discovery, is the environment where learners confront opportunities to learn. Learning opportunities span the whole spectrum from premeditated moments (for example, new employee orientation, or annual recertification training), to unplanned, unstructured, and uncontrolled moments, often manifested in the middle of a workflow."[1]

## COLLABORATION AS CURRENCY:

*"....the future of work is in learning and the future of learning is in the workplace"- FutureU.* [2]

## WHAT IS WORKPLACE INCIVILITY?

Workplace incivility is defined in part as deviant behaviors that are low in intensity (Andersson & Pearson, 1999). Low intensity, however, does not mean that incivility is of minor consequence and can safely be overlooked in organizations. Andersson and Pearson (1999) theorize that uncivil experiences in the workplace are like an accumulation of minor stresses. These may be more damaging than a single, major stressful event and spiral to a point where incivility transitions to overt aggression (Andersson & Pearson, 1999; Cortina, Langhout, Magley, & Williams, 2001). Andersson and Pearson's (1999) model of a conflict spiral from incivility to coercive behaviors that lead to workplace aggression is consistent with the "popcorn" model of aggression where repeated minor offenses or injustice eventually lead to an explosion of aggression (Folger & Skarlicki, 1998; Schat & Kelloway, 2005).

Examples of uncivil behaviors include writing nasty and demeaning notes or emails, undermining a colleague's credibility, treating another

---

1   http://www.learningsolutionsmag.com/articles/16/the-continuous-learning-environment-sur-viving-learning-solution-discovery-

2   http://www.futureu.com/business/learning_opportunities.html

like a child, berating one for an action in which he or she played no part, giving people the silent treatment, publicly reprimanding someone, making unfounded accusations, and spreading gossip (Johnson & Indvik, 2001; Pearson, Andersson, & Porath, 2000). Being uncivil also includes excluding someone from a meeting, neglecting to greet someone, cutting people off while they are speaking, not turning mobile phones off during meetings; listening in on another's phone call, ignoring a colleague's request, using demeaning language or voice tone, making inflammatory remarks; and writing rude or unnecessarily incendiary emails (Johnson & Indvik, 2001; Pearson, Andersson, & Wegner, 2001). Workplace incivility manifests itself in the work environment through a wide assortment of behaviors such as rude remarks, verbal attacks, wrongful blame, preferential treatment, and unfavorable work assignments (Carter, 1988; Marks, 1996; Neuman & Baron, 1997). Workplace incivility is generally verbal, passive, indirect and subtle as opposed to physical, active, direct, and overt (Baron & Neuman, 1996). Physical, active, direct, and/or overt behavior is more easily recognized as bullying and is more easily sanctioned by the organization. The very nature of incivility makes it less obvious, more difficult to recognize, and therefore more difficult to sanction or even to address.

What is considered acceptable workplace behavior depends on organizational norms and legal frameworks. For instance, less formal organizational cultures may accept conduct that would be unacceptable in a more formal organization. However, even these less formal organizations may find their "acceptable" conduct restricted by changes in the legal environment. New statutes or regulations may require changes in an organization's acceptable workplace standards and behaviors. Before sexual harassment laws came into effect, sexual harassment in the workplace did not constitute cause for complaint and legal action. Today it is acknowledged and accepted that sexual harassment creates a hostile work environment, and that a failure to address the issue can result in penalties imposed on the organization.

Johnson and Indvik (2001) suggested that workplace incivility may cause the development of a hostile work environment increasing the likelihood of harassment, intimidation and violence, which may lead to serious legal and economic ramifications.[3]

## ■ COST AND CONSEQUENCES OF INCIVILITY TO BUSINESS

General Statistics on Incivility

Recent study of a diverse occupational sample of 180 workers in the Canadian prairies found that 40% reported experiencing at least 1 of 45 specific acts indicative of psychological harassment or bullying on a weekly basis for at least 6 months. An additional 10% of the sample reported experiencing 5 or more such acts on a weekly basis for at least 6 months.[4]

What other problems does incivility cause in Canadian companies?

**90%** of HR professionals say it hurts collaboration

**78%** say it affects talent retention

**52%** say it affects brand reputation

Source: 2011 survey on workplace incivility by Bar-David Consulting and Canadian HR Reporter http://www.benefitscanada.com/benefits/health-wellness/benefits-column-the-impact-of-workplace-incivility-62273

In the fourth annual Civility in America[5] nationwide poll conducted by Weber Shandwick and Powerl Tate with KRC Research showed- of Americans surveyed:

» 50% have ended a friendship because another person was uncivil

» 48% have defriended or blocked someone online because of uncivil behavior

---

3    https://www.questia.com/read/1G1-397579873/taking-the-good-with-the-bad-measuring-civility-and

4    Lee & Brotheridge, 2005

5    http://www.webershandwick.com/news/article/civility-in-america-2013-incivility-has-reached-crisis-levels

» 43% expect to experience incivility in the next 24 hours

» 2.4 times per day is the average number of times Americans encounter incivility

» 24% have experienced cyberbullying

» 19% of parents have transferred their child to a different school because of incivility at school

» 26% have quit a job because it was an uncivil workplace

» One often cited source for insight into the cost of incivility is research conducted by Christine Pearson and Christine Porath. Over 14 years, the pair has polled thousands of workers about how they're treated on the job, in one survey where 800 managers and employees in 17 industries were polled, 98% reported experiencing uncivil behavior.[6] Additional findings are listed below.

Among workers who've been on the receiving end of incivility:

» 48% intentionally decreased their work effort.

» 47% intentionally decreased the time spent at work.

» 38% intentionally decreased the quality of their work.

» 80% lost work time worrying about the incident.

» 63% lost work time avoiding the offender.

» 66% said that their performance declined.

» 78% said that their commitment to the organization declined.

» 12% said that they left their job because of the uncivil treatment.

» 25% admitted to taking their frustration out on customers.

The National Institute for Occupational Safety (NIOSH) research found that 25 percent of businesses have issues with workplace bullying.[7]

Workplace incivility is damaging to organizations in the form of:

---

6    https://hbr.org/2013/01/the-price-of-incivility/

7    http://www.cdc.gov/niosh/updates/upd-07-28-04.html

» increased turnover intention (Cortina, Magley, Williams, & Lang-hout, 2001; Lim, Cortina & Magley, 2008; Giumetti, McKibben, Hatfield, Schroder, Kowalski, 2012),

» decreased job satisfaction (Cortina et al., 2001; Cortina and Mag-ley, 2003; Miner-Rubino & Cortina, 2004; Penney & Spector, 2005; Lim, et al., 2008; Lim & Lee, 2011; Morrow, McElroy & Scheibe, 2011)

» decreased performance (Porath & Erez, 2007; 2009; Estes & Wang, 2008), decreased organizational commitment (Blau & An-dersson, 2005)

» decreased organizational citizenship behavior (Porath & Erez, 2007).

» Additionally, Andersson and Pearson (1999) discuss the spiraling effect of incivility. The spiraling effect states that in the presence of incivility a retaliation of sorts occurs, possibly leading to much higher intensity aggressive behaviors.[8]

» 91% of people in a US poll said they believe incivility leads to vi-olence.[9]

» 75% of adults admit to texting or talking while driving even though they know it's dangerous to themselves and others.[10]

» 92% of teens say they feel social media, e.g., Facebook and Twitter is making us a less civil society.[11]

A 2011 poll of more than 5,000 drivers for the Canadian Automobile Association found 73 per cent of people believed road users were exhibiting more rude habits than in the recent past. And in a 2013 survey by B.C.-based Insights West, the majority of respondents had, over the previous month, witnessed public swearing (87 per cent), a child

---

8   https://www.questia.com/read/1G1-397579873/taking-the-good-with-the-bad-measuring-civili-ty-and

9   http://www.roca.org/OA/143-144/143r.htm

10  http://ansonalex.com/infographics/poor-cell-phone-etiquette-statistics-infographic/

11  http://bit.ly/I9MzoY

misbehaving without parental intervention (76 per cent), public spitting (72 per cent), and the use of cellphones during a movie (53 per cent).

Poor parenting was cited as a culprit by 93 per cent of respondents, followed by the influence of technology, at 84 per cent. Among Canadians 18 to 34, 70 per cent said someone had written something rude on their Facebook page, directed a mean tweet at them, or been disrespectful to them elsewhere online.

Prior to the Vancouver Olympics, volunteers participated in a kind of civility bootcamp, aimed at fostering such skills as attentive listening and conflict management. And looking to the nation's bleachers, more than 65,000 Canadians have participated in Respect in Sport's parent program, a behavioral training initiative – made mandatory by many sport bodies – designed to prevent infighting among overzealous moms and dads.[12]

### Reduced Stress Management and Health.

"35% of the U.S. workforce (an est. 53.5 million Americans) report being bullied at work; an additional 15% witness it. Half of all Americans have directly experienced it." [13]

Psychologists and other researchers are finding that rudeness does more than just make life unpleasant. It also has an impact on our ability to concentrate, our well-being and the bottom line.[14]

6,850 complaints launched in Quebec since introducing 'psychological harassment' legislation in June 2004.[15]

6% of women are sexually harassed at work per year[16] Research in the UK shows that 1/3 to 1/2 of stress-related illness is due to workplace bullying. According to a

---

12   Compiled, written and published by Misty Harris, http://o.canada.com/life/rudeness

13   http://workplacepsychology.net/tag/incivility/

14   http://www.apa.org/monitor/2013/11/rude.aspx

15   http://www.sharonebardavid.com/wp-content/uploads/2012/01/Business-Case-Respect-Web-site-Version-Dec-2011-2.pdf

16   Statistics Canada, in HR Reporter, Dec 3, 2007

In a report tabled in the British parliament, it is estimated that 40 million working days are lost each year because of bullying. In addition, 25% of targets of bullying will leave that job, and 20% of witnesses will leave, 35% of those who leave do so very quietly, without any feedback.[17]

## INCREASED COSTS

According to a study conducted by Accountemps and reported in Fortune, managers and executives at Fortune 1,000 firms spend 13% percent of their work time—the equivalent of seven weeks a year—mending employee relationships and otherwise dealing with the aftermath of incivility.[18]

A 2011 survey by Bar-David Consulting and *Canadian HR Reporter* shows incivility affects key business indicators. Nearly all (92%) Canadian HR professionals agree incivility has negative effects on productivity. Eighty "percent" (again, remember to choose just one way to write 'percent' and stick with it) report an impact on absenteeism. And 72% say customer service suffers as a result.[19]

U.S. academic research from 2011 focusing on both Canadian and U.S. companies shows two out of three employees experienced a decline in performance after an incivility incident. Four out of five lost time worrying about the incident. And nearly half (47%) of employees purposely lowered their effort or decreased their time at work due to incivility.[20]

A sample of costs that are associated with stress in the workplace[21]:

» 19% of absenteeism costs

---

17  http://www.gov.mb.ca/labour/labmgt/emp_standards/submissions/lee.pdf

18  http://www.roberthalf.com/accountemps/free-resources

19  http://www.benefitscanada.com/benefits/health-wellness/benefits-column-the-impact-of-workplace-incivility-62273

20  http://www.benefitscanada.com/benefits/health-wellness/benefits-column-the-impact-of-workplace-incivility-62273

21  Joan Burton, IAPA (Industrial Accident Prevention Association, 2006)

- » 40% of turnover costs
- » 10% of drug plan costs
- » 60% of workplace accidents
- » 100% of stress related lawsuits (e.g., Bank of Montreal vs. Zorn-Smith, Honda, RCMP) Chrysalis Performance Inc. Research (text size inconsistency)

## NEGATIVE IMPACT TO CUSTOMER RETENTION

Public rudeness among employees is common, according to our survey of 244 consumers. Whether it's waiters berating fellow waiters or store clerks criticizing colleagues, disrespectful behavior makes people uncomfortable, and they're quick to walk out without making a purchase.[22]

## REDUCED CREATIVITY AND INNOVATION:

Witnesses to rudeness also suffer a loss of cognitive powers and the ability to be creative, says a study[23] by Amir Erez, a psychologist at the University of Florida's school of management. It's just bad business, he says: One toxic employee can poison a whole office with a few angry outbursts and four-letter words.

"Managers should be very concerned because the negative consequences of rudeness on the job are not limited to the person who happens to be the victim," he said. "If five other people are watching, the effects are going to spill over into the rest of the organization." In an experiment Pearson and Porath conducted with Amir Erez, a professor of management at the University of Florida, participants who were treated rudely by other subjects were 30% less creative than others in the study.

---

22  https://hbr.org/2013/01/the-price-of-incivility/

23  *www.wharton.upenn.edu/bakerretail/files/**Amir_Erez**_Paper_2.pdf*

In an experiment we conducted with Amir Erez, a professor of management at the University of Florida, participants who were treated rudely by other subjects were 30% less creative than others in the study. They produced 25% fewer ideas, and the ones they did come up with were less original. For example, when asked what to do with a brick, participants who had been treated badly proposed logical but not particularly imaginative activities, such as "build a house," "build a wall," and "build a school." We saw more sparks from participants who had been treated civilly; their suggestions included "sell the brick on eBay," "use it as a goalpost for a street soccer game," "hang it on a museum wall and call it abstract art," and "decorate it like a pet and give it to a kid as a present."[24]

## PERFORMANCE AND TEAM SPIRIT DETERIORATE.

Survey results and interviews indicate that simply witnessing incivility has negative consequences. In one experiment we conducted, people who'd observed poor behavior performed 20% worse on word puzzles than other people did. We also found that witnesses to incivility were less likely than others to help out, even when the person they'd be helping had no apparent connection to the uncivil person: Only 25% of the subjects who'd witnessed incivility volunteered to help, whereas 51% of those who hadn't witnessed it did.[25]

## REDUCED TRUST AND DISENGAGEMENT

Nearly 1 in 4 of all employees suffer chronic anger on the job. Workplace anger is on the upswing, because people feel betrayed by their employers... one element of this perceived betray is constant uncertainty about the future of their jobs, *The Marlin Co. & Yale School of Management.*

---

24  https://hbr.org/2013/01/the-price-of-incivility/
25  https://hbr.org/2013/01/the-price-of-incivility/

## REDUCED MORALE AND LOWER PRODUCTIVITY

Ralph Fevre, a professor of social research at Cardiff University said his research showed that incivility in the workplace translates into increased turnover, more sick days, lower morale and poor productivity. But remedying this situation isn't as straightforward as it would seem. *"Managers and supervisors are the single most important source of incivility in the workplace and some of this occurs as they pursue the objectives their employer has given them. This in turn suggests that companies sometimes lose sight of the fundamentals because they are determined to follow a particular strategy,"* Mr. Fevre said. According to his research, incivility is most often demonstrated by shouting, insults, treating others disrespectfully, intimidating behavior and persistent criticism. He said that there is a substantial overlap between incivility at work and other forms of ill treatment in the workplace, including violence.

Naturally, some offices are worse than others but those that consider their work "super intense" are prone to problems of all types. The most reliable predictors of a troubled workplace? When employees feel they need to compromise their principles or when organizations put their own needs ahead of their employees' well-being, Mr. Fevre said.[26]

## EXAMPLES OF CIVILITY INITIATIVES WE CAN LEARN FROM:

## CAMPUS CIVILITY INITIATIVES

1. ***Civility and Community and the University of Tennessee***

http://civility.utk.edu/ Principles of Civility and Community -
The University of Tennessee, Knoxville affirms the value of each member of the university community and recommends that all UTK community members adhere to the following Principles of Civility

---

26  http://sites.cardiff.ac.uk/ahss/no-easy-remedy-for-incivility-at-work/

and Community. Inclusivity, Diversity, Dialogue, Collegiality, Respect, Knowledge, Integrity, Learning, Awareness, Response. http://civility.utk.edu/ Bias Incident Protocol and Reporting: http://bias.utk.edu/ The University of Tennessee, Knoxville, is committed to providing students, faculty, staff, and campus visitors an environment that is safe, as well as civil, and one that encourages the exchange of ideas through discourse in every aspect of campus life. All members of the campus community are encouraged to report bias motivated incidents or crime.

## CIVILITY INITIATIVE

In the spring of 2010, Chancellor Jimmy G. Cheek assembled a Task Force on Civility and Community and asked its members to define civility and come up with a list of guiding principles and recommend ways we can further civility on our campus. Video:

https://www.youtube.com/watch?feature=player_embedded&v=bX-OObdcUmNU

Ready for the World:

http://rftw.utk.edu/

The University of Tennessee is involved on an ambitious plan to help students gain the international and intercultural knowledge they need to succeed in today's world.

Ready for the World is part of a long-range plan to transform the campus into a culture of diversity that best prepares students for working and competing in the 21st century. Are you ready?

2. **Commitment to Civility, University of Southern Maine**

https://usm.maine.edu/nursing/commitment-civility

The concepts of community and social justice are central to the mission and philosophy of the USM CONHP. Faculty, students, staff are committed to promoting a healthy and just environment that supports transformative learning, academic integrity, open communication, and personal and professional growth among the diverse members of our academic community. We believe that these commitments are grounded in intellectual openness, in personal and professional accountability, and in the democratic values of inclusivity and mutual respect which are guided by rational discourse and by a relational ethic of care.

3. *Fashion Institute of Technology – Civility Initiative*

https://www.fitnyc.edu/14264.asp

FIT's emerging civility initiative is aimed at engaging our community in a discussion of respectful ways of living and learning in a higher education environment.

In 2012, a committee made up of faculty, staff, students, and administrators was formed to champion the FIT Civility Initiative. The committee was charged with developing a road map for a civility campaign and creating a civility mission statement for the FIT community.

Following the success of the first Civility Week that took place in April 2013, Enrollment Management and Student Success rolled out the **WEAR it Monday** campaign to re-engage the student community during the fall 2013 semester. To continue building momentum for the FIT Civility Initiative, the FIT community will be celebrating **Kindness Week** in partnership with PTK (Phi Theta Kappa) and Student Ambassadors in spring 2014. **Kindness Week** will be a joint effort throughout the FIT community in future years to come as part of the overall FIT civility program. More events will be planned for fall 2014, including a joint kick-off sponsored by the President's Office and the United College Employees.

4. *Indiana, Purdue, Fort Wayne Universities Civility Initiative Statements*

http://www.ipfw.edu/committees/diversity/initiatives/civility-statement.html

Indiana University–Purdue University Fort Wayne is committed to the goals and ethics of academic investigation and education. The foundation of academic pursuit is the process of free inquiry, in which individuals may openly explore and express ideas. Free inquiry requires an environment that encourages open investigation, as well as the educational growth and positive social development of individuals. Therefore, it is important to state explicitly the ethics that define our academic community.

Safe Zone - What is a Safe Zone? A Safe Zone is a place where students can talk freely about being lesbian, gay, bisexual, or transgender without fear of criticism or hatred, where LGBT students will not only be supported, but affirmed and valued. http://www.ipfw.edu/offices/cwra/programs/safe-zone.html

Diversity Showcase - The IPFW Chancellor's Council on Diversity celebrated a record-setting Diversity Showcase November 15, 2012. This year's celebration marked the first Showcase for Chancellor Vicky Carwein. Dr. Carwein expressed that a key and central component of her leadership includes the expectation for diversity to be achieved and appreciated throughout the campus. Dr. Carwein shared her vision with a record number of attendees that included faculty, students, staff and community members. http://www.ipfw.edu/committees/diversity/initiatives/diversity-showcase.html

5.  *University of San Diego – Restoring Respect*

https://www.sandiego.edu/restoringrespect/

Restoring Respect is community initiative promoting greater civility in San Diego civic dialogue. The initiative is supported by a consortium of San Diego area academic institutions and community groups including the Catfish Club of San Diego, the San Diego Community College District and the University of San Diego.

On Civility - https://www.sandiego.edu/restoringrespect/about-us/on-civility.php

What is Civility?

Civility, which comes to us from the Latin word for citizen, includes not only the notions of courtesy and politeness, but also such matters as social relationships and proper conduct in human relationships. For some, civility is the essential glue that holds society together, and it involves such important issues as friendship, altruism, responsibility, dignity, and justice.

6. *George Mason University – The Civility Project*

http://civilityproject.onmason.com/

**Mason Civility Project** has been inspired by the same fabric that is at the heart of our university and defines the Mason Spirit. Allow me to share with you a little bit of history to bring some light into these words. George Mason University was named after George Mason, a Virginian, who is described in the history of the United States as the central genius of the American Revolution. He is known as the primary author of the Virginia Declaration of Rights, a document that he wrote in 1778, which served as the bedding to the Constitution of the United States of America.

http://civilityproject.onmason.com/abou/civility-project-proposal/

The civility project aims to promote civility at George Mason University. This project will assess the benchmarks in the field of promoting civil engagement across colleges and universities in the US. Specifically, we are interested in learning and promoting the core values of civil interactions in highly diverse communities. Through this project we are hoping to initiate a dialogue across different constituencies to be able to establish and promote new standards of civil behavior across the university. Potential methods for implementing these standards include development of: programming initiatives around the topic, Mason guidelines for civil behavior, protocols for uncivil behavior, curriculum focused on civility as it relates to various disciplines, etc. - See more at: http://civilityproject.onmason.com/abou/civility-project-proposal/#sthash.l8KBUon5.dpuf

### 7. *Rutgers Project Civility*

http://projectcivility.rutgers.edu/about-project-civility

History and vision - In 2009, Dr. Kathleen Hull, the Director for the Byrne Family First Year Seminars and Dean Mark Schuster, Senior Dean of Students, had a conversation that would create the foundation for what became to be known as **Project Civility at Rutgers**. Based on the timing of events last fall 2010, many believed the two-year initiative was reactive and a response to specific events last fall. However, it was almost two years in the planning. Dr. Hull was teaching a Byrne Seminar called "Ain't Misbehavin," using Dr. P.M. Forni's book *Choosing Civility: The Twenty-five Rules of Considerate Conduct*. Dean Schuster oversaw the Dean of Students Office and the newly named Office of Student Conduct in 2009.

### 8. *UCDavis Humanities Institute – The Civility Project*

http://dhi.ucdavis.edu/archive/civilities

Drawing upon our campus's strengths in research across the disciplines, the **Humanities Institute's *Civility Project*** engages with questions around civility on UC campuses, asking how we might better develop or refine a shared notion of civility, and foster the conditions necessary to nurture it.

### 9. *Western Michigan University – Campus climate for Diversity, Equity, and Inclusion tactical action community*

http://wmich.edu/diversity/initiatives/campus-climate-diversity-equity-inclusion-tactical-action-community

**Campus-wide Equity and Civility Initiative Project Action Team (CECI PAT)**

This PAT seeks to promote and ensure an environment that is equitable and civil for all members of the University community.

**Mission**

To ensure equitable access for all, the Office of Diversity and Inclusion provides leadership by working collaboratively with the University community to identify and overcome institutional barriers and affirm the dignity, value, and uniqueness of each member of our community.

10. ***Plattsburgh state university of New York – Class uses Civility initiative***

http://www.plattsburgh.edu/about/profiles/programs/civility.php

A semester-long project ensued, culminating in what she called a communication audit, in this case using the SUNY Plattsburgh Civility Committee's civility survey.

Class members launched a student survey that mirrored the faculty/staff survey with questions adjusted to students' circumstances. For instance, instead of asking about workplace civility, the students' survey asked about classroom civility issues. In addition to the survey, Isgro asked her students to interview a faculty member, a staff member and a student independently of the survey. From this information, they were required to ultimately present their findings to the civility committee as a final project.

---

**COMMUNITY CIVILITY INITIATIVES**

1. ***Choose Civility Portland***

http://www.portlandlibrary.com/highlight/choose-civility/

Portland Public Library invites the Greater Portland community to enhance our public life by choosing civility! PPL is pleased to announce **Choose Civility Portland**, modeled on the work of the Howard County Library System. With generous funding from the Lerner Foundation, the Library aims to position itself as a community center where citizens can gather to discuss issues important to our community. - See more at: http://www.portlandlibrary.com/highlight/choose-civility/#sthash.DoZCVwRb.dpuf

---

2. *Civility Initiative Org*

http://www.civilityinitiative.org/

MISSION - The Civility Initiative aims to engage Rye citizens of all ages to work towards a greater culture of caring, respect, and integrity in our community and beyond.

More information/Articles/resources - The path to civility is thornier than one might think. People don't typically yell and swear in our community (except at sports games!), children are taught to say please and thank you, and cars stop (most of the time) for pedestrians at the cross walk. However, there were a few incidents over the last year and a half that gave us pause and left many of us feeling unsettled about the way we treat each other in Rye. In the depth of difficult and at times heated exchanges, we discovered that we had an opportunity to come together and reflect on what our core values are as a community and what we want them to be going forward.

3. *Choose Civility Washington County*

http://www.wcps.k12.md.us/parents_community/civil_behavior.html

As part of the Choose Civility initiative in Washington County, a Hagerstown/Washington County Chamber of Commerce Eggs & Issues meeting segued into a Choose Civility Washington County Symposium on Tuesday, March 9, 2010. The keynote speaker was Dr. P.M. Forni, Johns Hopkins University professor and co-founder of the Johns Hopkins Civility Project in 1997. Other speakers for breakout sessions covered issues such as ethics, civility and mediation, character counts, and civility in sports.

Our Vision - http://www.wcps.k12.md.us/our_vision/

**Building a community that inspires curiosity, creativity, and achievement.**

The BOE and WCPS staff compiled input from Washington County community members, including students, parents, and staff of WCPS, as the school system looks to establish the new vision for public education. According to a public letter issued by BOE President Dr. Justin Hartings at the start of the process, it had been more than ten years since the BOE last developed a vision statement for WCPS. This new vision statement will guide WCPS in creating the educational experiences that students will need to thrive in a 21st Century environment.

### 4. *The Oshkosh Civility Project – A Community based Initiative*

http://www.oshkoshcivilityproject.org/

The **Oshkosh Civility Project** has been advancing the cause of civility since 2010. It began as an ad hoc community-based effort. Walter Scott brought the idea for this initiative from his travels to Truckee, California, where he discovered the "Speak Your Peace" campaign developed by the Truckee-Tahoe Community Foundation. That campaign from California was developed based on work originally done in Duluth-Superior using as a reference authority *"Choosing Civility"* by P.M. Forni. Dr. Forni advised the Oshkosh effort and many other groups on the formation of civility improvement efforts. Dr. Forni was brought to Oshkosh by the Oshkosh Civility Project and delivered several community presentations during the formal launch of the initiative in February 2011.

In his discussions with representatives from the Oshkosh Community Foundation and the University of Wisconsin Oshkosh, a small planning group was formed that was comprised of representatives from a number of community-based organizations, including the Oshkosh Chamber of Commerce, the Oshkosh Public Library, the Oshkosh Area School District and other related individuals and organizations.

### 5. *Public Libraries Online – Choose Civility*

http://publiclibrariesonline.org/2013/04/choose-civility-public-libraries-take-center-stage/

Choose Civility is a community-wide initiative that invites everyone in Howard County to choose respect, empathy, and consideration at every opportunity when interacting with others—at work and in their personal lives.

Why focus on civility? Because in an increasingly fragmented world where relationships tend to be conducted through social media, civility connects and unites us on a personal level. Because civility is crucial to the very fabric of our community's quality of life—especially for our youth, who represent the next generation of leaders.

6. *Incourage Community Foundation*

https://incouragecf.org/lead/initiatives/speak-your-peace/

We believe people with something to say should have the opportunity to express themselves—and the responsibility to deliver their message with kindness and respect. Practicing civility is how you get good—and how a community gets great. At the center of this initiative are Nine Tools of Civility and one wish: For the "peace" in "Speak your Peace" to be taken to heart.

7. *Diversity and Inclusion Office*

http://www.umassmed.edu/dio/initiatives/recognition-programs/chancellors-awards-program-overview/civility-award/

The University of Massachusetts Medical School is a large diverse community committed to a civil, respectful and humane workplace. Our commitment to civility contributes to the recruitment and retention of top talent: as a result, we uphold the dignity of the individual in the following ways: conducting ourselves with integrity, courtesy and respect toward fellow members of our UMMS community; holding individuals accountable for their actions and; promoting an environment where individuals feel safe and supported. Recognition Programs and Civility Award - http://www.umassmed.edu/dio/initiatives/recognition-programs/

8. *Utah Civility and Community*

http://www.utahcivility.org/

**Citizens' Five Steps to a More Civil and Caring Utah**

In Utah we are committed to respectful discourse and behavior toward all people. Further we are committed to being a welcoming, inclusive and caring community. Now is a great time to pass it on and start the five steps to a more caring Utah.

https://www.youtube.com/watch?v=Rn1kz8DuaFQ&feature=player_embedded

9. *Finneytown Civic Association – Because it matters*

http://www.fcaontheweb.org/new/civility.htm

In 2008, Marilyn Dainoff, then a Finneytown resident, brought the subject of Civility to the FCA board. She had seen a television commercial in Florida that described a program called Because it Matters. Since it looked to be a program aimed at bettering a community through positive action, we devoted FCA's May 2008 general meeting to exploring the subject in an audience-participation meeting. As a result of the discussion, Marilyn Dainoff and Debbie Ohl organized and conducted two summer workshops aimed at carrying forward the civility momentum generated at the May meeting.

10. *Beverley Hills Human Resources – Embrace Civility Initiative*

http://www.beverlyhills.org/citygovernment/commissions/humanrelationscommission/?NFR=1

The Human Relations Commission promotes positive human relations in all aspects of community life. We invite every member of this community to support an environment where civility, respect and responsible actions prevail.

The primary objective of the Beverly Hills Human Relations Commission is to actively establish our city as a model of a just and equitable society. The Commission recognizes the benefits inherent in a diverse community, fosters understanding and acceptance of all its citizens, and promotes civil discourse and conduct.

## CIVILITY INITIATIVES IN POLITICS

### 1. *Prize for civility in Public Life*

http://sites.allegheny.edu/civilityaward/

The Allegheny College Prize for Civility in Public Life – the nation's leading effort to positively reinforce civility in contemporary American politics – will take a different approach this year. In this its bicentennial year, Allegheny is engaging nationally renowned historians to help the College identify and award the most important moments of civility in American history.

"Civility has played an essential and under-appreciated role in American history," said Mullen. "It is our hope that by helping people to appreciate the profound, essential and positive role that civility has played in American history, we can in some small way inspire current politicians to recommit to civility. And perhaps most importantly, we hope to inspire young people to see politics as a vocation worthy of their aspirations."

### 2. *College of Arts and Sciences  - Institute for Civil Civic Engagement – Campaign Civility Project*

http://www.sandiego.edu/cas/institute-for-civil-civic-engagement/initiatives/campaign-civility-project/

Who We Are

The Campaign Civility Project is a partnership between **KGTV 10NEWs, The Independent Voter Network** and the project **Restoring Respect**, an initiative co-sponsored by the San Diego Community College District, the University of San Diego School of Leadership and Education Sciences and the Catfish Club of San Diego.

What We Seek to Do

The Campaign Civility Project seeks to create greater awareness amongst citizens and elected officials concerning the levels of civility and incivility in local political campaigns.

Initiatives - http://www.sandiego.edu/cas/institute-for-civil-civic-engagement/initiatives/all-initiatives.php

### 3. *National Constitution Center – Civility and Democracy*

http://constitutioncenter.org/experience/programs-initiatives/civility-and-democracy/

As the country examines the tone of political dialogue, the National Constitution Center hosted an interactive, interdisciplinary forum titled *Can We Talk? A Conversation about Civility and Democracy in America.* The forum explored the current state of public discourse and the issue of civility in the context of the roles that dissent and protest play in American politics.

### 4. *The institute for Civility in Government – Civility Leadership*

http://www.instituteforcivility.org/who-we-are/civility-leadership/

While leading legislative conferences to Washington, DC in the 1990's, Cassandra Dahnke and Tomas Spath became increasingly concerned with what they perceived to be a decline in civil discourse in politics and government, and with the impact of that decline on policy and community life. Finding no national organization devoted to addressing the issue of civility at the grassroots level at the time, they launched the Institute for Civility in Government in 1998. The Institute interacts directly with elected officials, staff, and constituents, offering models that cut through partisan noise by emphasizing active listening, tolerance, and the importance of claiming one's own needs without degrading the needs of others.

### 5. *Journal Sentinel – Civility initiative aims to ease rhetoric from Madison to Israel*

http://www.jsonline.com/news/religion/118280594.html

A coalition of Jewish groups is launching a civility initiative meant to ratchet down the rhetoric around hot-button issues, from the political wrangling in Madison to what's best for state of Israel.

———

The effort, modeled after a national program begun last year by the New York-based Jewish Council for Public Affairs, initially will target Milwaukee's Jewish community. But organizers hope eventually to engage a wider interfaith audience.

"As a society, and not just in the Jewish community, we've allowed the shrillest voices to dominate," said Elana Kahn-Oren, director of the Milwaukee Jewish Federation's Community Relations Council, one of the sponsoring organizations.

### 6. *The Good Government Initiative – Civility in Government*

http://www.goodgov.net/community-conversation-civility-in-government-can-it-happen-in-south-florida/

Can there be civility in politics? That was the question considered by Ambassador Sue Cobb, Senator Rene Garcia, former Senator Dan Gelber, and Pauline Winick of The Protocol Centre in the first of a series of Community Conversations organized by the Good Government Initiative. The panel was moderated by Katy Sorenson, president and CEO of the initiative on March 2 at the Biltmore.

### 7. *Tennessee Bar Association – Balancing Civility and Free Expression*

http://www.tba.org/programs/balancing-civility-and-free-expression

Can civility co-exist with free speech in today's world? That's just one topic that will be explored in a series of public conversations presented across the state this fall and spring by the Tennessee Bar Association. The initiative is designed to encourage a public conversation about the tensions between civility and free speech, the state of our public square and the challenges of maintaining civil discourse in a democracy.

### 8. *Indiana Fore Front – Civility in Government*

http://www.indianaforefront.com/civility-in-government/

There's a new effort underway to encourage civility in the General Assembly.

Let's begin this discussion with the fact that things are not as civil as they used to be inside the Statehouse. R's and D's socialize together less frequently than they did in the past. Campaigns are tougher and hard feelings last longer.

It's a situation that was recognized recently when over 100 retired legislators from both parties got together at the State Fairgrounds to form a new organization, the Association of Retired Members of the Indiana General Assembly, or ARMIGA.

That gathering prompted an initiative to give out civility awards to deserving legislators. They would be the first awards of this kind in the country.

An organizational meeting was held today and a number of details are still being worked out. The idea is to encourage good behavior.

### 9. *NCDD Community Blog – Next Generation Initiative*

http://ncdd.org/14335

We're pleased to be able to highlight The Next Generation Initiative, a fantastic project driven by NCDD supporting member and former Ohio state representative Ted Celeste of the National Institute on Civil Discourse. Next Generation is trying to help state legislators find ways to be more civil with each other as they create legislation, and we think it's fundamentally important work. To get a sense of what the initiative is about, check out this great article from Akron Legal News that recently covered Ted's work. You can read more below or find the original piece here *and on NICD's blog* here.

VIDEO – Building trust through Civil Discourse: https://www.youtube.com/watch?v=fkmvfh9DUtg&feature=player_embedded

### 10. *Center for Municipal research and Innovation – Ethica and Civility resources*

http://www.floridaleagueofcities.com/Resources.aspx?CNID=656

The Florida League of Cities has compiled resources on ethics and civility for municipal elected officials and their employees, in whom citizens have placed their trust. Florida has very broad laws related to ethics, public meetings and public records, and many cities have adopted additional standards for their officials and employees. Many local governments have also adopted civility pledges to ensure that the public, elected officials and staff follow reasonable rules for public conduct.

## WORKPLACE CIVILITY INITIATIVES

### 1. *U.S Department of Veteran Affairs – CREW*

http://www.va.gov/ncod/crew.asp

What is CREW?

Civility, Respect, and Engagement in the Workplace (CREW) is a VA-wide culture change initiative. First launched in 2005 by the VHA National Center for Organization Development (NCOD) in response to employee feedback that low levels of civility affected their level of job satisfaction, it has since been utilized by over 1,200 VA workgroups to establish a culture of respect and civility in their organization.

### 2. *Bar-David Consulting*

http://www.sharonebardavid.com/services/real-training-solutions/

These sessions equip your leaders and employees with practical tools for creating civil, respectful work environments. They'll learn how to diagnose, prevent and respond to any type of respect-related situation (we'll cover everything from social cliques and moody personalities, right up to outright targeted bullying).

We have become widely recognized for our workplace civility training sessions (in fact, Sharone Bar-David is a leading Canadan expert on workplace incivility). Our clients have consistently offered rave reviews about our service. In these incivility-focused inspirational sessions, leaders and staff learn how to identify and deal with those seemingly insignificant behaviors that are rude, discourteous, or disrespectful, where it is unclear if the person engaging in these behaviors actually intends any harm.

### 3. *The professional Institute of the Public Service of Canada*

http://www.pipsc.ca/portal/page/portal/website/groups/nureg/081213?_template=/website/t_printerfriendly

"A collaborative workplace is an environment where civility and the CNSC values underpin our interactions, where leaders value and listen to those who work for them, where excellence is robustly encouraged, and where well-being in all forms is actively promoted."

## Introduction

As a steward for the past eight years, I have assisted members dealing with incidences of incivility and disrespect, sometimes perceived as harassment. Often the conflict is low-level and doesn't quite meet the threshold for harassment. Yet this low-level conflict is disruptive and undermines efforts to establish a collaborative workplace.

With the introduction of the CNSC Code of Values and Ethics and the launch of the Collaborative Workplace Initiative, CNSC employees have a golden opportunity to create a collaborative workplace where civility and CNSC values underpin our interactions. Every CNSC employee has a responsibility to treat others with civility and respect and has the right to be treated in the same way.

### 4. *The Delaware Employment Law Blog*

http://www.delawareemploymentlawblog.com/2009/07/nows-a-great-time-for-workplac.html

Workplace civility is a value that all organizations should strive to achieve. For those employers who may need a bit more motivation to implement a workplace-civility initiative, now is the time! August is "Win With Civility" month. Chase's Calendar of Events includes a list of causes to which August has been dedicated as a "special month."

Noting that it is a national dedication, I thought the dedication must warrant certain recognitions, so I did a Google search for ways employers celebrate, observe, or at least acknowledge the special dedication. Surprisingly, a Google search uncovered little more than other websites noting the dedications of August and companies selling promotional materials. Although I was disappointed at the search results, I assume the results reflect a lack of interest in the special dedication rather than a lack of interest in "winning with civility" as a general principle. To help readers who want to "win with civility" in August I have included a reminder of what civility means and some suggestions on how a person can behave to "win with civility."

5. *Acadia University – Centre for Organizational Research and Development*

http://cord.acadiau.ca/crew-interventions.html

**What is CREW?**

CREW stands for Civility, Respect and Engagement at Work. It is an intervention program based on a series of meetings focused on improving issues of civility, respect and work engagement within a specific group. Each group completes a survey before and after their participation in CREW. The group uses this baseline data to assess their specific areas of focus related to civility. In this way, each group is able to determine the actions they will take to improve their overall civility as well as their own methods for improving their work environment. The 'after-CREW' survey provides an objective measure of the group's work during CREW.

Download the **You're so Rude App**

Free on iTunes and upgrade for $1 to get
10 Free Business Etiquette Briefs.

For **50%** off ***30% Solution online course***
with exclusive insights from author, Lew Bayer,
use code **#302016**
at **www.the30percentsolution.com**

CPSIA information can be obtained
at www.ICGtesting.com
Printed in the USA
FFHW010846051118
49183399-53398FF